Introduction to
THEOLOGY

Revised Second Edition

John D. Laurance, S.J., Editor
Department of Theology, Marquette University

PEARSON
Custom
Publishing

Cover Art: "12th century Mosaic of Christ from the Church of Hagia Sophia, Istanbul (Constantinople), Turkey." Photo taken by John D. Laurance, S.J.

Printed in the United States of America

10 9 8 7 6 5 4 3 2 1

ISBN 0-536-50294-3

2007440046

MT/MR

Please visit our web site at *www.pearsoncustom.com*

PEARSON CUSTOM PUBLISHING
501 Boylston Street, Suite 900, Boston, MA 02116
A Pearson Education Company

In every individual human being everything is present (<u>homo quo-dammodo omnia</u>), and the whole achieves a unique manifestation of itself in each particular individual. The community of humankind for its part is not the agglomeration of the many—all too many, but the unity in love of those each of whom is unique in his or her own right, a love which sets each free for his own, which assembles all this and so once more unifies it.[1]

—Karl Rahner, S.J. (1904–1984)

[1] Karl Rahner, "Marriage as a Sacrament," pp. 199–221 in: *Theological Investigations, X,* David Bourke, Tr. (New York: Seabury, 1977), p. 210. English rendered gender inclusive—Ed.

Introduction

This present volume is a second expanded revision of *Introduction to Theology* which was first published in 1995. The original edition resulted from meetings held during the 1994–95 academic year in the Department of Theology of Marquette University in order to redesign its basic undergraduate course, "THEOLOGY 001: Introduction to Theology." There was need for a common text which would (a) provide students with an awareness of the key personages, events, and concepts, as well as the overall historical development, of the Catholic and wider Christian traditions; and thus (b) furnish the common background presupposed in all upper-division theology* courses at Marquette. Since no textbook available at the time accomplished these goals, the department chose readings from both the Bible and church tradition* to provide this common text to be used by all sections of the introductory course.

Obviously any selection of texts for a single course needs to be very limited. Nevertheless, the set of readings the Department of Theology settled on represents a wide spectrum of theological sources across the whole span of salvation* history, thereby offering a surprisingly comprehensive introduction to theology. This, the latest, revision with its additional readings allows instructors a rich variety of readings to choose from, representing different theological sources. In addition, as an aid to both instructor and student, many of the existing introductions to individual readings were expanded and some new ones created in order to draw out some of the theological implications of the texts and bring out their underlying theological unity. Since theology is not only a "science," as St. Thomas Aquinas indicates in reading #20, but also an art, the "Discussion Questions" newly added to each reading require the student, not to simply report on the reading's contents, but to begin practicing the art of theologizing, to think *theologically* on the text and on the basis of the text.

A proper use of the book does not demand that all the readings be covered or studied in the precise order in which they appear, although because of the expanded introductions to each text and the newly added "Discussion Questions," doing so is an excellent strategy. Since as a study in specifically *Christian* theology its unity derives from the person, words and actions of Jesus Christ, its cardinal, defining selection is the Gospel of Mark. All other readings can be found either to anticipate or burgeon forth from this fundamental New Testament understanding of Christ as the culmination and fullness of God's self-revelation in human history. Within this christological unity, then, each instructor is free to arrange the readings, and supplement them with other background material, according to his or her own theological synthesis.

As editor I am particularly indebted to both present and past members of the Department of Theology at Marquette, along with one doctoral graduate (Dr. Silviu Bunta), who generously composed the fuller introductions to readings throughout the book, and whose names appear subscribed to their respective compositions. The hope is that this textbook will prove valuable as an introduction to theology in many Christian colleges besides Marquette.

John D. Laurance, S.J., Ph.D.
Department of Theology
Marquette University
June 1, 2006

Contents

TIME LINE

B.C.* (B.C.E.)*—*B.C. dates are mostly approximate:*

1800	Abraham
1250	The Exodus
1000	King David
950?	*J* (Yahwist source for **Genesis, Exodus**)
850	*E* (Elohist source for **Genesis, Exodus**)
742–701	Isaiah
722	Fall of the Northern Kingdom
650	**2 Samuel**
650	*D* (Deuteronomist source for **Genesis, Exodus**)
620	King Josiah's Reform
587–537	Fall of Southern Kingdom, Temple destroyed; Babylonian Exile
550	Second Isaiah **(Isaiah 40–55)**
550	*P* (Priestly source for **Genesis, Exodus**)
563–483	Siddhartha Gautama, the "Buddha"
551–479	Confucius, Chinese philosopher
470–399	Socrates, Greek Philosopher
450	Editing of **Isaiah 1–12**
427–347	Plato, Greek Philosopher
384–322	Aristotle, Greek Philosopher

A.D. *(C.E.):*

ca. 4 B.C.–A.D. 30 ***JESUS***

ca. 46–58	St. Paul's three missionary journeys
ca. 54	St. Paul, **Letter to the Galatians**
ca. 55	St. Paul, **First Letter to the Corinthians**
ca. 64	Sts. Peter and Paul martyred in Rome
70	Destruction of the Temple in Jerusalem
ca. 70	**Gospel of Mark**
ca. 70–100	Four **Gospels**
ca. 90	**Hebrews**
ca. 117	St. Ignatius of Antioch, **To the Magnesians**
ca. 100–165	St. Justin Martyr, **The First Apology**
ca. 120–200	St. Irenaeus, bishop, theologian, first Patristic writer
ca. 170–236	St. Hippolytus of Rome, **The Apostolic Tradition**
ca. 185–254	Origen, priest,* theologian
ca. 210–258	St. Cyprian of Carthage, **On the Unity of the Catholic Church**
ca. 290–347	St. Pachomius, founder of coenobitic monasticism
306–337	Reign of Constantine
313	The Edict of Milan
325	Council of Nicaea, rejection of Arianism
ca. 330–95	Sts. Basil the Great, Gregory Nazianzen, Gregory of Nyssa
381	Council of Constantinople I, **Nicene-Constantinopolitan Creed**
339–397	St. Ambrose of Milan, bishop, theologian
345–420	St. Jerome, the Latin "Vulgate" Bible
347–407	St. John Chrysostom, Patriarch of Constantinople, theologian
354–430	St. Augustine, bishop, theologian;
397–401	**The Confessions**
431	Council of Ephesus, rejection of Nestorianism
?–461	Pope St. Leo I, "the Great," 440–461
451	Council of Chalcedon, rejection of Monophysitism
ca. 480–ca. 550	St. Benedict, "Father of Western Monasticism"

ca. 540–604	Pope St. Gregory I, "the Great," 590–604
570–632	Muhammad, founder of Islam
787	Council of Nicaea II, **Against Iconoclasm**
800	Charlemagne crowned Holy Roman Emperor
927–1156	The Cluniac Reform
1033–1109	St. Anselm of Canterbury **Cur Deus Homo**
1225–1274	St. Thomas Aquinas **Summa Theologiae**
1342–ca. 1420	Julian of Norwich **Revelations**
1483–1546	Martin Luther **Preface to Romans** (1522)
1491–1556	St. Ignatius of Loyola, **Autobiography, Spiritual Exercises**
1540	Founding of the Society of Jesus
1506–1552	St. Francis Xavier, Jesuit, "Apostle of the Indies"
1545–1563	Council of Trent
1570	Missal of Pope St. Pius V: Tridentine Mass*
1515–1582	St. Teresa of Avila, Carmelite mystic
1596–1650	René Descartes, French philosopher
1724–1804	Immanuel Kant, German philosopher
1790	John Carroll consecrated first Catholic bishop in the U.S.
1869–1870	Vatican Council I declares papal infallibility.
1810–1903	Pope Leo XIII, 1891 **"Rerum Novarum,"** first social encyclical
1909	Beginning of the "Liturgical Movement"
1876–1958	Pope Pius XII (Eugenio Pacelli), 1943 "Mystici Corporis," 1943 "Divino Afflante Spiritu," 1947 "Mediator Dei"
1886–1948	Dom Odo Casel, O. S. B., theologian
1939–1945	The Second World War
1947–1960	Dead Sea Scrolls discovered
1948	World Council of Churches established
1929–1968	Martin Luther King, Jr., 1963 **Letter from Birmingham Jail.**
1962–1965	Vatican Council II, 1963 **Constitution on Sacred Liturgy;** Vatican Council II, 1964 **Constitution on the Church**

1965	Patriarch Athenagoras I (1886–1972) and Pope Paul VI (1897–1978) jointly deplore the mutual anathemas of 1054.
1969	Missal of Pope Paul VI
1904–1984	Karl Rahner, S.J., theologian
1999	Catholic/Lutheran Agreement on Justification* by Faith

I
Sacred Scripture

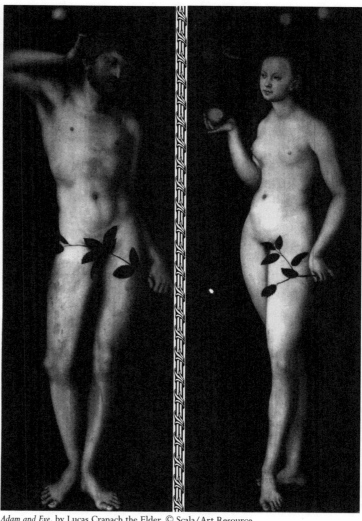

Adam and Eve, by Lucas Cranach the Elder, © Scala/Art Resource

The Bible as God's Revelation

Note: *Asterisks (*) marking words indicate that their explanations, along with those of many others, can be found in the Glossary at the end of the book.*

God's Revelation*

Christians believe that God chose to reveal himself and the mystery of his will. This revealed will is his decision to bring us into a fellowship with him that saves us from sin and death and gives us a share in his eternal nature. God makes this revelation because he loves us. God reveals himself and his will to save us by talking to people as to his friends and by living among them. God does this especially through the history of his people Israel, from the time of Abraham until the life, death, and resurrection of Jesus Christ, who is the mediator and fullness of God's revelation.* God's revelation through Israel and through Christ occurs in a small part of the world and during a very few centuries. So how can all people in all the other places and times benefit from this revelation?

Transmitting God's Revelation

After his resurrection Christ gave to his apostles* the divine gifts they needed to fulfill a mandate he gave them. By this mandate he commanded them to preach the Gospel as a source of all saving truth and right living. In their preaching and example and in the institutions that they set up, the apostles handed on this Gospel, which was the revelation* they had received from living with Christ, hearing him, and seeing him act, as well as from the Holy Spirit's instruction after Christ's resurrection. Under the inspiration of the Holy Spirit, apostles and others associated with them wrote down the message of salvation* in books. The Church later gathered these books into what it calls the New Testament. In doing this, the Church joined these books to the Old Testament books it had already venerated because Jesus, his disciples, and their fellow Jews had also considered them God's word. The teaching, life, worship, and study of the whole Church continue to pass on what is received from the apostles and to deepen Christians' perception of it.

Bible, Tradition,* and Bishops*

Therefore, the Church's tradition* and its Bible have the same divine source: God's revelation. They also have the same goal: the transmission of that revelation to all times and places. In fact, the Church's tradition and its Bible flow together, as it were, into a single reality that functions as the supreme standard for what Christians should believe. On one hand, the Bible *is* God's word *unchangeably* put into writing by the inspiration of the Holy Spirit. On the other hand, the tradition *transmits* God's word (including the Bible), and tradition *grows and deepens.* It is the Church's tradition that has made known which books belong in the Bible and which books do not, and the tradition deepens and updates the Church's understanding of the Bible. The leading role in interpreting the Bible and the Church's tradition belongs to the teaching authority of the Church's bishops. This authority goes all the way back to the mandate Jesus gave to his apostles. The bishops exercise this authority only as servants subordinate to the Bible and to the tradition.* Thus, each of these three—the Church's Bible, its tradition, and its bishops' teaching authority—needs the other two to fulfill its own role in the transmission of God's revelation.

Inspiration of the Bible

Christians believe that the things in the Bible that are divinely revealed were put into writing under the inspiration of the Holy Spirit. This means that God chose certain people in whom and through whom God acted in order that they might write only what God wanted them to write. To do this, God worked through these authors' use of their own faculties and powers. Thus, these people were functioning as true authors of the Biblical books they were writing. Therefore, God is *author* of the Bible, but God did not *write* it because God worked on a plane higher than that of the human authors who actually wrote the Biblical books. Still, whatever the human authors assert in the Bible is asserted by the Holy Spirit. For this reason, Christians believe that the Bible teaches without error the truth that God wanted put in it for our salvation.

Truth and Interpretation

Thus, the Bible is about God's saving truth. Therefore, it is only this sort of truth that Christians should expect the Bible to communicate with divinely guaranteed reliability. Of course, people can be saved without knowing the truth about many sorts of issues investigated by modern science, for instance, how old the universe is and what physical processes were at work in its first moments of existence, whether some biological species evolved from others, whether all people descended from a single human couple. Thus, Christians should not expect the Bible's divinely guaranteed reliability to help us answer such questions. But the Bible does transmit God's revealed saving truth through the work of human beings acting as true authors. This fact implies that we must know what the Bible's human authors meant so that we can discover what God's revelation in the Bible means. To discover what these authors meant, we need to find out—just as we would for any author—about the literary genres, the forms of thinking and of expression, and the historical contexts of the time and place in which Biblical passages or books were written. At the same time, we should interpret the Bible in the same Holy Spirit that inspired its human authors. Therefore, we will look for how any part of the Bible fits in with the rest of the Bible which that Spirit inspired and how that part of the Bible is related to the rest of what the Christian tradition transmits to us of God's revelation.

—*Rev. Joseph G. Mueller, S.J.*

The Books of the Old Testament

Note: Books whose titles are printed in *italics* are not regarded as canonical, i.e., normative, by most Protestants. They often appear in Protestant Bibles but only under the term, "Apocrypha."

THE PENTATEUCH:

Genesis

Exodus

Leviticus

Numbers

Deuteronomy

THE HISTORICAL BOOKS:

Joshua

Judges

Ruth

1 Samuel

2 Samuel

1 Kings

2 Kings

1 Chronicles

2 Chronicles

Ezra

Nehemiah

Tobit

Judith

Esther

1 Maccabees

2 Maccabees

THE WISDOM BOOKS:

Job

Psalms

Proverbs

Ecclesiastes (Qoheleth)

Song of Songs

Wisdom

Sirach (Ecclesiasticus)

THE PROPHETIC BOOKS:

Isaiah

Jeremiah

Lamentations

Baruch

Ezekiel

Daniel

Hosea

Joel

Amos

Jonah

Micah

Nahum

Habakkuk

Zephaniah

Haggai

Zechariah

Malachi

The "Pentateuch"

The book of *Genesis* stands at the beginning not only of the Bible as a whole, but also of one of its major units, the first five books known alternately as **Torah** (Hebrew: "teaching"), **Pentateuch** (Greek: "five [book] containers"), and **Law**: *Genesis, Exodus, Leviticus, Numbers,* and *Deuteronomy*. The remainder of the Bible is traditionally divided into the Historical Books, the Prophets, and Wisdom Literature. The Pentateuch presents the background and content of the foundational event in the life of the ancient Israelites: God's delivering the Hebrew tribes from slavery into a Promised Land and establishing them as his people Israel around the year 1250 B.C.,* doing so by means of a covenant* sacrifice and the gift of the Law.

As a single unit, the Pentateuch was traditionally thought to have been written or dictated by the prophet Moses, the central figure of this founding period. It was only in the eighteenth century that this presumption first became questioned. In the spirit of the Enlightenment, scholars then began to scrutinize the text more closely, noticing not only that Moses' own death is recorded in *Deuteronomy* 34, but that within the same books there exist different vocabularies and narrative styles. For example, whereas in some narrative passages the sacred name *Yahweh* is used for God, in others the generic name *Elohim* is found; and these Yahwist and Elohist passages differ also, as we shall see, in their theological interests and emphases. From such evidences it was concluded that, not only were the five books *not* written or dictated by a single person, but different parts were composed at different times and places and assembled finally into a single text only much later in Israel's history. It was through discoveries such as these that the various Historical-Critical methods were developed (Redaction* Criticism, Form Criticism, Literary Criticism, etc.) to provide fuller and more accurate understandings of biblical texts within their original horizons of meaning.

In the nineteenth century Julius Wellhausen (1844–1918) proposed a "documentary hypothesis" that the Pentateuch was formed in the period after the Babylonian Exile (c. 587–538 B.C.) by the combination of four preexistent written sources. These sources or traditions soon bore the names **"Yahwist"(J), "Elohist" (E), "Priestly" (P), and "Deuteronomist" (D)**. Until recently "J" (10th c.?) and "E" (9th c.?) were universally thought to be the earliest of the four. The text of **J** suggested that it was written by a lay author in the Jerusalem court of David or Solomon. **E** is seen as a northern document, probably composed after Solomon's kingdom was divided by his two sons into two separate kingdoms: Israel in the north and Judah* in the south. Whereas J features anthropomorphisms, vivid story telling, and a promise-to-fulfillment theological vision, E emphasizes morality, faith,* and fear of the Lord, presenting God as totally awesome and strictly transcendent. E begins in *Genesis* 12 with the story of Abraham and envisions the Mosaic covenant* as the highpoint in human history.

D, found mostly in the Books of *Deuteronomy* and *Joshua*, is probably also a northern kingdom document, the core of which was written in the eighth century and then brought down and further developed in the south (possibly the law discovered by King Josiah in 621). In the spirit of the eighth century prophets, Amos, Hosea, and Isaiah, it insists on the fear/love of God and constantly exhorts to obedience to divine commands, especially a loving care for the poor.

Finally, **P**, reflecting the interests of the temple priesthood, is concerned mostly with genealogies and matters of worship and ritual (e.g., *Leviticus*), and was probably compiled during or soon after the period of the Exile (587–534 B.C.) when most of Judah's* inhabitants were carted away in slavery to Babylonia. Influenced by this traumatic event, P teaches that just as God is holy, so must Israel be holy, set apart from and uncontaminated by any man-made cult. It does so by presenting the whole history of Israel and creation itself in liturgical terms.

Thus, according to P, God created the world in six "days" and rested on the seventh, thereby grounding the Sabbath observance as intrinsic to the divine ordering of the world itself. P also re-interprets preexistent agricultural feasts into celebrations of God's great deeds in Israel's history. The winter barley harvest becomes the pilgrimage feast of Passover, and the wheat harvest celebrated seven weeks later is transformed into the yearly feast of Pentecost, memorializing the covenant sacrifice and giving of the Law at Mt. Sinai.

In recent decades some biblical scholars have postulated that J is actually the latest of the four traditions, composed after the exile (post 538 B.C.). They argue that J, haunted by Israel's continual failure throughout its history to live up to the covenant, sought to correct the Priestly tradition's excessively optimistic view. Thus, for example, where in *Genesis* 1 the P account repeatedly emphasizes the goodness of creation, J in chapters 2–3 adds its own version of creation followed almost immediately by Adam and Eve's fall from grace.*

Whatever the order of J,E,P,D, the very fact that the first two chapters of *Genesis* contain two separate accounts of creation, each written in a decidedly different style and with a different theological approach, is clear evidence that the Pentateuch is not only the work of more than one human author or redactor (interpreting editor), but actually the compilation over a long period of Israel's history of a variety of sources into a final, quilt-like unity. Indeed, evidence that the Pentateuch had a final redactor—someone who arranged all the sources according to a unified faith vision—are four teachings which pervade the whole work: (1) God acts in human history; (2) He has chosen Israel to be his people in a special way; (3) He is personal, not some blind irrational force; and (4) He acts throughout history in a pattern of promise, election, covenant, and law.

—*Rev. John D. Laurance, S.J.*

1

Creation and Fall

GENESIS 1–11

INTRODUCTION

The God of History

The Bible opens with the words, "In the beginning . . ."(1:1). By God's word, then, time itself was set in motion. True, according to scholars the original human authors of *Genesis* probably envisioned God fashioning creation out of some pre-existing materials. However, later, under the guidance of the Holy Spirit, these same divinely inspired texts were seen in the light of the whole of Scripture* to reveal how the universe exists only as God's self-expression, wholly symbolic of him, in which he offers himself. As such, creation also implies a dialogue partner, calling for personal, self-giving response in return, so that it begins to be complete in its meaning only when, on the sixth "day," *"God created man in his image; in the divine image he created him; male* *and female He created them* (1:27)." The God who created all things is thus also the God of history, the fundamental meaning of everything that happens in the world. And according to *Genesis,* human beings are to share in God's work of giving meaning (1:28; 2:19-20). In addition, since the absolute goodness of God is evident in all he has made (c. 1), in order to be true to themselves they must love God in all things and all things in God, giving themselves completely to him in return. Whatever there is of evil (moral disorientation) in the world, then, is the result solely of humankind's refusal to do so, its history of sin (cc. 3–11).

Theological Stories Interpreting History

Although the stories in *Genesis* 1–11 of creation and humanity's fall from God's grace* are just that: *stories,* they are no less true than if they were eye witness accounts of actual events. No written history can ever be purely objective. Because it is impossible to record *all* human events, historians must *choose* from among them, deciding which they deem worth remembering. However, in addition to recording past events in the life of Israel and its relationship to God, divinely inspired biblical authors also sometimes create stories to convey the God-given, deeper meanings of those events. For example, the story of the six "days" of creation reveals how the God who ordained the Sabbath rest for Israel also created and gave order to the whole universe (see *Isaiah* 40). That is why any purely physical inconsistencies are unimportant, such as the fact that, even though a day is measured by the rising and setting of the sun, the sun itself is not created until the fourth "day." Similarly, the forbidden tree "in the middle of the garden" teaches how *all* creation as God's gift belongs ultimately to God and not to humans, so that Adam and Eve's eating the tree's fruit reveals how sin is actually humankind's attempt from the very beginning to deny the gift-nature of creation and to claim totally independent dominance over it. Their attempting to be their own gods results only in self-alienation (nakedness), alienation from others (e.g., male dominance), and alienation from the rest of creation (pain and hard work). Finally, just as Eve is formed out of Adam's rib, so are their progeny also one flesh with them, sharing in their same alienations, as symbolized in the remaining stories of *Genesis* 1-11. The Bible, therefore, is not history in the modern sense of that word, but *theo-logy* in its original sense: the "word of God" expressed in the faith* "word of (about) God."

The Community's Expression of Faith

Just as the Old Testament (OT) originates out of and expresses ancient Israel's fundamental faith-interpretation of the world, the New Testament (NT) represents the essential faith of the Church. However, whereas for ancient Israel the OT ("Hebrew Bible") was, and continues to be for the Jewish community today, the totality of Sacred Scripture*, Christianity includes both OT and NT within its scriptural "canon" (see *2 Timothy* 3:16). It does so because the NT is basically a reinterpretation of OT persons and events in light of the person, words, and actions of Jesus Christ as the full realization of God's eternal plan of creation and salvation (see *Ephesians* 1–3). The NT locates in Jesus himself the origin of this interpretation of salvation history (e.g., *Mark* 9:4; *Luke* 24:27, 44–46; *John* 5:46), and by affirming him to be the Son of God it proclaims that interpretation divinely normative for Christian faith.

Typologically Fulfilled in the New Testament

As part of this reinterpretation of the OT, the NT *Gospel of John* begins by imitating the opening of *Genesis:* "*In the beginning (En arche) was the word.*" It then goes on to identify Jesus Christ as the fullness of God's "word," the Word made flesh: "*all things came to be through him*" (*John* 1:1–3). To the degree, then, that other things in the world exist are they also participations in Jesus Christ as God's self-manifestation (see *Colossians* 1:15–16; *Hebrews* 1:1). Thus, Adam, the father of the human race, is a "type" of Christ—manifesting and making Christ already present in the world at humanity's very beginning—in that, through his loving death and resurrection, Jesus Christ, like Adam, also embodies in his humanity the whole of the human race: *"Just as through one man/humanity (anthropos) sin entered the world . . . who was a **type** of the one to come . . . much more have the grace* of God and the free gift in that grace of the one man/humanity Jesus Christ abounded for the many"* (*Romans* 5:12–15 *passim*). However, if by our created solidarity with Adam, the "old man" (*Romans* 6:6; *Ephesians* 4:22; *Colossians* 3:9), we human beings inherited unwanted tendencies toward sinful excesses (*Romans* 7:13–25), much more are we in solidarity with the "new man," Jesus Christ, because it was in his obedient victory on the cross over sin and death that we have been at once both originally created and re-created, i.e., fully redeemed (*Colossians* 1:15–20).

—*Rev. John D. Laurance, S.J.*

DISCUSSION QUESTIONS

1. According to *Genesis* 1–11, based on the evidence of creation God is to be revered and adored. Is this because of his power and dominance, or because of his goodness, or both? If both, in your judgment is there an intrinsic connection between God's power and his goodness, and if so, what is it?

2. In your judgment, do the *Genesis* creation accounts support, stand neutral to, or contradict the modern scientific theory of evolution? Explain.

3. Why, according to the two creation accounts in *Genesis* 1–2 taken together, did God create humanity male and female?

4. If the current trend continues, one day the whole world will speak a common language: English. According to *Genesis* 11 would this necessarily be a bad thing, or what is meant by the story of Babel?

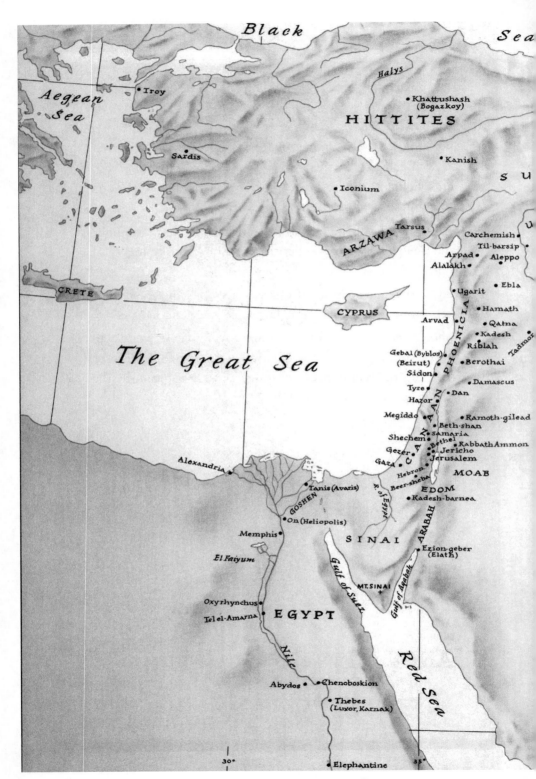

Black Sea

Aegean Sea

Troy

Sardis

HITTITES

Khattushash (Bogazkoy)

Halys

Kanish

SU

Iconium

CRETE

ARZAWA Tarsus

Carchemish
Til-barsip
Arpad · Aleppo
Alalakh

Ebla

Ugarit

CYPRUS

The Great Sea

Arvad

Hamath

Qatna
Kadesh
Riblah

Gebal (Byblos)
(Beirut)
Sidon

Berothai

Tadmor

PHOENICIA

Damascus

Tyre

Dan

Hazor

Megiddo

Ramoth-gilead

Beth-shan
Samaria

Shechem
Gezer
Gaza

Bethel
Jericho
Jerusalem

Rabbath Ammon

CANAAN

Hebron
Beer-sheba

MOAB

Alexandria

Tanis (Avaris)

GOSHEN

On (Heliopolis)

R. of Egypt

EDOM

Kadesh-barnea

Memphis

SINAI

ARABAH

El Faiyum

Ezion-geber
(Elath)

MT. SINAI

Gulf of Suez

Gulf of Aqabah

Oxyrhynchus
Tel el-Amarna

EGYPT

Nile

Red Sea

Abydos · Chenoboskion

Thebes
(Luxor, Karnak)

30°

35°

Elephantine

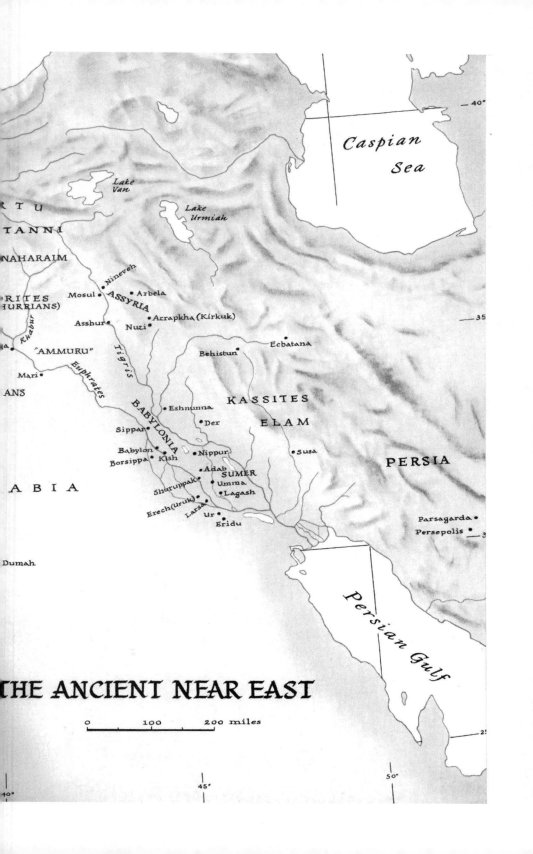

Caspian
Sea

—40°

Lake
Van

Lake
Urmiah

—35

RTU

TANNI

NAHARAIM

RITES
HURRIANS)

Nineveh

Mosul • ASSYRIA • Arbela

Asshur • Arrapkha (Kirkuk)

Nuzi

Ecbatana

Behistun

Khabur

"AMMURU"

Euphrates

Tigris

Mari •

ANS

KASSITES

Eshnunna

ELAM

Der

Sippar BABYLONIA

Babylon • Nippur

Borsippa • Kish

Susa

PERSIA

ABIA

Adab
SUMER
Umma

Shuruppak • Lagash

Erech (Uruk) Larsa

Ur

Eridu

Parsagarda •

Persepolis • 3

—3

Dumah

Persian Gulf

—25

THE ANCIENT NEAR EAST

0   100   200 miles

40°   45°   50°

2

Abrahamic Tradition

GENESIS 12–24

INTRODUCTION

Historical Background

The historicity of the stories of *Genesis* 12–24 is generally contested among scholars. These narratives are not simply about individuals with interesting destinies and complicated and intriguing family plots, but they are primarily sagas about nations in their incipient and rudimentary stages where they are still aggregates of persons and families. In these tales groups within ancient Israel define their nation in terms of personal and familial ancestry. *Genesis* 12–24 is also meant to establish essential distinctions between ancient Israel and its neighboring nations, while explaining their indubitable common past and culture. Certain persons and families become representative of nations. The depictions of the ancestors establish the collective characters and the destinies of the nations emerging from them and outstanding deeds. Personal incidents often foreshadow national events of later times. A classic example is the migration of Abraham to Egypt, so evidently foretelling the later story of the exodus. *Genesis* 12–24 is the story of Israel's own identity and of the ethnographic structure of the world known to the chosen people, the world in which Israel stands out in its unique covenant* with God. Within this worldview, the "personal" story of ancient Israel is a narrative of faith* and divine providence. *

Ancestral Covenants

The relation of God to the ancestors and specifically to Abraham is mostly expressed in covenants. *Genesis* 12–24 is permeated with them (e.g., 12, 15, 17). The repetition of promises builds up an expectation for fulfillment initially realized in the exodus, ancient Israel's foundational event.

Christianity and Abraham

As in the case of Adam, these ancestral stories provide background for the New Testament where they are directly associated with Jesus' identity and mission. From the early Christian perspective the momentum of expectation built in the repeated promise to Abraham is extended beyond the event of the exodus to the ultimate fulfillment of the promise in Jesus' person and mission. According to *Galatians* 3:6–29, the covenant with Abraham is fulfilled in the faith* of the Christian community. The promise to Abraham of an offspring (singular) is fully realized in the person of Jesus Christ in and through whom all of humanity is united to God (*Galatians* 3:26–29). According to *John* 8:39–59, Jesus claims to be not only the realization of the promise to Abraham, the "personal" realization which the patriarch foresaw and in which he rejoiced, but also to be the God of Abraham (and of the other ancestors), the claim for which the bewildered crowd is ready to exact the punishment for blasphemy.

—*Dr. Silviu Bunta*

DISCUSSION QUESTIONS

1. The stories of *Genesis* 12–24 locate the origin of the Hebrew people in Abraham as their primogenitor. Are there any indications they also originated through divine choice, as God's *chosen* people from the very beginning, that God's power was at work here?

2. God calls Abram, as he does many others throughout the Bible (e.g., Adam, Samuel, Jeremiah, Peter, Paul, etc.). What might this pattern of calling tell us, if anything, about the author's understanding of God and of how we are to come to know him? With Abram's call comes a new name. What biblical significance might there be in the giving of a new name?

3. In chapter 14 the shadowy figure of Melchizedek, seemingly unconnected to the rest of the narrative, suddenly appears and then disappears. On reading through this section, why, do you suppose, the final redactor of *Genesis* included this episode?

4. Abraham has become synonymous with faith in God (e.g., *Romans* 4). What examples can you find in the text where he especially demonstrates that faith? Can you identify any changes or fluctuations in his faith?

3

Mosaic Covenant

EXODUS 1–20

INTRODUCTION

The Identity of Israel

Exodus 1–20 describes the foundational events of ancient Israel as they are conceived later by the authors and editors of these stories. According to these authors Israel comes into being by deliverance from slavery in Egypt and the gift of both the law and of Canaan, the promised land. Scholars today generally agree that *Exodus* 1–20 does not depict actual historical events. Ancient Israelites are most probably indigenous to Canaan, emerging as an increasingly distinctive Semitic nation among other Canaanite populations in the later centuries of the second millennium B.C.E.* Rather than conveying mere historical facts, *Exodus* 1–20 communicates manners in which groups within ancient Israel define their nation and answer essential identity questions, such as: Who are we? How did we come to be what we are? Where are we coming from? Who is our God? How did we come to have the laws that we have? *Exodus* 1–20 answers with a fascinating story of national identity and unity, of collective liberation from Egypt, of ethnic and theological distinction from and superiority to other Canaanite populations, of divine laws provided so exceptionally to a whole nation in a public and astonishing manner, and of a national God superior to other national gods. As in the case of the stories of Genesis, the non-historical character of *Exodus* 1–20 paradoxically only enhances its theological value.

The Ten Commandments

The ten commandments are preserved in two slightly different forms, namely in *Exodus* 20 and *Deuteronomy* 5. The numbering of these commandments does not coincide in Judaism and major Christian denominations.

Exodus and Sinai Retold

The central theological value of *Exodus* 1–20 is explored and developed in early Christian communities. It is not surprising that this text, defining national and religious identity for the Judaism of the first century C.E., becomes a narrative of identity in early Christianity. Early Christians saw themselves as witnesses to the spiritual meaning of the Sinai covenant* (*2 Corinthians* 3:1–6). According to *Acts* 2:1–13, the foundational event of the Christian community occurs during the Jewish feast of Pentecost, a festival commemorating the foundational value of Sinai for Judaism. *Ephesians* 4:7–16, which directly quotes *Psalm* 68:18 (19 in Hebrew), associates God's ascent on Sinai and giving of the law to the ascent of Jesus and the giving of the Spirit. Within this parallelism Jesus is not simply a Moses figure, a recipient of the law, but he corresponds to the divine giver of the law. Jesus' repetitive use of "I am" in self-revelatory sayings in the Gospel of John also suggests an identification of Jesus with the God appearing to Moses in *Exodus* 3 where God states, "I am who I am." Jesus Christ is not simply typologically foreshadowed in the *Exodus* narratives, but he is present in these events in his divinity.

The Manna and the Water from Rock

According to early Christian theology*, Jesus Christ is the God appearing to Moses and the pillar of cloud and fire leading the Israelites through wilderness. He is also the water-producing rock and the spiritual food or manna on which subsisted the ancestors (*1 Corinthians* 10:3–4), just as the Church today subsists on him in his fullness through the Eucharist* (*John* 6:48–51). Jesus is the life-sustaining power of the wandering Israel, of its exceptional identity, and of the Church itself through the new manna, the Eucharist. Subsequent Christian theology would further develop the parallelism between manna and the Eucharist by emphasizing that, like the Eucharist, manna loses its essential spiritual dimension and function, when reduced to mere nourishment of the body.

—*Dr. Silviu Bunta*

DISCUSSION QUESTIONS

1. Throughout *Exodus* 1–20 human interests and concerns interfere with God's intent. Inevitably God's intent prevails. From your perspective, do the stories of divine success treat all humans involved fairly? What does the manner in which God's intent is imposed on people reveal about the authors' understanding of justice?

2. What does *Exodus* 1–20 reveal about the authors' conception of the nature and authority of law? How does this concept compare to modern understandings of law, both secular and biblical?

3. God identifies himself to Moses as "the God of Abraham, . . . Isaac, . . . Jacob" (*Exodus* 3:6, 15). Why identify himself in such a limited way? Why not rather as "God," or "the God who created the universe"?

4. In the story of manna from heaven (c. 16), why, do you suppose, when the Israelites tried to store and hoard this gift from God (except when they did so for the Sabbath), it turned wormy and

rotten? Why in c. 17 did God choose, from of all places, to bring water out of a rock? What for the authors might be the deeper theological significance of these two details, applying possibly to all kinds of situations in human life?

NUMBERING OF THE TEN COMMANDMENTS

From: *Exodus 20:2–17:*	*Catholic & Lutheran* #	*Orthodox & Reformed* #	*Jewish* #
"I am the Lord your God, who brought you out of the land of Egypt . . ."	1	1	1
"You shall have no other gods before me."	1	1	2
"You shall not make for yourself a graven image, or any likeness of anything . . ."		2	2
"You shall not take the name of the Lord your God in vain . . ."	2	3	3
"Remember the Sabbath day, to keep it holy."	3	4	4
"Honor your father and your mother . . ."	4	5	5
"You shall not kill."	5	6	6
"You shall not commit adultery."	6	7	7
"You shall not steal."	7	8	8
"You shall not bear false witness against your neighbor."	8	9	9
"You shall not covet your neighbor's wife" (See *Deut* 5:21)	9	10	10
"You shall not covet your neighbor's goods"	10	10	10

4
Israel's Response

DEUTERONOMY 26:1–11

INTRODUCTION

For a brief textual introduction to the Book of Deuteronomy, see "The Pentateuch," page 9.

Why Sacrifice?

Notice that this passage from *Deuteronomy* is not only a declaration of faith, but one directed personally to God as a "You," in the grammatical second person. Through this faith declaration, then, those gathered for worship enter into relationship with their God.

In their accepting the whole Promised Land in the form of its fruits, the ancient Israelites are also accepting God as *their* God, present as Giver in the gifts he has given them. And, correspondingly, through these same symbolic words and acts of acceptance they are also—in the giving back of the land's first fruits in a ritual sacrifice—offering themselves whose whole lives so depend on the land and the fruits of its soil.

But just as God presumably did not give the Promised Land in the first place in order to "buy" the love of his people, but simply out of love for them, so too, by their gift of thanksgiving, are the people of God here invited *out of pure graciousness* to recognize God in his independent goodness, and not as someone they seek to manipulate by a strategic buying of favor. Both parties, then, as it were, give "something for nothing," and in doing so recognize the inalienable otherness and goodness of the other—the basis for true personal love.

Yet one might ask, "If this is an engagement of love, then why is it commanded?" The answer is that all true love has an element of obligation to it. If, for example, someone you know greets you, "Hello, how are you?," you sense immediately the obligation to return that *gift* of greeting. You do so because the very sacredness of the other person (grounded ultimately in that person's sacredness to God) demands to be recognized. That is why Jesus could *command* that we love and greet (*Matthew* 5:27) even those who hate us.

Jules Breton, *The Song of the Lark,* 1884, oil on canvas, 110.6 x 85.8 cm, Henry Field Memorial Collection, 1984. 1033.
© Art Institute of Chicago

Thanksgiving as Love is Creative

In its sacrifice of first fruits not only does Israel here gratefully recognize God's original act of love but, by that very recognition, actually allows it to take place and have its effect in them. That is to say, God *effectively* loves Israel—and Israel experiences that love—only in and through Israel's own sacrificial return of loving gratitude. By his love God not only allows Israel to exist as inalienable persons in his sight, but in his accepting Israel's gift in return He bestows on them the personal power and dignity of their actually letting Him *be* God in their world.

Scripture Born from the Liturgy*

According to scholars, this brief liturgical prayer provides evidence of how early biblical—especially patriarchal—traditions originated as credal declarations proclaimed aloud in gatherings of public worship. At shrines such as Shechem, Gilgal, and Shiloh, the priests* who offered sacrifices were also entrusted with guarding and amalgamating the oral and written faith traditions of their communities. The Bible was born, then, out of "liturgical" activity, at least in this broader sense.

This short declaration of faith in *Deuteronomy* 26 also demonstrates how the whole Bible is actually a single confession of faith (first by the ancient Israelites, and then by the Christian Church with the addition of the New Testament), a confession of all God has done for them throughout salvation history, just as later on in this book St. Augustine makes his *Confessions* of faith to God in a spirit of gratitude for all God has done in his life. Thus, the whole Bible is fundamentally prayer—some parts, like the *Psalms,* more intensely and explicitly so than others. That is why the Medieval monks referred to the reading of Scripture* as *lectio divina,* "divine reading," because when one reads it with faith, it actually deepens one's faith-relationship with God.

—*Rev. John D. Laurance, S.J.*

DISCUSSION QUESTIONS

1. Notice how the one addressing the *Deuteronomy* 26 confession switches from first person singular, "My," to first person plural, "us," and then back again to "I." What might be the theological reason why the prayer requires the use of both singular and plural in this way?

2. Why, do you suppose, that after making the offering the one who does so is commanded then to celebrate, as if that were part of the liturgical event? And why celebrate not only with family and Levite (priest*), but also with any aliens in their midst?

3. "Eucharist*," as you know, means "thanksgiving." In comparing the basic dynamic of this grateful offering of first fruits to what takes place in the offering of bread and wine at a Christian Eucharist or Lord's Supper, what similarities do you find? What differences? (*If you are unfamiliar with the Eucharist, see readings #13 and #14 below.*)

4. If you were to make a brief, grateful confession of faith to God for all of his goodness to you in your past life, what would you write? If you were to change "I" to "we" in your confession of faith (see question #1), what would you write?

5
House of David

INTRODUCTION

Background

2 *Samuel,* one of the historical books of the Bible, concentrates mostly on King David's reign in Jerusalem during the 10th century B.C.* The story of David starts in *1 Samuel,* where the origins of monarchy as an institution in Israel are presented. *1 Samuel* begins by illustrating with stories the Israelites' desire for a king, then moves to the selection of Saul as king, Saul's fall from favor, the choice of David as the Lord's anointed or "*messiah**," and finally the struggle between Saul and David for the leadership of Israel. *2 Samuel* opens with the defeat and death of Saul, and then moves into reports on David's military and political successes: David (a) unites the 12 tribes who proclaim him king (chapter 5), (b) conquers Jerusalem and makes the city the center of his kingdom (chapter 5), and (c) brings in the important religious relics from the desert experience: the Ark of the Covenant* and the Tent of Meeting, relics that had been the focal point for the

33

The Young David, Andrea del Verrocchio (1435–1488).
© Erich Lessing/Art Resource

worship of the Lord during the time of the settlement, 1200 B.C.–1000 B.C. (chapter 6). These chapters all form the backdrop to *2 Samuel 7*. Chapters 11 and 12 of *2 Samuel* present the story of David's adultery with Bathsheba, the wife of Uriah the Hittite, and the tragic aftermath of that adultery. These two chapters make the point that David, while favored, was also flawed, and that he paid a price for his transgression. (For example, David's family life suffers a series of crises: in chapter 13, one of David's daughters, Tamar, is raped by her half brother, Amnon; this rape is avenged by Tamar's brother Absalom, who engineers Amnon's murder.)

Davidic Covenant

Chapter Seven marks the height of David's power and prestige. This chapter begins with a statement about David's desire to build a temple for the Lord—he has brought in the religious relics from the desert experience, the Ark of the Covenant and the Tent of Meeting, but he wishes to construct a permanent place for the worship of the Lord. His prophet, Nathan, at first tells him that this is a good plan but later rescinds the Lord's permission. In the oracle delivered by Nathan, David is told that he is not to build a "house" for the Lord—the Lord will build a "house" for David! There is a word play here: "house" is used both in the sense of a permanent structure and of a dynasty, progeny to continue David's line. The text assures that David's dynasty will continue as the chosen agent of God's salvation. This text is the basis for the tradition of the *Davidic covenant,* the tradition that God has made a covenant with His anointed, David.

"Covenant"

A *covenant,** in the Bible, has the particular meaning of an agreement, a bond, forged between God and His people or God and one individual. In the Old Testament books preceding *2 Samuel,* we have already encountered the *Abrahamic covenant,* the covenant God made with Abraham (*Genesis* 12, 15, 17) and the *Sinai covenant,* also known as the *Mosaic covenant,* the agreement forged at Sinai between

God and the people of Israel, with Moses acting as the representative of the people. According to *2 Samuel* 7, God has made a special covenant with David. David is promised two things: land and dynasty. David had wanted to build a "house" (a temple) for God; God announces, through Nathan, that He will build a "house" (a dynasty) for David. A descendent of David will always be on the throne in Jerusalem. God commits Himself to David—the covenant is an eternal, unconditional one, one that cannot be broken.

The importance and strength of this tradition, this idea that God has made special promises to David, is evident throughout the Old Testament: *Isaiah* 2:2–4; *Isaiah* 8:23–9:6; *Isaiah* 11:1–9; *Psalms* 2 and 72. The promise of a dynasty to David becomes the basis for the *messianic expectation,* the hope for a *messiah** that develops after the destruction of Jerusalem and the end of the Davidic dynasty in 586 B.C.

Faith Significance

For Christians, *2 Samuel* 7 is one of the most theologically important texts in the Old Testament. The *Davidic covenant* first presented here is of central importance in the New Testament. Jesus is the son "descended from David according to the flesh" (Paul's Letter to the Romans, 1:3). When Christians proclaim that Jesus is *Christ* (= *Messiah**), they are affirming their belief that the *Davidic covenant* has reached its culmination in Jesus. See, e.g., *Mark* 8:29: "*And [Jesus] asked them, 'But who do you say that I am?' Peter said to him in reply, 'You are the Messiah.' "*

—*Dr. Deirdre A. Dempsey*

DISCUSSION QUESTIONS

1. Why do you think that the Lord chooses David as His anointed? What does this choice have to say about David? About God?

2. What do you suppose prompted David so scantily clothed to leap and dance before the ark, especially since Michal thought it such an embarrassing thing for a king to do? The author then vindicates David. How then should the reader imitate David's example?

3. You have read, in the selections from *Genesis* and from *Exodus,* about two other covenants, the Abrahamic covenant and the Sinai, or Mosaic, covenant. Does this covenant with David, described in chapter seven of *2 Samuel,* take precedence over the other two covenants? Does it negate those covenants?

4. In the *Chronicles,* two biblical books that are later re-workings of the material we have in the books of *Samuel* and *Kings,* no mention is made of David's adultery with Bathsheba. Why then, if it didn't nullify God's choice of David as king, do you suppose the author here decided to include it? Are there possibly some deeper meanings he thought it conveyed? If so, what might they be?

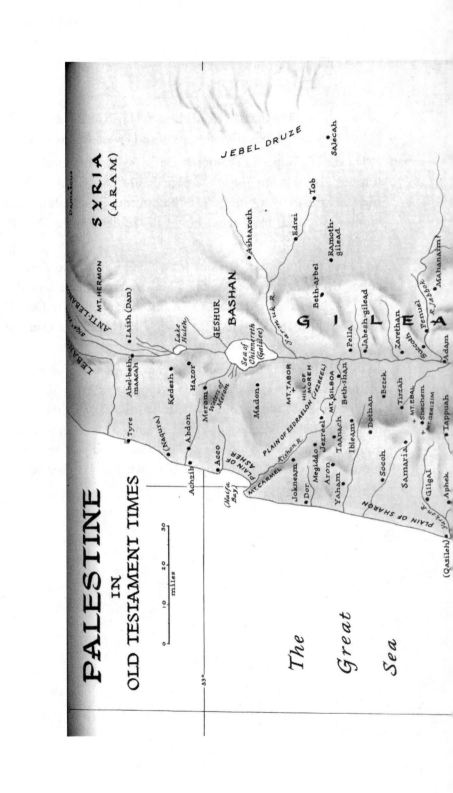

PALESTINE
IN
OLD TESTAMENT TIMES

miles
0   10   20   30

The

Great

Sea

SYRIA
(ARAM)

JEBEL DRUZE

Salecah

Damascus

Tob

Ashtaroth

Edrei

Ramoth-
gilead

MT. HERMON

Beth-arbel

ANTI-LEBANON

BASHAN

Laish (Dan)

Lake
Huleh

GESHUR

Penuel

G   I   L   E   A   D

Pella

Jabesh-gilead

R. Jabbok

Mahanaim!

Sea of
Chinnereth
(Galilee)

Yarmuk R.

Zarethan

Succoth

Adam

Abel-beth-
maacah

Kedesh

Hazor

Merom
Waters of
Merom

Madon

Jabbok R.

MT. TABOR

HILL OF
MOREH

(Naqura)

Tyre

Abdon

Aceo

Achzib

(Haifa
Bay)

MT. GILBOA

Bezek

Tirzah

MT. EBAL

(JEZREEL)

Beth-shan

PLAIN OF ESDRAELON

Kishon R.

Jezreel

Taanach

Ibleam

Dothan

Shechem

MT. GERIZIM

Tappuah

Jokneam

Dor

Megiddo

Aron

Yaham

Socoh

Samaria

Gilgal

Aphek

PLAIN OF SHARON

(Qasileh)

Yarkon R.

MT. CARMEL

PLAIN OF
ASHER

33°

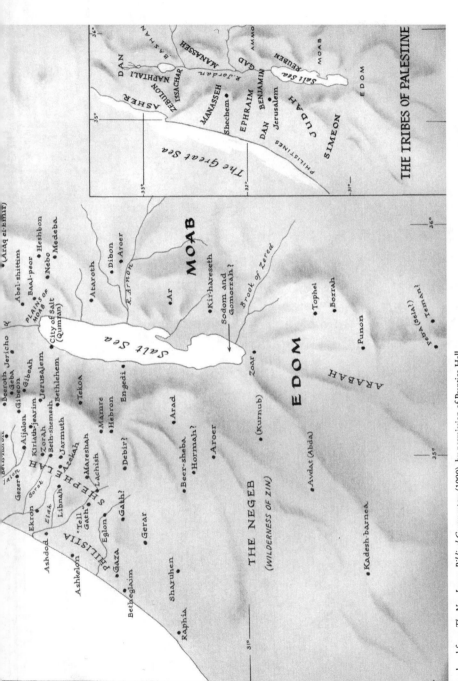

Reproduced from *The New Jerome Biblical Commentary* (1990), by permission of Prentice-Hall.

6
Messianic Prophecies

ISAIAH 5–12

INTRODUCTION

The Prophetic Tradition

The Prophets of Ancient Israel spoke to their contemporaries about their own times. Their words, however, lived on and became tools for understanding new experiences of God. Classical Israelite prophecy begins in the eighth century, B.C.E. Amos and Hosea preach in the Northern Kingdom of Israel about the social injustice in their society and about the people's infidelity to God. At roughly the same time in the Southern Kingdom of Judah, the prophet Isaiah begins to preach in Jerusalem about his own society. Understanding these prophets historically can be complicated by many factors.

History of the Book

The book of *Isaiah* was compiled over five hundred years. To understand the text, it is helpful to sort out what goes back to the eighth century prophet and what have been expansions, further insights, and further applications. This is not an easy and obvious task. Sometimes even ideas that are completely different from the historical Isaiah have become part of the book traditionally attributed to him.

The awareness that the book comes from many voices and hands came slowly and over centuries. Already in the 11th century, C.E., Rabbi Abraham ibn Ezra (1040–1105) pointed out that the second half of the book of *Isaiah* was addressed to the Jerusalemites who had been deported to Babylon in the 6th century, B.C.E. By the early 19th century, most critical scholars understood *Isaiah* 1–39 and *Isaiah* 40–66 as First and Second Isaiah.

"First Isaiah"

Isaiah of Jerusalem is distinctive as a prophet because he focused on Jerusalem's city traditions with idea of the sacred city and a chosen dynasty rather than on the story of Israel with ideas of Exodus and covenant.* In the section of *Isaiah* included for discussion in this textbook, chapters 5–12, there are many different ideas, events, and voices. The next paragraphs offer comments on only selected ideas in some of the texts.

Chapter 5. After a parable* condemning Jerusalem's leadership for religious infidelity and social injustice, accusations are given regarding specific crimes of oppression of the poor by foreclosures of mortgages, luxurious living at the expense of those in need, neglect of the unfortunate in the community, and arrogance in the face of the sufferings of others.

Chapter 6. The vision in the temple depicts an awe-inducing experience of God as the source of all known to the author. Scholars have used this scene as a basic model of an encounter with the Sacred. In the text, Isaiah seems to have entered the Holy of Holies in the temple of Solomon and seen the stationary symbols on the Ark move within this confined space.

Chapter 7. The setting is the historical threat of invasion of Jerusalem and Judah by the Northern Kingdom (sometimes called Ephraim) in alliance with its neighbor the Kingdom of Aram/Syria, an event sometimes called the Syro-Ephraimite war. Just as the prophet is depicted in various other places in *Isaiah* 1–39, here Isaiah demands of the king complete trust in God (rather than trust in military strength and in alliances). King Ahaz's lack of faith and trust in God occasions Isaiah's oracle to the king about the birth of a child and the future destruction of the Northern Kingdom (which happened in 722) and the capture of Damascus, the capital of the Kingdom of Syria (in 732). Later on, Christians read the Immanuel ("God with us") prophecy in *Isaiah* 7:14 as a prediction of Jesus. Over the centuries, there was debate between Jews and Christians on the meaning, even the original wording, of the text. *Matthew* 1:23 quotes the verse in its Greek translation as *"a virgin shall conceive."* Thus, the text, in this way, is seen to anticipate both the Incarnation* and the Virgin Birth.

Chapters 9 and 11. Both chapters begin with sections (9:2–7; 11:1–9) that describe a new ruler. It is unclear whether these words come from the eighth century and portray a contemporary descendant of David. Or whether they are from a later century and perhaps describe a hoped-for true king that God would use for the fulfillment of the hope that the Davidic dynasty raised.

Christian Interpretation

These texts in *Christian usage* point out not only the demand for social justice but also the need for reflection on the nature of God. These chapters of *Isaiah* have also aided Christian thought about Jesus. Jesus is "God with us." This expression facilitates the idea of God coming in a human nature and walking with fellow human beings. The Christian understanding of Jesus as Messiah* involves the ideas of prophet, priest,* and king. The prophetic role might be seen in Chapter 9. The priestly role is connected with the Temple scene in chapter 6. And the royal function is etched in Chapter 11.

—*Dr. John J. Schmitt*

DISCUSSION QUESTIONS

1. Should religious texts like these, in which a prophet speaks against unjust governments on the basis of religious faith, provide support for our doing the same today? Why or why not?

2. To what degree does the depiction of God in chapter 6 resonate with your image of God or that of others you know? Why do you think Isaiah chose to recount this dramatic experience in the temple?

3. What, if anything, in these texts might help foster Jewish-Christian relations today? In what way?

4. Many texts in chapters 9 through 12, foretelling a brighter future, have become part of the Church's liturgy,* especially in the Advent and Christmas seasons, seasons of hope. Do you sense from the text that God will bring about this new age totally without human cooperation, or are we to be involved in some way?

7
Universal Salvation

ISAIAH 40; 52:13–53:12

INTRODUCTION

"Second Isaiah"

The name of the prophet in *Isaiah* 40–55, the prophet who speaks to the exiled Jerusalemites about the coming liberation from Babylon, is unknown. The prophet is called "Second Isaiah" because his words sometimes echo those of Isaiah of Jerusalem two centuries earlier and are part of that collection. Some Bible readers have said that the poetry of Second Isaiah is of the highest level in the Old Testament. The prophet repeats some of the themes of First Isaiah, especially the chosenness and holiness of the capital city of the former southern kingdom, Jerusalem or Zion.*

Because of the poetic structure of most of the material in Isaiah 40–55, the names Jerusalem and Zion* are often found in coupled lines. The group might be addressed as Jerusalem in one line of the couplet and as Zion in the next, or vice versa. It is also interesting to note that the dominant image and the way of addressing the audience changes within these sixteen chapters. In chapters 41–48, the predominant image and addressee is Israel/Jacob while in chapters 49–55 the theme and direct address is Zion/Jerusalem.

Chapter 40

Chapter 40 opens the combined two sections and offers themes that will recur in the following chapters, 41–55. These chapters also use themes from earlier parts of the book. The setting in chapter 40, a divine council, echoes chapter 6 and the reaction of the prophet there. The first two verses of chapter 40 depict God speaking and commanding others to comfort the exiles who, under the imagery of Jerusalem, have paid the price of their previous infidelity. The others that God addresses are the heavenly messengers who carry God's word. God is now going to deliver the exiles and lead them back to the holy city. The prophet's reaction is hesitation to take on this commission of preaching.

Zion* herself becomes the herald who proclaims that God is leading the people home. Yet God leads the people not as a king but as a shepherd. The tenderness of God is seen in v. 11, but the majesty of God is apparent in the following verses. This creating and liberating God is not like the god-statues of Babylon, man-made and in need of being carried around. The prophet, thus, employs and applies the theme of creation—this coming liberation is a new creation. In later chapters the theme of exodus is invoked—this future liberation is a new exodus.

In 40:27–31, there is focus on the faint-hearted, those in the exile who could not believe that any change would happen. Some were so dejected that hope seemed too remote. The prophet uses enormous energy to convince his hearers/readers that God will send deliverance. In the following chapters, the prophet names the instrument that God will use to bring about this salvation.* Cyrus is declared the anointed *(mashiach)* of the Lord.

Servant Songs

Within Isaiah 40–55, there is a sequence of four songs that present a mysterious figure, the servant of the Lord. These passages have been singled out by many for particular analysis. In the first song, 42:1–4, God is depicted as presenting the servant as God's prophet who will bring justice to many people and will care for the weak and faint-hearted. The second song, 49:1–6, has the servant speak about his acceptance of this special vocation to preach deliverance for the people and a light to all nations. In the third song, 50:4–11, the servant reports the difficulty of his vocation. Opposition against this figure is severe, but the servant knows that God will see him through this ministry of speaking truth and helping those discouraged.

The Suffering Servant

The final servant song, 52:13–53:12, tells an amazing story in a new literary structure. The depicted speaker in 52:13–15 is God. A chorus of observers recites 53:1–11. The last speaker is God, 53:12. The scene tells the tale of overwhelming opposition to the servant, the rejection, failure, persecution, and defeat of the servant. Yet the servant succeeds in his efforts: his word lives on and his victory is assured. The passage contains the Old Testament's only statement of an individual suffering for the sins of many others, becoming the sin-offering for others.

The identity of this servant has been a major debate over the millennia. Already in the New Testament, the question is asked, "*About whom does the prophet say this, about himself or about some one else?*" (Acts 8:34). What indeed did the text refer to when it was written? The answers have covered the range from an individual person to collective figure, from someone past to someone future, from king to prophet. Some today see the figure as the prophet of the exile; others see him as the great prophet of the past, Moses. Traditional Jewish interpretation understands the figure to be a personification of the people Israel.

Fully Realized in Jesus Christ

Christianity sees that the role of special prophet and of one who suffers ignominiously for others is ultimately fulfilled in Jesus and his sufferings. Indeed, the New Testament writers were greatly influenced by this passage. Paul had received the tradition about Jesus as one whom God had destined for this role of suffering and death and victory. It could well be that when the followers of Jesus continued the table fellowship of Jesus, they read passages such as these to ponder and to assist them in thinking about their risen Lord.

Thus, the *Christian significance* of these readings from Second Isaiah includes ideas of salvation* and liberation, re-creation and fulfillment, as in Chapter 40. In chapter 53, one sees a savior who suffered the depths of human nature and remained true to God, and whom God brought through victoriously.

—Dr. John J. Schmitt

DISCUSSION QUESTIONS

1. How does the depiction in chapter 40 of the heavenly council presided over by God correlate with any other biblical passages or with the experiences of most people?

2. In chapter 40 and in the chapters that follow, one sees the world transformed. What does it mean to participate in the transformation of the world?

3. How does the view of Jesus as the servant of the Lord fit with contemporary presentations of Jesus?

4. Does the success of the servant resonate with most images of public service or of prophecy today?

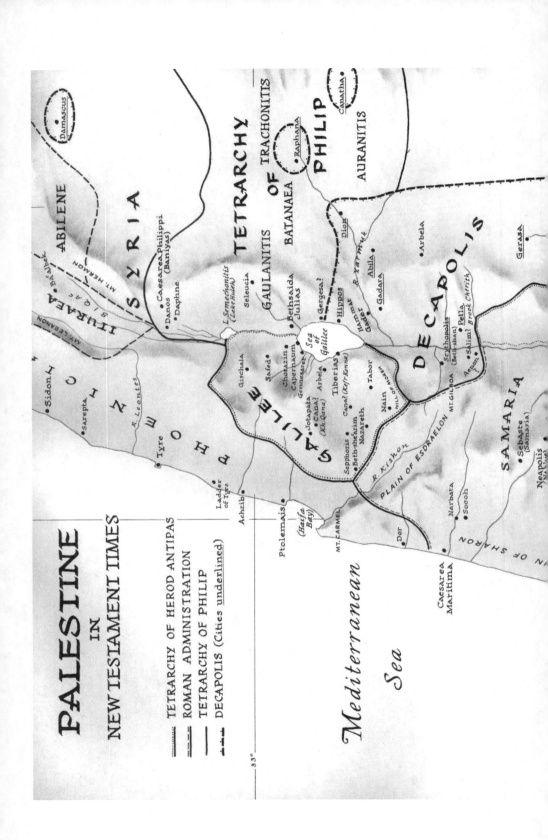

PALESTINE
IN
NEW TESTAMENT TIMES

.... TETRARCHY OF HEROD ANTIPAS
– – – – ROMAN ADMINISTRATION
———— TETRARCHY OF PHILIP
–·–·– DECAPOLIS (Cities underlined)

33°

Mediterranean Sea

PHOENICIA

SYRIA

ABILENE

ITURAEA

GALILEE

GAULANITIS

TETRARCHY OF TRACHONITIS

BATANAEA

PHILIP

AURANITIS

DECAPOLIS

SAMARIA

PLAIN OF ESDRAELON

PLAIN OF SHARON

Damascus
Baalbek
Mt. Lebanon
Mt. Hermon
Caesarea Philippi (Baniyas)
Danos
Daphne
Sidon
Sarepta
R. Leontes
Tyre
Ladder of Tyre
Achzib
Ptolemais
(Haifa Bay)
Mt. Carmel
Dor
Caesarea Maritima
Gischala
Safed
Chorazin
Capernaum
Gennesaret
L. Semechonitis (Lake Huleh)
Seleucia
Bethsaida Julias
Sea of Galilee
Gergesa?
Hippos
Hammat Gader
Jotapata
Canal (Kh. Qana)
Sepphoris
Beth-she'arim
Nazareth
Arbela
Cana? (Kefr Kenna)
Tiberias
Nain
Hill of Moreh
Tabor
R. Kishon
Narbata
Socoh
Sebaste (Samaria)
Neapolis
Raphana
Canatha
Dion
R. Yarmuk
Abila
Gadara
Arbela
Gerasa
Scythopolis (Beth-shan)
Pella
Salim
Aenon
Brook Cherith
Mt. Gilboa

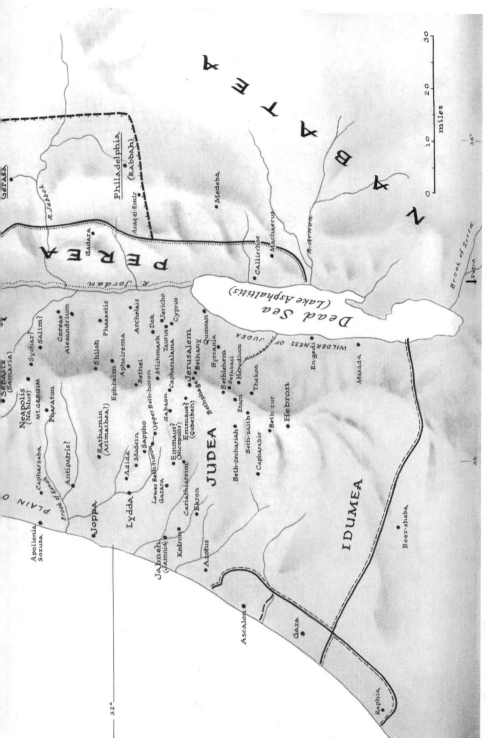

Reproduced from *The New Jerome Biblical Commentary* (1990), by permission of Prentice-Hall, Inc.

8

The Faith of Jesus

HEBREWS 1; 5; 10–13

INTRODUCTION

A Christological Sermon

This selection from *Hebrews* is located at this point in the book because it provides an ideal transition from OT to NT. Of all NT writings *Hebrews* offers the most extensive treatment of the OT, and is also most respectful of continuity. Traditionally known as *The Letter to the Hebrews,* scholars today agree that on the basis of its rhetorical devices and structure this mysterious document is not a letter at all, but a homily intended to be proclaimed aloud in various venues. Dating it anywhere from A.D.* 60 to 90, many surmise that it has, if not a Roman, at least an Italian origin (see 13:24). It may have been directed to Asia Minor churches, in any event to Jewish converts who after leaving Judaism were anxious about forgiveness of sins. The author teaches that Jesus Christ offered a once-for-all sacrifice (10:10) for sin which is fully and eternally effective before God in heaven, unlike Levitical Temple sacrifices which were offered daily but ineffective (10:11). The OT itself prefigures this priesthood of Christ in Melchizedek, "*king of Salem and priest of the most high God*" who blessed Abraham (7:1; see *Gen* 14:17–20), to which God himself witnesses in Psalm 110:4 (7:17). Not only Melchizedek, but Moses (3:1–6) and Abraham (11:17–20) as two founders of the Jewish faith are also presented as types which Jesus brought to their fulfillment in his own person through his life, death, and resurrection.

God Spoke Through a Son

According to *Hebrews* 1:1–2, the God who "spoke" himself outwardly in the past—not only in the beauty, order, power, and goodness of the world (*Gen* 1), but also in the words and deeds of the OT prophets—has now said himself completely in a Son through whom he created the world. All things exist, then, only by their participation in this fulness of God's self-manifestation: his Word made flesh. But *how* has God spoken through Jesus Christ? For *Hebrews* the answer can be expressed in a single word: "faith"—Jesus' faith in God the Father. Although the beginning chapters of the document stress the *obedience* of Jesus more than his faith, the author makes clear that the two are the same (3:18–19), so that Jesus' faith consists in his always doing the Father's will, even unto death (10:9–10). *Hebrews* therefore encourages its readers to live lives of obedience to God's will as Jesus did, no matter what sufferings may come in the process (e.g., 12:3–11; 13:12–13). Indeed, it is only through suffering that faith will be made perfect in them as it was in Christ (5:9).

Jesus' Saving Faith: As we know, to believe in someone is to trust, or to *en*trust one's self to them. Consequently faith in God is more than mere *notional* assent to revealed truth. It is the giving of one's whole life over to God who is wholly Other. For *Hebrews*, Christian faith is a participation in Jesus' own faith, his loving obedience to the Father's will throughout his life, his learning to conform all of his own desires to the Father's heart (5:7–10). Therefore, although it includes sincere confession with the mouth (*Rom* 10:10), because its "source" or principle is the death-conquering sacrificial faith of Jesus himself, Christian faith is primarily the hearing and responding to God's will, his own mind and heart, in all of one's actions. According to *Hebrews*, therefore, all that is needed for human beings to attain the salvation* won in Christ is to open themselves up to receive and allow him to realize in their lives (5:9: "*who obey him*") the victorious faith he enacted in his own humanity on earth, by their offering themselves in his "*once-for-all*" (10:10) self-offering to the Father.

OT Witnesses of Jesus' Saving Faith

As proof of this fact, the author spends a whole chapter (11) recalling "*a cloud of witnesses*" (12:2) to Jesus' faith, from Abel to David and the prophets, to demonstrate that Jesus' faith was already present and realized in their lives of obedience, and how God spoke and continues to speak himself today in Christ through those very same lives of faith (11:4). At the end of this litany of holy Old Testament witnesses, the author concludes by saying that Jesus is "*the originator and the fulfiller of faith*" (12:2b). That is to say, through his life, death, and resurrection Jesus *originated* and *brought to fulfillment* in his own person that single, *faith*ful humanity into which people throughout history by their lives of faith are taken up and united to God.

Unity in Christ

Here we see that for *Hebrews*, God the Father speaks himself out fully to the world in the Son's own fully giving himself back to the Father in his sacrificial death on the cross. Furthermore, anyone who by the gift of the Holy Spirit truly believes in Christ—by their own offering of faith—is united to the Father by virtue of Jesus' sacrificial faith acting within them, so that God continues to "speak" in Christ through them as well. *Hebrews* stresses, however, that all who are truly united to Christ in his historically saving faith in the Father must by that very fact also be united to one another. Indeed, their oneness with Christ is not only expressed but also enacted precisely through their union to one another in the Church, the community in Christ's faith, particularly in its liturgical celebration as highpoint of its enactment of that faith (10:23–25; 13:14–15).

—*Rev. John D. Laurance, S. J.*

DISCUSSION QUESTIONS

1. What similarities in theology*, if any, are there between *Genesis* 1 and the beginning of *Hebrews?* Explain.

2. Are there any indications in the text of *Hebrews* 1; 5; 10–13 that the author sees Jesus prefigured in the Servant described in *Isaiah* 52:13–53:12? Explain.

3. *Hebrews* 11:1 states that "*faith is the assurance of things hope for, the conviction of things not seen,*" and yet the document itself seems to state that faith was clearly to be seen in many OT witnesses and most fully in Jesus. How would you explain this seeming discrepancy?

4. What does the author mean by his saying, "*let us go forth to him outside the camp*" (13:13)? What is the OT origin of this image, "*outside the camp*"? And in light of its context here in *Hebrews*, what might it suggest about how to live authentic Christian life today?

9

The Good News of Salvation

THE GOSPEL OF MARK

INTRODUCTION

Authorship, Place, and Date of Writing

Ancient tradition attributes this Gospel to "John Mark," the companion of Paul and Barnabas mentioned in *Acts* (12:12, 25; 13:5–13; 15:37–39) and elsewhere (*Colossians* 4:10; *Philemon* 24; *2 Timothy* 4:11), and holds that this Mark was acquainted with Peter (see, e.g., *1 Peter* 5:13), perhaps acting as his amanuensis or secretary. Tradition also holds that Mark's Gospel was written in Rome. None of this can be confirmed by external or internal testimony, that is, from separate independent witnesses or from clues in the text itself. There is a strong consensus, however, that this Gospel was composed around the year 70 C.E., during the Jewish Revolt against Rome and possibly right after news of the Temple's destruction had reached the author.

It is commonly held that Mark's Gospel was known to and used by *Matthew* and *Luke*, who incorporated large parts of it—often word-for-word—into their Gospels. The various theories as to which

Gospel was written first and who copied from whom and in what order comprise "The Synoptic Problem," since these "Synoptic" Gospels "see" (Greek: *opt-*) together or "in the same way" *(syn-).*

An Outline of the Gospel

All four New Testament Gospels have been referred to as "Passion* Narratives with long introductions," and this rightly emphasizes the primary goal of these writings: to portray Jesus Christ as crucified, died, and risen. They are, therefore, depictions of the *kerygma,* the preached message of Good News. Consequently, the "plot" of each provides explicit and implicit answers to such questions as What did Jesus say and do? Who killed him? Why? What did his followers think and do? What are the Gospel's readers/hearers to do? And each of the Gospel-writers (or Evangelists) has a discernible point of view—a specific theology*, including various estimates as to the respective roles of the divine and human will in the events of salvation.*

There is no Birth Narrative, such as we find in *Matthew* and *Luke,* and no extensive Prologue, as in *John.* Broadly, the first half of the Gospel, *Mark* 1–8, concerns the "public ministry" of Jesus; in *Mark* 9–16, though public activities continue, the emphasis is more and more on "private instruction," as Jesus prepares his followers for his death. The central section of the Gospel includes the following:

8:27–30 Peter's confession of faith;

8:31–33 The first prediction (of three) of the Passion* (suffering);

8:34–9:1 Conditions of discipleship ("If anyone would come after me . . .");

9:2–9 The Transfiguration: an anticipation of glory.

Framing the whole narrative are accounts of Jesus' *baptism* and *death,* which seem to be composed as a deliberate pair (in literary criticism: an *inclusio*) marking the beginning and ending of his earthly, Spirit-led mission:

(Mark 1:16–20) The Call of Simon Peter and Andrew. Late Fifth-Century Mosaic, The Church of San Apollinare Nuovo, Ravenna, Italy.
© Scala/Art Resource

Jesus' baptism (1:9–11)	Jesus' death (15:37–39)
1:10a Heavens split open (Greek: *schizomai*)	15:38a Temple curtain split in two (Greek: *schizomai*)
1:10b The Spirit descends (Greek: *pneuma*)	15:37 Jesus "expires" (Greek: *ek-pneuo*)
1:11 Voice from heaven: the "beloved Son . . ."	15:39 Human voice: "God's Son"

We know from contemporary sources that the huge Temple curtain was embroidered with the sun and moon and stars (but *not,* of course, the zodiac); it thus imitated the actual heavens. Likewise, the "voice" at Jesus' death is human—and Gentile (non-Jewish)! This is one of many clues that *Mark* was addressing a chiefly Gentile audience and expected missionary work among Gentiles to continue.

Mark's Understanding of Jesus

Mark's Christology* (his understanding of Jesus' humanity, divinity, and mission) is often described as "low" in comparison with, say, the "high" Christology of the Gospel of *John.* But perhaps it is fairer to describe it as relatively undeveloped, especially in its metaphysical aspect. The cry from the cross, "My God, my God, why have you forsaken me?" is sometimes cited as evidence of Jesus' sense of abandonment in death. But it is more appropriately seen as modeling a faithful, even pious, response to a personal crisis: the quotation of Scripture (here, *Psalm* 22:1) as the word and power of God. The continuation of this Old Testament "lament" psalm leaves no doubt that the one who prays it trusts God to deliver the soul from eternal death.

Mark's favorite title for Jesus is "Son of Man," which at first sight appears to stress only Jesus' humanity. There is a continuing debate as to what this title likely meant *before Mark* wrote his Gospel (e.g., simply "every person," or "I, myself," or perhaps an apocalyptic figure, whether individual or collective; see *Daniel* 7:13). But in *Mark,* Jesus as "Son of Man" has three tasks or roles:

- he forgives sins—see 2:1–12, especially 2:7: only *God* can forgive!;
- he will come again—see 14:62, in response to the high priest's question;
- he suffers—see especially 10:45: "to give his life as a ransom for many."

Not surprisingly, Jesus is endowed with many special powers. He can read people's minds, perform miracles, and predict the future; he knows the Scriptures just as his life is shaped by them. For example, the brief Temptation story (1:12–13) echoes both the Israelites' forty years of wandering in the wilderness after the Exodus and the creation narrative in *Genesis* 2. But in him everything is also being renewed: for *Mark,* this Son of Man is without precedent (9:7), and he brings "a new teaching" (1:27).

The Parables*

Most characteristic of Jesus' public ministry in *Mark* is his teaching "in parables." This is in contrast to his later private instruction, which (ironically) is spoken "plainly" or "openly" (8:32). A parable* (Greek: *parabol*)is a story that compares two things, "placing" (from the verb *ballo,* "to put, place, throw") the one "next to" or "alongside" *(para-)* the other. For *Mark,* the parables at the same time reveal and conceal something about the Kingdom of God. In any case, as *Mark* sees it, the parables defy the popular modern understanding of them as "simple illustrations of faith" or the like. Instead, they are a window onto reality as God sees it—a vision of a new world.

The parables also create or make plain a distinction between "insiders" and "outsiders," a theme in *Mark* that naturally makes some readers uncomfortable. In 4:10–12, for example, right after the Parable of the Sower, Jesus speaks of himself as re-enacting the ministry of the prophet Isaiah (see *Isaiah* 6): he says he speaks in parables not only to *include* but also to *exclude* in light of the imminent and unavoidable judgment of God. (Not surprisingly, both *Matthew* and *Luke* "soften" this apparently deterministic teaching.)

Other Markan Themes:

- the disciples are regularly depicted as lacking understanding or faith—see, e.g., 4:40; 8:33;
- Jesus keeps his mission and identity secret—see, e.g., 3:12; 8:30; 9:9;
- but the demons know who he is—see, e.g., 1:34; 3:11;
- Galilee (in northern Israel) is regarded positively, Judea (in the south) negatively;
- trusting in Jesus will include experiencing persecutions— see, e.g., 4:17; 10:30;
- "the Kingdom of God is at hand!"—see, e.g., 1:14–15; 13:1–37.

The Ending of Mark

Mark's Gospel ends abruptly, by ancient or modern reckoning (see 16:8). The last few words do "make sense" grammatically, but there is no summing up, no final command, no hint as to what might happen next in the life of the young Church. It was therefore common in previous eras to consider the book incomplete, perhaps because of an accident of some sort: Mark's premature death, or the loss of a page or two of a codex (book) copy of the text. But with few exceptions, the consensus of modern authorities is both that Mark *intended* to end at 16:8 and that someone else later *added* 16:9–20, the extra twelve verses supplying a post-resurrection narrative (appearances, instructions) much like those in *Matthew, Luke,* and *John.*

—*Dr. Julian V. Hills*

DISCUSSION QUESTIONS

1. What is "good" about the Good News in *Mark* (see 1:1)? What would a "Markan" congregation look like, then or now?

2. Few western Christians believe in the imminent (or even relatively near) end of the world. To what extent can we separate *Mark*'s overall message from his eschatological* urgency?

3. Who, do you think, is the mysterious "young man" who flees naked in 14:51–52? (The same Greek word, *neaniskos,* "youth," reappears in 16:5.) An angel? A hypothetical believer? Mark?

4. What reason(s) can you think of why Mark presents the disciples as so slow to understand who Christ is (e.g., 6:52; 8:21; 8:33; 10:37)? Would Mark say the same thing of most Christians today? Why or why not?

THE WORLD OF THE NEW TESTAMENT
ROME AND THE EASTERN MEDITERRANEAN

Boundary of the Roman Empire   Provincial boundaries   + Seven Churches of Asia

| 0 | 100 | 200 | 300 | 400 | 500 miles |

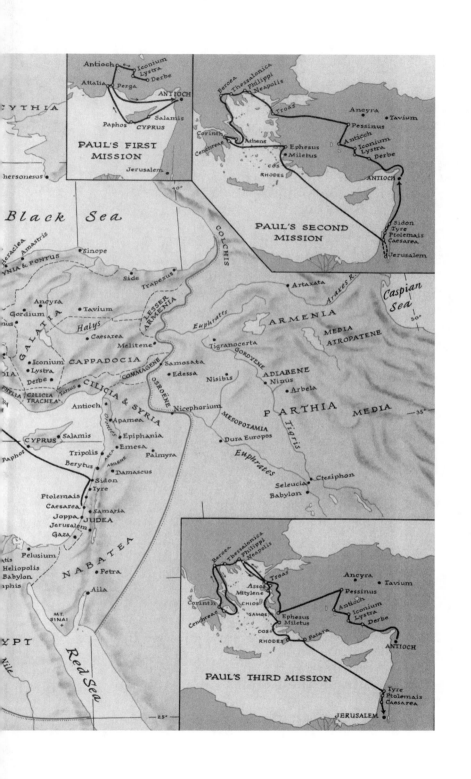

PAUL'S FIRST MISSION

PAUL'S SECOND MISSION

PAUL'S THIRD MISSION

10

The Grace of Christ

GALATIANS

INTRODUCTION

Paul's Writings

The Apostle* Paul is the only individual of the New Testament era from whom we have original, personal writings. In terms of New Testament literature, Paul is clearly the most influential apostolic figure. He is responsible for thirteen of the New Testament letters, although many scholars think that only seven of these *(Romans, 1 and 2 Corinthians, Galatians, Philippians, 1 Thessalonians and Philemon)* were written by Paul himself. The others *(Ephesians, Colossians, 2 Thessalonians and the Pastoral Epistles: 1 Timothy, 2 Timothy and Titus)* are often called the pseudo-Paulines and may have been written by disciples of the apostle, following his death, in order to carry on his literary and theological tradition. Paul's personal writings are also the earliest literature which we possess from the Christian movement. Paul wrote letters to his fledgling churches during the late forties and throughout the fifties of the first century, and so his writings antedate our written gospels by several decades. *1 Thessalonians* is often thought to be his earliest letter, written in about 48 C.E. Again, because of their antiquity, Paul's writings are of unparalleled importance for understanding early Christianity's history and theology.*

Paul's Life

The most reliable information for writing a biography of Paul comes from the letters he himself wrote, and much of this kind of information can be drawn from the *Epistle to the Galatians.* Paul was a Jew born in the Hellenized atmosphere of the *diaspora** at the very beginning of the Common Era. He was educated as a Pharisee, that is, an expert teacher and interpreter of the Jewish scriptures. He was also well educated in Greek grammar, rhetoric and philosophy, spoke Greek as his everyday language and used the Greek translation of the Old Testament for purposes of study, although he probably also knew Hebrew. He was not a disciple of the earthly Jesus and was, in fact, personally involved in persecuting early Christian believers as heretical to Judaism. In approximately 35 or 36 C.E. Paul had a visionary experience, a revelation,* as a result of which he came to accept Jesus as Messiah* and Son of God and experienced himself called by God's grace* (1:15) to be an apostle (a Christian missionary preacher) to the Gentiles in particular. He became associated with an established missionary effort toward the Gentiles, and went on numerous journeys through Greece and Asia Minor.

During his career as an apostle, Paul had contact with those who had followed Jesus during his earthly career and who were leaders of the mission to the Jews of the older Christian community in Jerusalem. He received the tradition about Jesus from those who had known him during his earthly life, and he mentions his encounters with Peter, James, and John especially. However, Paul also had some serious disagreements with these individuals, as *Galatians* 2 shows.

On his missionary journeys Paul worked as a craftsman to support himself, preaching in synagogues and in work places, gradually gathering converts. He remained in a city or town long enough to establish a viable community with local leadership, and then he moved on. Often his new churches had questions and insecurities about their new beliefs and community life. Sometimes other Christian missionaries, bringing different versions of the new Christian story, would enter these Pauline churches, causing great confusion and distress. Paul kept in contact with his churches by writing letters, which served as a vehicle for his presence and his teaching, answering their questions, admonishing, warning, correcting and comforting them.

At the end of his life Paul collected a sum of money from his Gentile churches for the support of the Jewish Christians in Jerusalem. This "collection" expressed the unity of Jews and Gentiles as believers. However, it is uncertain whether this collection was accepted, since this unity was disputed at the time. Paul was probably arrested in Jerusalem, and he may have been taken to Rome. He probably died a martyr around A.D. 60. We have no certain knowledge of the time and manner of his death, but tradition has it that he died by the sword.

The Epistle

The Epistle to the Galatians was written during the 50's of the Common Era to a church founded by Paul, but ready to accept "another gospel" preached by other missionaries who arrived after Paul had left. Whereas Paul's gospel emphasizes how salvation* comes to human beings as *grace,** a free gift from God through faith in Jesus Christ and his suffering, death, and resurrection to overcome sin and death, that "different" gospel added circumcision and observance of the law of Moses to faith in Christ.

The Galatian Christians were converted by Paul from paganism. They had not previously been observant Jews. However, they were impressed with the authority and knowledge of the newly arrived Jewish missionaries. The message and status of these missionaries challenged Paul's authority over the Galatian community. In response to their challenge and to the Galatians' rejection of Paul and his gospel, Paul presents a strong scriptural argument in support of his understanding of salvation in Jesus Christ from those same Jewish scriptures. For this reason, the *Epistle to the Galatians* is especially useful for appreciating the continuities and contrasts between the Jewish faith and Christianity or between the Old and New Testaments. It was Paul's intention to explain that very thing to his confused converts.

—*Dr. Carol L. Stockhausen*

DISCUSSION QUESTIONS

1. What do you think Paul means when he writes in chapter 2: "*I have been crucified with Christ; it is no longer I who live, but Christ who lives in me*"? (Paul was still alive and so had obviously not *literally* been crucified.)

2. In chapter 3 Paul scolds his readers: "*O foolish Galatians! Who has bewitched you, before whose eyes Jesus Christ was publicly portrayed as crucified*!" Jesus had long since died and rose from the dead by the time the Galatians first heard of him. So, then, what do you think Paul means here by "*before whose eyes*"?

3. "*You're goina havta serve somebody,*" sings Bob Dylan in one of his songs. Before their receiving faith in Jesus Christ, according to Paul whom or what were the Galatians forced to serve? In what way? And why, do you think, St. Paul refers to the service of Christ as "freedom"—the opposite of slavery?

4. Explain in your own words, arguing on the basis of the text, what you think St. Paul means in this epistle by the word "flesh."

11
The Body of Christ
1 CORINTHIANS 10–15

The Corinthians

During his missionary travels, Paul had founded the Christian community at Corinth. Subsequently, through oral reports and in a letter sent him by the community, he became aware of problems there. *1 Corinthians* consists of responses to the reports and letter. The problems Paul addresses reflect at root a selfish individualism or factiousness in the community. Many of the Corinthian Christians believe that all that is important is to "know" the fact of their salvation,* and that this knowledge in fact liberates them from duties of love to their fellow Christians or even to Christ.

The Gospel

Paul therefore begins his letter by reminding the Corinthians of the message he preached to them. This message was the message of the Cross. Contrary to all worldly wisdom and all expectations, God's power is manifested in Christ's humbling of himself and finally acceptance of death. Christians must imitate Christ in living not for themselves but for their fellow Christians—together, Christ's Body. The supreme gift of the Holy Spirit to Christians is therefore love, loving service and self-sacrifice to Christ's Body. Paul's own work as an apostle exemplifies such love, and his authority is exercised through a call to the Corinthians to imitate him in imitating Christ. (This last point is developed further in *2 Corinthians* in response to more explicit challenges among the Corinthians to Paul's authority).

Problems

These principles are applied to the specifics of the Corinthian problems. Major points from your reading are as follows:

(1) **Meat from pagan sacrifices** (10). Just as most of the Israelites in the desert on the Exodus from Egypt came to grief through their lack of fidelity, even as they were being saved *("baptized . . . in the cloud and sea")* and nourished with *"supernatural food and drink"* (10:3–4), so will the Corinthians perish if they are not faithful to Christ who nourishes them in the Eucharist* with his own body and blood.

(2) **The Eucharist and Christian life** (11:17–34). The Eucharist or Lord's Supper is a proclamation of Christ's death, by which he gave himself up for us to establish a covenant* relationship with us. To celebrate it in a context of selfishness and division is to violate its very nature, to reject the Christ who at the Last Supper and in his death shared himself completely. Such a violation results in condemnation rather than blessing.

(3) **Spiritual gifts and love** (12–14). The work of the Spirit is to affirm Jesus Christ. Spiritual gifts such as wisdom, knowledge, faith, healing, miracles, prophecy, discernment of spirits, praying in tongues and their interpretation (12:8–10) manifest God's presence and power and love and are not given for self-aggrandizement but for the good of the entire Body of Christ. The greatest such gift is therefore love.

(4) The resurrection (15). The Corinthians already believe that Christ is risen—this was the faith Paul received and passed on to them; if it is not true, their faith is in vain and they who have lived and died for Christ are pitiable. But if Christ is risen, then the members of his Body will also rise. In response to skepticism about bodily resurrection, Paul insists that resurrection is not mere resuscitation of a corpse but will change their corruptible (mortal) bodies into an incorruptible (immortal) form, as different from their present bodies as a plant is from its seed. Their transformation, not yet complete, can only be completed after death or when Christ returns at the end of time if they subject themselves to the Father in Christ.

—Rev. William S. Kurz, S.J.

DISCUSSION QUESTIONS

1. In chapter 10 what do you suppose St. Paul means when he says, "*that rock was Christ*"? Surely he doesn't mean that Christ was literally a rock.

2. What do you suppose St. Paul means in chapter 11 by eating "*without recognizing the body?*" What "body" does he have in mind, and how is one to "recognize" the body? (Or bodies?) What is your evidence in the text?

3. Within the theology* of St. Paul presented in these chapters why does it make perfect sense that love is the greatest of all the gifts? (Chapters 12–13).

4. Why is it, according to St. Paul, that Christ's resurrection is so important for us? Just because Christ rose from the dead why should we think that those who believe in him will rise as well? (Chapter 15).

II
Christian Tradition

Assumption of the Virgin, by Titian. © Scala/Firenze

12

Bishops, Presbyters, and Deacons

To the Magnesians 1–9

ST. IGNATIUS OF ANTIOCH (CA.117)

INTRODUCTION

Ignatius' Life

We know nothing of Ignatius of Antioch other than what can be deduced from the seven letters he wrote to Christian communities as a prisoner en route to Rome. He is also called Theophorus, which means "God-clad" or "bearing God." He was a bishop* in Antioch who was arrested by Roman authorities and brought to Rome for death in the amphitheatre where he was martyred about 117, probably during the reign of Trajan. During his journey, Ignatius made a lengthy stay at Smyrna, where he met with representatives of a number of Christian communities in Asia Minor and sent letters to the Christians of Ephesus, Magnesia, and Tralles. The general message was to beware of heretics and to submit to ecclesiastical authority.

From Smyrna he also sent a letter to Rome telling the Christians there not to try to save him, saying *"I am the wheat of God, and I must be ground by the teeth of wild beasts that I may become the pure bread of God"* (4.1). From Troas he wrote to the churches of Philadelphia and Smyrna as well as a letter to Polycarp. The first use of the word "catholic" to refer to the universal church is attributed to Ignatius (*Letter to the Symrnaeans*, 8:2).

Theological Themes

The major themes in Ignatius' writings are: (1) the importance of maintaining Christian unity in love and sound doctrine,* (2) the role of the bishop*, presbyters, and deacons* in maintaining Christian unity, (3) the Eucharist* as the "medicine of immorality," and (4) Christian martyrdom. The overarching theme is unity. Mutual love and correct doctrine* serve this unity. Obedience to church authority ensures unity of belief.

Ignatius stressed the real humanity and historical existence of Jesus against the teaching of the Docetists, the heretics about whom he warned in his letters to the Christian communities. Ignatius insisted that Jesus Christ was *truly* born, was *truly* persecuted, was *truly* crucified, *truly* died, and was *truly* raised from the dead. The Docetists believed that Jesus only appeared to suffer and was not really human. Ignatius wrote to the Trallians, *"But if, as some godless people, that is, unbelievers, say, he suffered in mere appearance—being themselves mere appearances—why am I in bonds?"* (*Letter to the Trallians*, 9–10). Ignatius viewed his impending violent death as a testimony to his belief in the true reality of Jesus Christ as fully human and fully divine.

The Eucharist also reflects the unity of the church. *"Take care, then, to use one Eucharist, so that whatever you do, you do according to God: for there is one Flesh of our Lord Jesus Christ, and one cup in the union of His Blood; one altar as there is one bishop with the presbytery and my fellow servants, the deacons"* (*Letter to the Philadelphians*, 4:1). That Eucharist is valid which is offered by the bishop or by one authorized by the bishop (*Letter to the Smyrnaeans*, 8:1). The Eucharist reflects the true teaching about Jesus full humanity. Ignatius says that "*the heretics abstain from Eucharist because they do not allow that the Eucharist is the flesh of Christ*" (*Letter to the Smyrnaeans*, 6).

Ignatius embraced martyrdom as a way of uniting himself to God. In his letter to the Romans he writes: "*I bid all men know that of my own free will I die for God, unless ye should hinder me . . . Let me be given to the wild beasts, for through them I can attain unto God.*" (Rom. 4)

Historical Questions

Ignatius' description of a church order reflecting a threefold office of bishop, presbyters, and deacons* raises questions for historians because no other source unequivocally corroborates this threefold order until Hermas and Irenaeus in the middle of the second century. Thus historians question the extent to which Ignatius' description of church order represented church order as it existed in his day, although this threefold order did develop into the present hierarchal structure of the church. At any rate, these terms do not exactly mean what they do for us today. For example, in Ignatius' day, a bishop was more the equivalent of what we know as a pastor of a church. Ignatius description of the episcopacy does not include the idea of apostolic succession*, which would be prominent in Irenaeus. Nor is the bishop described in priestly terms he is in the *Apostolic Tradition* (ca A.D. 215). The major role of the threefold authority for Ignatius was to protect the unity of the church in its doctrinal teaching. The age of the apostles* had passed and the church was threatened by heretical teaching. Obedience to the authority of the bishop ensured purity of doctrine.*

For Ignatius the bishop represented the Father, the presbyters were councilors advising the bishop and represented the council of the apostles, and deacons were entrusted with the service of Jesus Christ. In our own day bishops are seen to represent Christ the High Priest and govern an area of the church called a diocese, presbyters are priests and co-workers with the bishop, and deacons assist bishops and priests in the ministry of the word, the liturgy*, and works of charity.

—*Dr. Susan K. Wood, SCL*

TEXT

Michael W. Holmes, editor and revisor of 1891 J. B. Lightfoot translation. *The Apostolic Fathers: Greek Texts and English Translations.* Grand Rapids, MI: Baker Books, 1999. ("To the Magnesians" pp. 151–155)

Ignatius, who is also called Theophorus, to the Church at Magnesia on the Maeander, which has been blessed through the grace* of God the Father in Christ Jesus our Savior, in whom I greet her and wish her heartiest greetings in God the Father and in Jesus Christ.

5   **1.** When I learned how well-ordered your love toward God is, I rejoiced and resolved to address you in the faith of Jesus Christ. For inasmuch as I have been judged worthy to bear a most godly name, in these chains which I bear I sing the praises of the churches, and I pray that in them there may be a union of flesh and spirit that comes

10   from Jesus Christ, our never-failing life, and of faith and love, to which nothing is preferable, and—what is more important—of Jesus and the Father. In him we will, if we patiently endure all the abuse of the ruler of this age and escape, reach God.

2. So, then, I was permitted to see you in the persons of Damas,

15   your godly bishop, your worthy presbyters Bassus and Apollonius, and my fellow servant, the deacon* Zotion; may I enjoy his company, because he is subject to the bishop as to the grace of God, and to the presbytery as to the law of Jesus Christ.

3. Indeed, it is right for you also not to take advantage of the youth-

20   fulness of your bishop, but to give him all the respect due him in accordance with the power of God the Father, just as I know that the holy presbyters likewise have not taken advantage of his youthful appearance, but yield to him as one who is wise in God; yet not really to him, but to the Father of Jesus Christ, the Bishop of all. For the

honor, therefore, of him who loved you it is right to be obedient with- 25
out any hypocrisy, for it is not so much a matter of deceiving this bishop
who is seen, but of cheating the One who is unseen. In such a case he
must reckon not with the flesh but with God, who knows our secrets.

4. It is right, therefore, that we not just be called Christians, but
that we actually be Christians, unlike some who call a man "bishop" 30
but do everything without regard for him. Such men do not appear
to me to act in good conscience, inasmuch as they do not validly meet
together in accordance with the commandment.

5. Seeing then that all things have an end, two things together lie
before us, death and life, and everyone will go to his own place. For 35
just as there are two coinages, the one of God and the other of the
world, and each of them has its own stamp impressed upon it, so the
unbelievers bear the stamp of this world, but the faithful in love bear
the stamp of God the Father through Jesus Christ, whose life is not
in us unless we voluntarily choose to die into his suffering. 40

6. Since, therefore, in the persons mentioned above I have by faith
seen and loved the whole congregation, I have this advice: Be eager to
do everything in godly harmony, the bishop presiding in the place of
God and the presbyters in the place of the council of the apostles* and
the deacons, who are most dear to me, having been entrusted with the 45
service of Jesus Christ, who before the ages was with the Father and
appeared at the end of time. Let all, therefore, accept the same attitude as God and respect one another, and let no one regard his
neighbor in merely human terms but in Jesus Christ love one another
always. Let there be nothing among you which is capable of dividing 50
you, but be united with the bishop and with those who lead, as an
example and a lesson of incorruptibility.

7. Therefore as the Lord did nothing without the Father, either by
himself or through the apostles (for he was united with him), so you
must not do anything without the bishop and the presbyters. Do not 55
attempt to convince yourselves that anything done apart from the
others is right, but, gathering together, let there be one prayer, one
petition, one mind, one hope, with love and blameless joy, which is

Jesus Christ, than whom nothing is better. Let all of you run together as to one temple of God, as to one altar, to one Jesus Christ, who came forth from one Father and remained with the One and returned to the One.

8. Do not be deceived by strange doctrines* or antiquated myths, since they are worthless. For if we continue to live in accordance with Judaism, we admit that we have not received grace*. For the most godly prophets lived in accordance with Christ Jesus. This is why they were persecuted, being inspired as they were by his grace in order that those who are disobedient might be fully convinced that there is one God who revealed himself through Jesus Christ his Son, who is his Word which came forth from silence, who in every respect pleased him who sent him.

9. If, then, those who had lived in antiquated practices came to newness of hope, no longer keeping the Sabbath but living in accordance with the Lord's day, on which our life also arose through him and his death (which some deny), the mystery through which we came to believe, and because of which we patiently endure, in order that we might be found to be disciples of Jesus Christ, our only teacher, how can we possibly live without him, whom even the prophets, who were his disciples in the Spirit, were expecting as their teacher? Because of this he for whom they rightly waited raised them from the dead when he came.

The complete texts of the letters of St. Ignatius of Antioch are available online at: http://www.earlychristianwritings.com/ignatius.html.

DISCUSSION QUESTIONS

1. How is Ignatius' concern for the unity of the church reflected in this text?

2. What are the roles of bishop, presbyters, and deacons according to this text? What are the responsibilities of the people toward their pastoral leaders?

3. What is the meaning of suffering and persecution for Ignatius? Find lines in the text which support your answer.

4. Comparing this text to *Hebrews* 11:24–27 and *1 Peter* 1:10–11, what do you think Ignatius means in paragraph 9 by asserting that the OT prophets, who lived before the birth of Jesus Christ, were already "*his disciples in the Spirit?*"

13

The Sunday Eucharist
The First Apology 1, 65–67

ST. JUSTIN MARTYR (165)

INTRODUCTION

Background

This selection from *The First Apology* of St. Justin Martyr belongs to that era in church history known as the "Apostolic Fathers," the time between the death of the last Apostle, St. John the Evangelist (ca. A.D. 96), and the "Patristic* Age" beginning with the first "Father of the Church," St. Irenaeus of Lyons (ca. 185). A philosopher and Christian apologist, Justin (ca. 100–165) was born of pagan parents at Flavia Neopolis (ancient Shechem, modern Nablus) in Samaria. In his search for truth, he first tested out the teachings of the Stoics, then the Peripatetics, and finally the Pythagoreans before encountering an old man by the seashore who revealed to him the wisdom of Christianity (ca. 130). Baptized, Justin became a teacher of Christianity, first at Ephesus and then at Rome where he founded a school, arriving there during the reign of Emperor Antoninus Pius (138–161). It was probably during the prefecture of Junius Rusticus (163–167) that he refused to offer sacrifice to the Roman gods, and so was scourged and then beheaded for the faith.

Structure of the Eucharistic Celebration

"Apology" here means an *explanation* directed to non-Christians, especially those in power, of the reasonableness of the Christian faith and of the probity and good citizenship of Christians. *The First Apology* was composed sometime between A.D. 148 and 161 and, as is evident from its opening chapter, addressed mainly to the Roman emperor, Antoninus Pius, in whose hands lay the physical safety of the Church. Chapters 65–67 of *The First Apology* describes first the Christian liturgy* of baptism culminating in a eucharistic celebration, and then the Eucharist* of a typical Sunday. From these two descriptions one can discern various elements in the order of a eucharistic celebration at the time: (1) the continual reading through of one biblical book at a time *(lectio continua)*; (2) a homily by the presider on the readings; (3) prayers of the faithful (as prescribed in *1 Timothy* 2:1–4); (4) the kiss of peace; (5) the offertory procession of gifts; (6) the presider's spontaneous rendering—according to a traditional pattern—of a eucharistic prayer, responded to with an "Amen" by the assembly; and (7) finally the distribution of the eucharisted bread and wine: the body and blood of the Lord, both to those present and absent.

Eucharist and Christian Life

In these selections from *The First Apology,* Justin also supplies his own theological understanding of Christ's real presence, and teaches how the liturgy is related to the ethical demands of ordinary Christian life. In addition to its being a thanksgiving to the Father for salvation* in Christ, the Eucharist* in the early Church was also understood as a solemn pledge to live a life of sacrifice for God and neighbor. This is clear from a contemporary document, *The Martyrdom of Polycarp* (ca. A.D. 155), where St. Polycarp of Smyrna prays just before his

Byzantine Mosaic, Three Angels at table under the Oak of Mamre and the Sacrifice of Isaac, from San Vitale Church in Ravenna, Italy.

© Scala/Art Resource

martyrdom by fire. In it the 86-year-old bishop of Smyrna prays, "*I give you thanks that you have counted me worthy . . . [to] . . . have a part in the number of your martyrs*," language similar both to the liturgical language used here by Justin: "*. . . for our being counted worthy to receive everything from him,*" and to that of eucharistic prayer of the 3rd century *Apostolic Tradition,* the next reading in this book: "*. . . giving you thanks that you have held us worthy to stand before you and give you priestly worship.*"

—*Rev. John D. Laurance, S.J.*

TEXT
Chapter 1—Address

To the Emperor Titus Ælius Adrianus Antoninus Pius Augustus Caesar, and to his son Verissimus the Philosopher, and to Lucius the Philosopher, the natural son of Caesar, and the adopted son of Pius, a lover of learning, and to the sacred Senate, with the whole People of the Romans, I, Justin, the son of Priscus and grandson of Bacchius, natives   5 of Flavia Neapolis in Palestine, present this address and petition in behalf of those of all nations who are unjustly hated and wantonly abused—myself among them.

Chapter 65—Sacraments of Initiation

After washing the one who believes and having joined him to our ranks, we then lead him to those who are called "brothers" to where they are assembled, in order to make communal prayers for ourselves and for the enlightened (baptized) one, and for all others everywhere, that through our works we may be counted worthy, now that we have learned the truth, to be considered good citizens and guardians of the commandments—that thus we be saved with an everlasting salvation.* After ending the prayers, we welcome one another with a kiss. There is then brought to the one who presides over the brothers bread and a cup of water and of mixed wine; and taking them, he sends up praise and glory to the Father of the universe through the name of the Son and of the Holy Spirit, and he makes a prolonged eucharist for our being counted worthy to receive everything from him. And when he has concluded the prayers and the eucharist, all the people present agree by saying "Amen." This word Amen in the Hebrew language signifies the *Genoito* ("Let it be so"). After the presider has made eucharist and all the people agreed, those whom we call "deacons" distribute to all present a sharing in the eucharisted bread and wine and water, and they carry [it] to those who are absent.

Chapter 66—Christ's Real Presence

And we call the food itself Eucharist, of which no one is allowed to partake except the one believing that what we teach is true—one who has been washed with the washing for remission of sins and regeneration, and who is living as Christ taught. For we do not take these to be ordinary bread and ordinary drink; but just as Jesus Christ our Savior, who was made flesh through the Word of God, possessed flesh and blood for our salvation*, so likewise have we been taught that the food which has

been eucharisted by the prayer of his word—and from which by metab-
olism our own blood and flesh are nourished—is the flesh and blood of
that Jesus who we have been taught was made flesh. For the apostles, in
the memoirs they composed called Gospels, handed on to us what they
were taught in the same way (1 Cor 11:23): that Jesus took bread and,   40
when he made the eucharist, said, **"Do this in remembrance of me,
this is my body;"** and that, in the same way, having taken the cup and
made the eucharist, he said, **"This is my blood;"** and to them alone did
he give it. The wicked devils in the mysteries of Mithras have taught
people to imitate this. For as you either know or have the power of find-   45
ing out, in their mystic rites of initiation bread and a cup of water are set
forth with certain incantations.

Chapter 67—The Sunday Eucharist*

Now after all this is over, we continually remind each other of these
things. And those who are well provided for come to the aid of all the
needy; and we are always present to each other. Over everything that we
offer we bless the Maker of all things through his Son Jesus Christ, and   50
through the Holy Spirit. And on the day named after the sun, there is a
gathering of all who live in cities or in the country into one place, and
the memoirs of the apostles or the writings of the prophets are read as
long as there is time; then, when the reader stops, the presider makes a
verbal exhortation that we imitate all these beautiful things. Then we all   55
stand up together and send forth prayers; and, as we said before, after we
stop our prayers, bread and wine and water are brought forward, and the
presider sends up prayers and makes eucharists in the same way, as much
as he is able to do, and the people assent, saying the Amen; and there is
a distribution and participation in what has been eucharisted, and   60
through the deacons some is sent to those absent. And they who are well
off and willing give what each in his own judgment decides, and what is
collected is set by the presider, and he gives aid to orphans and widows
and those who have need because of sickness or some other reason, and
to those in chains and strangers passing among us—simply put, [the
presider] cares for all who are wanting. Indeed, we all assemble together

on the day of the sun, because it is the first day, the day on which God changed darkness and matter and made the ordered world; and Jesus Christ our Savior rose from the dead on this same day. For they crucified him on the day before the day of Kronos (Saturn); and on the day after the day of Kronos, which is the day of the sun, in his appearance to his apostles and disciples he taught them all that I have entrusted to your consideration.

DISCUSSION QUESTIONS

1. In light of what Justin says about who were allowed to participate in communion at the time, what do you think his stance today would be in regard Christians of different denominations sharing communion in common: the practice known as "intercommunion?"

2. Precisely how, in Justin's theology stated here, do bread and wine become the body and blood of Christ? If you also believe in Christ's real presence in the Eucharist, is that the way you understand its taking place? If not, how does your understanding differ?

3. As is evident from this text, the cult of Mithras was very popular in Rome at the time. Using the library or the internet, what can you find out briefly about its origin and nature, and what led to its popularity in Rome?

4. Notice that Justin gives two reasons why Christians celebrate the Eucharist on Sundays. From what you have learned previously in this book, do you see a possible theological connection between his two reasons and, if so, what might it be? Also, do you think that even today a regular *Sunday* Eucharist might be very important? If so, why? And if not, why not?

14

The Eucharistic Prayer

The Apostolic Tradition 4

ST. HIPPOLYTUS OF ROME? (CA. 170–CA. 236)

INTRODUCTION

The Apostolic Tradition

The Apostolic Tradition (AT) in its 43 chapters, originally written in Greek, is an example of a "church order," that is, a book of instructions on how to run a local church. Other such "church orders" include *The Didache* (ca. AD. 100), *The Didascalia Apostolorum* (ca. A.D. 235), and *The Apostolic Constitutions* (ca. A.D. 385). This document was actually lost to the Church for more than 1,000 years, reappearing only when a Bohairic translation of it was published in 1848. Then it was known simply as "The Egyptian Church Order." Later in the 19th century Sahidic, Coptic, Arabic, Ethiopic, and Latin manuscript versions of the work were also discovered. In 1906 E. von der Goltz suggested that this treatise was in fact the lost *Apostolic Tradition* attributed by historians at the time to St. Hippolytus of Rome. Studies by W. Schwartz in 1910

91

and R. H. Connolly in 1916 confirmed his theory. Finally, critical editions of the work were produced, first in 1937 by the Anglican Benedictine liturgical scholar Dom Gregory Dix, and then in 1946 (Paris) and 1962 (Münster) by the Belgian, Dom Bernard Botte, OSB.

Since, as its name implies, the AT claims to derive its instructions from the apostles themselves, in order for it to have been accepted in any way as traditional during Hippolytus' time, its core substance would have had to represent Roman church practice at least as far back as A.D. 150, before third century living memory. In addition to providing ordination prayers and a eucharistic prayer, it also gives directions on how to recognize the offices of confessor, virgin, widow, reader, and subdeacon in the church. Next it deals with baptism, beginning with a list of professions one must give up before becoming a Christian, e.g., actor or brothel-keeper. Finally, the AT sets down norms for daily prayer and other aspects of good, ordered Christian living.

A Presbyter in Rome

To the degree that the AT may in fact owe its compilation to St. Hippolytus, a word about this saint is in order. Hippolytus was a highly influential presbyter and theologian in the Roman church of the early 3rd century. In his understanding of the Trinity,* however, he did not ascribe to the Son and the Holy Spirit that same full, eternal, and personal divinity belonging to the Father in the way that was later defined by the Council of Nicaea (A.D. 325). As a result, his teaching on the Trinity* differed from that of Popes Zephyrinus (198–217) and Callistus (217–222). He also had other points of disagreement with these popes, possibly leading him into schism* for a time. Tradition has it, however, that he died, fully reconciled with the Roman church, as a martyr in Sardinia along with Pope Pontianus during the persecution of the Roman emperor Maximin (235–238).

Mosaic of Abel and Melchisedek Offering Sacrifices, from San Vitale Church in Ravenna, Italy.
© Scala/Firenze

The Eucharistic Prayer

In Catholic tradition the "eucharistic prayer" is the highpoint in the celebration of the Eucharist.* The presider—a bishop or a priest—blesses the bread and cup of wine in the name of the whole Catholic Church, especially those members gathered around the altar but also all throughout the world, by recalling and giving thanks for God's self-gift in Jesus Christ, through which blessing the bread and wine become the body and blood of Christ for reception by the faithful.

The eucharistic prayer of the AT begins by alluding to *Hebrews* 1:1, thanking God through Jesus Christ *"whom in these end times you sent as our savior and redeemer and messenger of your will."* It then goes on to recall how, in obedience to the Father, Jesus underwent his passion and death for our salvation, and how as part of those saving events Jesus at the Last Supper commanded that the ritual offering of bread and wine continue to be done as his memorial. In obvious obedience to the Lord's request, the prayer continues: *"Remembering, therefore, his death and resurrection, we offer you this bread and cup, giving you thanks that you have held us worthy to stand before you and give you priestly worship."*

This transitional sentence, as concluding the theology of the prayer *("therefore")*, clearly indicates that every eucharistic memorial of Christ's saving events throughout the ages, performed by the Church in obedience to his command, is itself an integral, intended part of his original fulfillment of God's will for our salvation: his passion, death, and resurrection. In other words, in their participation in the Church's Eucharist the faithful are actually being taken up by Christ into his own historical saving events. Furthermore, it is God the Father himself, through the Son's accepted performance of his will, who is the ultimate speaker and actor of the prayer for the salvation* of participants, doing so in their praying of this prayer as their own self-offering in faith through the ministry of the presider. In addition, the literary structure of this sentence *("offer," "remembering," "giving thanks")* also reveals that the participants' ritual offering of the bread and cup consists in a grateful recalling of what God has done in Christ which in turn is enacted, first in the ritual of the liturgical service itself, but also in their subsequent everyday lives of service to others in the world.

In the taking up of gifts of bread and wine as symbolic in a fully effective way of how all of God's blessings—both of creation and redemption*—come to humanity through Jesus Christ, the fullness of his word, the Church's Eucharist is strikingly similar in its dynamic to the liturgical prayer of *Deuteronomy* 26. There also, as we saw, ancient Israel enacts in its offering of the first fruits of the Promised Land a grateful recognition to God that the whole of its life is essentially a gift from his hands.

The recovery of these early Roman liturgical texts has had a huge impact on the Church in our own time. With the post-Vatican II Catholic liturgical reforms, the newly created "Eucharistic Prayer II" is modeled on this AT original. New Eucharistic prayers based on the same model have been created by, and come into use in, Lutheran, Episcopalian and other church denominations as well.

—*Rev. John D. Laurance, S. J.*

TEXT

P. The Lord be with you.
R. And with your spirit.
P. Lift up your hearts.
R. We have lifted them to the Lord.
P. Let us give thanks to the Lord. 5
R. It is proper and right.
P. We give you thanks, O God, through your beloved son Jesus Christ, whom in these end times you sent as our savior and redeemer and the messenger of your will. He is your inseparable Word through whom you made all things and who is well-pleasing to you. You sent him from 10 heaven into the womb of a virgin and, made flesh, he became manifest as your Son, born of the Holy Spirit and the Virgin. Doing your will and creating for you a holy people, he extended his hands in suffering in order to release those who trust in you. When he was betrayed into his voluntary Passion—in order to dissolve death, break the chains of the 15 devil, trample down hell, destroy its power, lead the just into the light, and typify the resurrection—, taking bread and giving thanks, he said, "Take, eat, this is my body which is broken for you." In the same way with the chalice, "This is my blood which is poured out for you. When you do this, do it as my memorial." 20

Remembering, therefore, his death and resurrection, we offer you this bread and chalice, giving you thanks that you have held us worthy to stand before you and give you priestly worship. And we ask you to send your Holy Spirit on the offering of your holy church. In gathering them together, let all who participate in these sacred mysteries 25 be filled with your Holy Spirit, in order to affirm their faith in the truth, that we might praise and glorify you through your son Jesus Christ, through whom be glory and honor to you with the Holy Spirit in your holy church both now and forever. Amen.

DISCUSSION QUESTIONS

1. If, according to the prayer, Jesus was *"betrayed"* into his Passion, in what sense was it *"voluntary?"* And why, do you think, is it important for the prayer to explicitly point out that it was voluntary?

2. What, if anything, does this prayer *as a source of theology* reveal about the inter-relationships among the Persons of the Blessed Trinity*?

3. What, if any, in the first sentence of the second paragraph are the causal inter-connections among: (a) the Church's *remembering* God's past saving activity in Christ, (b) its own present act of *thanksgiving* for those saving events, and (c) the *offering* it makes to God of the sanctified bread and wine?

15

Oneness in Christ
On the Unity of the Catholic Church (Selections)

ST. CYPRIAN OF CARTHAGE (CA. 210–258)

INTRODUCTION

Cyprian's Life

Thascius Caecilius Cyprianus was born into a rich and highly culti-vated pagan family between 200 and 210 in or near Carthage, an ancient city whose ruins lie just outside present-day Tunis, Tunisia. A renowned rhetorician, Cyprian grew disgusted with the immorality of his day and so, under the influence of the presbyter Caecilius, he became a Christian. Soon afterwards he was ordained a presbyter and then, in 248/249, he was made bishop of Carthage by popular accla-mation, much to the chagrin of some presbyters, including Novatus. As bishop, Cyprian wrote as he acted—with clarity, gentleness, and great authority, stressing especially the need for church unity and for the imitation of Christ. His written legacy includes 13 treatises and

81 letters. Under the persecution of Decius (249–251), in order to hold the Carthaginian church together, he went into hiding. However, in the later persecution of Valerian (257–261) he willingly surrendered himself and was martyred by beheading on September 14, 258.

Background to the Treatise

By circulating *On the Unity of the Catholic Church* in the spring of 251 just after the Decian persecution, Cyprian attempted to counteract a threatening schism* in his local church. In order to stay alive during the persecution most Christians committed apostasy either by sacrificing to Roman gods or by purchasing certificates *(libelli)* as false proof they had done so. Some presbyters later gave them sacramental reconciliation *without* the usual period of penitence for this grave sin, restoring them immediately to full communion. Cyprian strongly objected, arguing that by doing so those presbyters denied those who had lapsed *(lapsi)* the grace of penitence and weakened the Church's will to withstand any future persecutions. Opposition grew among some presbyters led by Novatus and by the deacon Felicissimus who also published a manifesto calling for such immediate reconciliation. Thus the unity which Cyprian writes about in this treatise of 27 chapters is not primarily the unity of the whole Church throughout the world, although he refers to that unity as well within the text, but the unity of the Church within each diocese around its duly established bishop as a realization of the universal ("catholic") Church.

Cyprian's Soteriology*

A helpful clue to Cyprian's fundamental theology of Church unity can be found in his Epistle 63, chapter 13. There he argues that it was through Christ's absolute, unconditional love for all human beings realized in his humanity on the cross that he saved the world. However, if that love is truly effective in us, uniting us to Christ, then it also unites us to all others so united in Christ. And just as that love was realized in Jesus' humanity, that is, in an embodied way, if we are truly united to Christ in his suffering, death, and resurrection, then we must also be united to all others united in Christ's love in an embodied way, that is, in the sacramental, visible Church throughout the world. As one scriptural basis for this teaching, Cyprian alludes to *Romans* 8:35 (*"What can separate us from the love of Christ?"*). He says, *"Nothing can separate the Church—that is, the people established in the Church, faithfully and firmly persevering in that which they have believed—from Christ, in such a way as to prevent their undivided love from always abiding and adhering."*

The Church as Sacrament* of Unity

For Cyprian, then, the question arises: where to find this Church? His answer: in union with the bishops united to each another as successors to the apostles upon whom Christ founded his Church, the "first" of whom was Peter. Thus in chapter 4 of *De Unitate Catholicae Ecclesiae* the "primacy" Cyprian attributes to Peter is not so much an authority of the Bishop of Rome *over* the other bishops in the Church, but Peter's being the first instance of Christ's entrusting to all the apostles the common care of his Church. As does St. Ignatius of Antioch (see *Magnesians* 2), Cyprian regards the bishop as a sacramental expression of Christ's love uniting the members of his local church to him and one another in the universal Church: *"the bishop is in the Church and the Church is in the bishop"* (*Epistle* 56:8). Therefore, obedience to the bishop is in fact obedience to the unifying love of Christ which binds the Church together, making it tangibly real and bodily effective in the world, allowing Christ to continue his work of salvation throughout history.

"Outside the Church . . ."

In chapter 6 Cyprian makes another famous statement: *"You cannot have God for your Father if you no longer have the Church for your mother."* Later church authors concluded from this that "outside the Church there is no salvation (whatsoever)" *(extra ecclesiam nulla salus)*. However, by "no longer" *(iam)* it is clear that Cyprian refers here only to those who, already members of the Church, knowing its unity is that of Christ's love necessary for salvation, nevertheless out of their own self-interests break it by setting up for themselves a rival bishop, thereby splitting the Church in two. In other words, Cyprian in fact is in agreement with the Vatican II teaching in *Lumen Gentium* 14 on this *relative* necessity of the Church for salvation, as we will see later on in this book.

TEXT

Translation by Maurice Bevenot, S.J., in *Cyprian: De Lapsis and De Ecclesiae Catholicae Unitate* (Oxford: At the Clarendon Press, 1971) revised.

1. Our Lord warns us by saying: *"You are the salt of the earth,"* and commands us to be prudent as well as simple in our efforts to be good. Accordingly, dear brothers, we must constantly be on our watch to know the snares of our crafty foe and to avoid them. . . .
5 We should fear not only the kind of persecution which in open warfare ranges abroad to overthrow and defeat the servants of God; the enemy is much more to be feared when, by feigning peace, he slithers himself through stealthy approaches, a strategy which has earned him the name 'serpent.'
10 **3.** With the coming of Christ, light had come to the gentiles and the lamp of salvation* was shining for the deliverance of humankind, so that the deaf began to hearken to the Spirit's call of grace, the blind to open their eyes toward God, the sick to recover their health unto eternity, the lame to hasten to the Church, and the
15 dumb to raise their voice aloud in prayer. Thereupon the enemy, seeing his idols abandoned and his temples and haunts deserted by the ever growing numbers of the faithful, devised a fresh deceit, using the Christian name itself to mislead the unwary. He invented heresies and schisms* in order to undermine the faith, corrupt the truth,
20 and destroy our unity. Those whom he has failed to keep in the blindness of their old ways he beguiles and misleads . . . They still call themselves Christians after abandoning the Gospel of Christ and the observance of his law.

4. But if anyone considers those matters carefully, he will not need a long discourse or arguments. The proof is simple and convincing, found in the summary of the truth the Lord speaks to Peter: *"I say to you, that you are Peter and upon this rock (petran) I will build my Church, and the gates of hell shall not overcome it. I will give to you the keys of the kingdom of heaven. And what you shall bind upon earth shall be bound also in heaven, and whatsoever you shall loose on earth shall be loosed in heaven."* And again after his resurrection he says to [Peter], *"Feed my sheep."* It is on him that he builds the Church, and to him that he entrusts the feeding of his sheep. And although he assigns an equal power to all the apostles, yet he founded a single Chair and, by his own authority, established the origin and continuance of the [Church's] unity. No doubt the other apostles were all that Peter was, but a primacy was given to Peter, and it is [thus] made clear that there is but one Church and one Chair. So too, even if they are all shepherds, there appears but one flock which is to be fed by all the apostles in common accord. Does anyone not holding on to the unity of Peter believe that he possesses the faith? Is the one who deserts the Chair of Peter, upon which the Church was founded, confident that he is in the Church?

5. The authority of the bishops forms a unity, of which each holds his part in its totality. And the Church forms a unity, however far she spreads and multiplies by the progeny of her fecundity; just as the sun's rays are many, yet the light is one, and a tree's branches are many, yet the strength deriving from its sturdy root is one. . . .

6. It is she who preserves us for God, she who seals for the kingdom the sons [and daughters] whom she has borne. Whoever breaks with the Church and enters on an adulterous union, cuts himself off from the promises made to the Church. You cannot have God for your Father if you *no longer* have the Church for your mother. . . . If one does not keep this unity, he is not keeping the law of God; he has broken faith with the Father and the Son, he is cut off from life and salvation.

7. This sacrament* of unity, this unbreakable bond of close-knit harmony is portrayed in the Gospel by our Lord Jesus Christ's coat,

which was not divided or cut at all, but when they drew lots for the
vesture of Christ to see which of them should put on Christ, it was
60   the whole coat that was won, the garment was acquired unspoiled
and undivided. . . . By the sacrament* of his garment was proclaimed the oneness of the Church.

13. For the same reason, when [Christ] was giving a rule for
prayer, He added: *"And when you shall stand for prayer, forgive if you*
65   *have aught against any man, that your Father also who is in heaven may*
forgive you your sins." And so, if one comes to the sacrifice (Eucharist)
with strife in his heart, he calls him back from the altar and bids him
be reconciled to his brother first, and then in peace of soul return and
make his offering to God. For the very gifts of Cain did not win
70   God's regard: such a man could not have God at peace with him
when he was torn with jealousy towards his brother and at war with
him. What sort of peace then do the enemies of the brethren promise
themselves? What sort to sacrifice do they think they offer in competition with the priests (bishops)? Do they think that Christ is with
75   them in their gatherings, when those gatherings are outside the
Church of Christ?

14. Nay, though they should suffer death for the confession of the
Name, the guilt of such men is not removed even by their blood. No
martyr can he be who is not in the Church: the Kingdom shall be
80   closed to anyone that deserts her who is destined to be its queen. Peace
is what Christ gave us; he commanded us to be united in heart and
mind: he enjoined us to keep intact and unimpaired the pledges of our
love and charity; no one can claim the martyr's name who has broken
off his love for the brethren. . . . Just as the devil is not Christ,
85   though he tricks people by the name, so a man cannot be reckoned a
Christian who does not abide in Christ's true Gospel and faith.

DISCUSSION QUESTIONS

1. Why, according to Cyprian's theology, does he say that the evil the Devil can do to the Church through schism* is much worse than what he can do through Roman persecutions?

2. To what does Cyprian refer in chapter 4 by the phrase "the Chair of Peter?" Why, do you think, if Cyprian is right that Christ assigned equal power to all the apostles, does Cyprian so emphasize the role of Peter?

3. To what is Cyprian referring in chapter 7 by the phrase, *"This sacrament of unity?"* If he is not talking about Baptism or Eucharist or one of the other seven sacraments* of the Catholic Church, explain what you think he means by the word "sacrament" here.

4. Explain in your own words what you think Cyprian means in chapter 7: *"By the sacrament of his garment was proclaimed the oneness of the Church."* Why "sacrament?"

16

The Church's Creed
The Nicene-Constantinopolitan Creed

THE COUNCIL OF CONSTANTINOPLE 1 (381)

INTRODUCTION

Origins

Properly called the creed of the Council of Constantinople, 381, this document is also known as the "Nicene-Constantinopolitan" creed because its roots, particularly in terms of its theology, go back to a council held in Nicaea (a town outside Constantinople, now present-day Istanbul). Since 381 this creed has functioned as the fundamental expression of Christian belief. It is recited, e.g., in the Roman Catholic Mass*, in the Lutheran Service, as well as in the services of most mainstream Christian denominations.[1]

---

[1]Some Free Church denominations have the creed printed in hymnals, but, it must be admitted, some Free Churches do not use the creed at all.

As a statement of the fundamental beliefs shared by most Christians, the Nicene-Constantinopolitan creed has played an important role in the modern Christian ecumenical movement. The creed has also functioned within each denomination that recites it as a document of self-definition, similar to the role the Constitution plays in American self-definition: 'This is who we are, what we believe, what keeps us who we are, what we test new developments against.'

Purpose of Creeds

"Creeds" in general perhaps originated with the very first generation of the Church as summaries of Christian beliefs. Such summaries functioned as teaching devices for new Christians: "This is what we believe, and to join our community you too must believe this." Or: "There's a lot of stuff to learn about, but this is what you really have to believe!" We know that by the middle of the second century Christian communities used such creedal summaries as part of baptism. The candidate for admission into the Church was asked a series of questions on their grasp of the faith, such as, "Do you believe in God the creator," to which the candidate was expected to answer, "Yes, I believe." Such statements of the faith were also used to test out claims to authority. If an argument was made by someone that some book was inspired and should be treated as "Scripture," then the content of the book was tested against the creed to see if it really was inspired and represented the beliefs of the community. Agreement wasn't necessary on a word for word basis, but the basic understanding expressed in the community's creed was the rule.

Typical Structure

Such creeds often followed a narrative or story form, usually divided into four "episodes" or "acts": (1) God, usually called the "Father" and always recognized as the creator; (2) the Son of God, who comes from (in both senses of that phrase) God the Father, and who comes to save us; (3) the Holy Spirit, who is very much associated with the origins and sustaining energy of the Church; and (4) an assortment of plot lines or details that further identify the believing community or the fate of that community. The core story of each of these episodes is developed in varying detail, but plot line number two, the Son, usually gets the most attention and development in the form of a summary of the key highlights from the life of Christ.

Historical Background

Whenever any of the four episodes of the creed are developed in any detail, that is because someone else is denying that particular element. For example, almost all the creeds that date from after the New Testament describe God as the maker of heaven and earth because there were people who believed that heaven and earth come not from God, but from some evil source. Similarly, creeds emphasize the reality of Jesus' birth from Mary because some people taught that Jesus wasn't really human (He was "better" than that!).

In the fourth century there was a major disagreement over whether the Son was "God" the way the Father was "God." The argument began around A.D. 318, when a priest named Arius taught that only God the Father was really "God" because only he was eternal and uncaused. The Son was not eternal because he was caused, and so he was not "God" in the full sense of the term. He was, in fact, a very special kind of creature. Not quite God, but God enough for us. Arius' bishop, Alexander, the bishop of Alexandria, Egypt, and Alexander's successor, Athanasius (a lot of *a*-word names here!) opposed Arius, and in 325, in Nicaea, a town outside the Emperor's new city, Constantinople, a group of bishops gathered from across the Greek-speaking part of the Empire to judge Arius' theology. The overwhelming majority of those bishops gathered in Nicaea condemned Arius' theology and he and some of his sympathizers were sent into exile. The Council produced a creed which stated, in no uncertain terms, that the Son was God as the Father was God. The fact was expressed using language which can be translated as "essence" or "substance" or even "being." The Son had the same "essence" as the Father.

"Person" and "Substance"

Arius' tendency to see the Son as a kind of "God-Lite," as it were, was condemned, but the creed went so far in stating divine unity that it left unsaid how the Father and Son were really different, and not just two appearances of this real existence, "God." Did the Father and the Son have the same substance the way Robin Williams and Mrs. Doubtfire have the same substance?

You have probably been taught, or at least heard, that "Trinity" means that God is "one in nature or being" *and* "three persons." This is the insight that most Christians came to by 381 and was signaled by the creed of Constantinople, 381. But the problem was that there was, when the argument started, no clear understanding of what it meant to be an individual. Your second grade teacher may have told you we are each as different as the little paper snowflakes you cut out and taped to your classroom window, but exactly how we were each different took some figuring out. In the ancient world the difference between this or that person was basically the difference between this hunk of human flesh and that hunk of human flesh. Difference was physically-based. That kind of difference could not apply to God who wasn't physical, so how were the real differences in God to be understood? Figuring out a way to articulate what it means to be a different person without depending on a material understanding took a while, as did finding a balance between a belief in God's unity and a belief in the different persons who were God. This development took from 318 until 381 and then some.

Basically, some Christians figured that one way to express the basis of the difference between Father and Son was to focus on their relationship(s). Relationships identify us as persons, make us persons. In the case of Father and Son the titles reflect their defining relationships (who they are), but those titles also express the basis for their unity. A son or daughter has the same nature as a parent. The Creed of 381 also recognized that Holy Spirit was divine and a person, but the scriptural language (e.g., "Father," "Son") for recognizing the relationships was not as clear and helpful. Spirit? Breath? The Creed of 381 uses the term "proceeds" to name the causal relationship that

identifies the Holy Spirit and which also serves as the basis for the Spirit's common divinity with the Father and Son. But the Council recognized that it wasn't as clear about how to understand that generative relationship, those "processions," and the distinct identity of the Holy Spirit. The language the creed uses of the Holy Spirit is not quite as confident as the language it uses of the Son.

—*Dr. Michel R. Barnes*

TEXT

Council of Constantinople I 381
Ecumenical II (against the Macedonians, etc.)

Condemnation of the Heretics

Can. 1. The faith of the three hundred and eighteen fathers who assembled at Nicea in Bithynia is not to be disregarded; but it remains authoritative, and all heresy* is to be anathematized: and especially that of the Eunomians or of the Anomians, and that of the Arians, or
5   that of the Eudoxians, and that of the Macedonians, that is to say of those opposing the Spirit, and that of the Sabellians, of the Marcellians and that of the Photinians and that of the Apollinarians.

The "Nicene-Constantinopolitan"[2] Creed
Reprinted from *Sources of Catholic Dogma,* translated by Roy J. Deferrari (1957), Herder & Herder

We believe in one God, Father omnipotent, maker of heaven and earth, and of all things visible and invisible. And in one Lord Jesus
10   Christ, the only begotten Son of God, born of the Father before all ages, light of light, true God of true God, begotten not made, consubstantial* with the Father, by whom all things were made, who for

---

[2]This creed, after the Councils of Ephesus (431) and Chalcedon (451), passed into the liturgical use of the Eastern Church, and this same thing took place in the West about the end of the eighth century through St. Paulinus of Aquileia against the Adoptianists.

us men and for our salvation came down and was made flesh by the Holy Spirit and of the Virgin Mary, and became man, and was cruci-fied for us by Pontius Pilate, suffered, and was buried and arose again   15 the third day, according to the Scripture, and ascended into heaven, and sits at the right hand of the Father, and is coming again with glory to judge the living and the dead; of whose kingdom there shall be no end. And in the Holy Spirit, the Lord, the giver of life, who proceeds from the Father,[3] who together with the Father and Son is   20 worshipped and glorified, who spoke through the prophets. In one holy, Catholic, and Apostolic Church. We confess one baptism for the remission of sins. We look for the resurrection of the dead, and the life of eternity to come. Amen.

DISCUSSION QUESTIONS

1. Although in the Latin version of the Catholic Mass* the Creed begins: "*Credo in unum Deum . . . ,*" that is, "*I* believe in one God . . ." the original Nicene-Constantinopolitan creed, as seen here, begins, "*We* believe in one God." Why do you sup-pose there is that difference?

2. The Nicene-Constantinopolitan Creed was specially formulated to counteract the false teaching of Arius. Where especially in the creed do you find evidence of this intention?

---

[3]The addition here of "and the Son" was first made in Spain. From here this cus-tom passed over into Gaul, then into Germany, as is clear from the Gallican liturgy of Moneius at the beginning of the fifth century, from the Synod of the Forum Julii 791, of Frankfurt 794, of Aquisgranum (Aachen), 809, which asked Leo III that it be reaccepted by the Roman Church. This, however, Leo refused, not because he rejected the dogma,* but because he feared to add anything to the traditional form. Afterwards, indeed, when St. Henry obtained from Benedict VIII his request that the creed be sung among the ceremonies of the Masses, the addition was accepted. This finally was admitted simultaneously by the Latins and the Greeks in the ecumenical Synods of Lyons II and of Florence.

3. In churches throughout the world some version of this creed is recited or sung every Sunday of the year by worshiping Christians. What possible benefit(s) do you think they derive in doing so?

4. *Canon 1* of the Council of Constantinople 1 in the text above makes reference to the heresy* of the Sabellians. On the basis of what you can find in the library or on the Internet, briefly explain the error they professed in regard to the nature of God. Why for some people would theirs have been an attractive teaching?

17

Prayerful Reminiscence

The Confessions: Book Eight

ST. AUGUSTINE OF HIPPO (354–430)

INTRODUCTION

Augustine (354–430) must certainly have a place in any list of people who have shaped Christian belief in a fundamental way.

Spiritual Autobiography

One of the most important of Augustine's many contributions is his invention of a type of book: the spiritual or psychological autobiography. No Christian, before the Confessions, had ever written an account of her or his life. Books about other Christians' lives, holy people who could serve as role models, had begun to gain popularity at about the time Augustine was born. The most famous and influential was The Life of Antony by Athanasius, bishop of Alexandria, Egypt. Quickly translated from Greek into Latin, this work influenced many young Christians, including Augustine himself and his friends.

The *Confessions* was a new kind of book for two reasons: It was about the person writing, and there is no presumption that the author is "holy," although there is still the idea that the story of what happened to Augustine can help other Christians in their lives (precisely because so much of Augustine's life seemed so unholy).

Family Background

Augustine was born into a family with a non-Christian father and a very pious Christian mother. His mother, Monica, was to remain a strong influence throughout Augustine's life, in part because his father died when Augustine was a teenager, and in part because she was a very special person who had great hopes for her son. Despite his mom's strong belief, Augustine was not much of a believing Christian when he was young. Until he was almost thirty he experimented with different beliefs, having, as a teenager, decided that Christianity was basically a religion for stupid people.

Milan and Ambrose

By profession Augustine was a rhetorician, that is, someone basically who trains public figures—like politicians and lawyers—in speaking and debate. In the culture in which Augustine lived this job was more important than it sounds as though it would be in ours. In addition, he was good at what he did and, although just a young man from "the sticks" of North Africa, he got a job teaching in Rome. Rome was officially still the capital of the western half of the Roman Empire, but the Emperor himself lived in Milan, and the government (and government groupies) followed the Emperor there. Augustine himself moved to Milan, and it was in that city that he came across Ambrose,* bishop of Milan, and a pretty bright guy himself. Ambrose* was able to help Augustine through his difficulties with what seemed like the stupid parts of Christianity. What Augustine came to see was that the problem he experienced was not so much with Christianity, but with himself. Augustine had a problem, and what the *Confessions* turns out to be about is his discovery of the problem and the solution.

Theology of the Confessions

Augustine begins his life story with childhood memories of events illustrating that there is something in people that drives them, not simply to doing bad things, but to enjoying doing bad things. There doesn't seem to have been a sentimental bone in Augustine's body because his portraits of being a baby, a child and a teenager are anything but cute and sweet. Augustine was not an uncommonly evil person; he was just more honest than most people about those moments which most of us try very hard to forget, or at least to hide. He was particularly bothered, as a young man, by feelings of lust. If he were living today he would be called a "womanizer." However, Augustine was not wanton with these feelings. As a young man he had a mistress to whom he was completely faithful for years (until his mom broke up the relationship because it wasn't going to help his career).

Augustine's desires were, for him, a window on to the fact that something deep down inside of him was basically broken: he knew what was best for him, he knew what was the right thing to do, and yet so many of his choices set him up to do the wrong thing. Augustine's insight was that on our own, our innate moral strength is too broken to overcome our own tendency to fail, but with God's help, with God's "grace," we can overcome our moral weaknesses and do the right thing. Augustine's "conversion" was not so much an experience of the fact that we all need God's help as it was the experience of receiving God's help.

—Dr. Michel R. Barnes

Church of St. Ambrose in Milan.
© Scala/Firenze

TEXT

I

Let me, O my God, remember with thanks to Thee and confess Thy mercies upon me. Let my bones be pierced through with Thy love, and let them say: *Who is like unto Thee, O Lord, Thou hast broken my bonds, I will sacrifice to Thee the sacrifice of praise.* How Thou hast broken them I shall tell and all who adore Thee will say as they listen: Blessed be the Lord in heaven and on earth, great and wonderful is His name.

5

Reprinted from *Confessions of St. Augustine,* translated by Frank J. Sheed (1943) by permission of Hachett Publishing Company

Your words had rooted deep in my heart and I was fenced about on all sides by You. Of Your eternal life I was now certain, though I saw it *in a dark manner and as through a glass* (1 Cor 13:12). All my former doubt about an incorruptible substance from which every substance has its being was taken from me. My desire now was not to be more sure of You but more steadfast in You.

But in my temporal life all was uncertain; my heart had to be purged of the old leaven. The way, our Savior himself, delighted me; but I still shrank from actually walking a way so strait. Then by You it came into my mind, and the idea appealed strongly to me, to go to Simplicianus whom I knew to be Your good servant, for Your grace* shone in him. I had heard that from his youth he had lived in great love of You. He was now grown old; and it seemed to me that from a long lifetime spent in so firm a following of Your way he must have experienced much and learned much. And truly so it was. I hoped that if I conferred with him about my problems he might from that experience and learning show me the best way for one affected as I was to walk in Your path.

For I saw the Church full; and one went this way, and one that. But I was unhappy at the life I led in the world, and it was indeed a heavy burden, for the hope of honor and profit no longer inflamed my desire, as formerly, to help me bear so exacting a servitude. These things delighted me no longer in comparison with Your sweetness and the beauty of Your house which I loved. But what still held me tight bound was my need of woman: nor indeed did the apostle forbid me to marry, though he exhorted to a better state, wishing all men to be as he was himself. But I in my weakness was for choosing the softer place, and this one thing kept me from taking a sure line upon others. I was weary and wasted with the cares that were eating into me, all because there were many things which I was unwilling to suffer but had to put up with for the sake of living with a wife, a way of life to which I was utterly bound. I had heard from the mouth of Truth itself that *there are eunuchs who have made themselves eunuchs for the kingdom of heaven (Matt 19:10–12)*; but Christ had said, *He that can take it, let him take it*. Certainly *all men are vain in whom there is not the knowledge of God and who cannot, by these good things that are seen, find Him that is (Wis 13:1).* Now I was no longer in that sort of vanity; I had gone beyond it and in the testimony of the whole creation 45 I had found You, our Creator, and Your Word who is with You and one God with You, by whom You created all things. But there is another sort of godlessness, that of the men who *knowing God have not glorified Him as God or given thanks (Rom 1:21).* Into this also I had fallen, but Your right hand upheld me and taking me out of it, 50 placed me where I might find health. For You have said to man: *Behold, the fear of the Lord is wisdom (Prov 9:10);* and again: *Be not desirous to seem wise, for those who affirm themselves to be wise become fools.* I had now found the pearl of great price, and I ought to have sold all I had and bought it. But I hesitated still. 55

II

So I went to Simplicianus, who had begotten Ambrose*, now bishop, into Your grace, and whom indeed Ambrose loved as a father. I told him all the wanderings of my error. But when I told him that I had read certain books of the Platonists* which had been translated into Latin by Victorinus, one time professor of Rhetoric in Rome—who 60 had, so I heard, died a Christian—he congratulated me for not having fallen upon the writings of other philosophers which are full of vain deceits, according to the elements of this world, whereas in the Platonists God and his Word are everywhere implied. Then to draw me on to the humility of Christ, hidden from the wise and revealed 65 to little ones, he began to speak of Victorinus himself whom he had known intimately when he was in Rome. Of Victorinus he told me what I shall now set down, for the story glorifies Your grace and it should be told to Your glory. For here was an old man deeply learned, trained in all the liberal sciences, a man who had read and weighed so 70 many of the philosophers' writings, the teacher of so many distinguished senators, a man who on account of the brilliance of His teaching had earned and been granted a statue in the Roman forum—an honor the citizens of this world think so great. He had grown old in the worship of idols, had taken part in their sacrilegious 75 rites, for almost all the Roman nobility at that time was enthusiastic for them and was ever talking of "prodigies and the monster gods of every kind, and of the jackal-headed Anubis—who all had once fought against the Roman deities Neptune and Venus and Minerva" and had been beaten: yet Rome was on its knees before these gods it had conquered. All this Victorinus with his thunder of eloquence had gone on championing for so many years even into old age: yet he thought it no shame to be the child of Your Christ, an infant at Your font, bending his neck under the yoke of humility and his forehead to the ignominy of the Cross.

O Lord, Lord, who dost *bow down Thy heavens and descend, dost touch the mountains and they smoke (Ps* 144:5), by what means didst Thou find thy way into that breast? He read, so Simplicianus said, Holy Scripture; he investigated all the Christian writings most carefully and minutely. And he said not publicly but to Simplicianus privately and as one friend to another: "I would have you know that I am now a Christian." Simplicianus answered: "I shall not believe it nor count you among Christians unless I see you in the Church of Christ." Victorinus asked with some faint mockery: "Then is it the walls that make Christians?" He went on saying that he was a Christian, and Simplicianus went on with the same denial, and Victorinus always repeated his retort about the walls. The fact was that he feared to offend his friends, important people and worshippers of these demons; he feared that their enmity might fall heavily upon him from the height of their Babylon-dignity as from the cedars of Lebanon which the Lord had not yet brought down. But when by reading in all earnestness he had drawn strength, he grew afraid that Christ might deny him before His angels if he were ashamed to confess Christ before men. He felt that he was guilty of a great crime in being ashamed of the sacraments of the lowliness of Your Word, when he had not been ashamed of the sacrilegious rites of those demons of pride whom in his pride he had worshipped. So he grew proud towards vanity and humble towards truth. Quite suddenly and without warning he said to Simplicianus, as Simplicianus told me: "Let us go to the Church. I wish to be made a Christian." Simplicianus,

unable to control his joy, went with him. He was instructed in the first
mysteries of the faith, and not long after gave in his name that he
might be regenerated by baptism, to the astonishment of Rome and
the joy of the Church. The proud saw it and were enraged, ground
their teeth and were livid with envy: but the Lord God was the hope   115
of his servant, so that he had no regard for vanities and lying follies.

Finally when the hour had come for his profession of faith—which
at Rome was usually made by those who were about to enter into
Your grace in a set form of words learned and memorized and spoken
from a platform in the sight of the faithful—Simplicianus told me   120
that the priests offered Victorinus to let him make the profession in
private, as the custom was with such as seemed likely to find the
ordeal embarrassing. But he preferred to make profession of salvation
in the sight of the congregation in church. For there had been no salvation in the Rhetoric he had taught, yet he had professed it publicly.   125
Obviously therefore he should be in less fear of Your meek flock when
he was uttering Your word, since he had had no fear of the throng of
the deluded when uttering his own. When therefore he had gone up
to make his profession all those who knew him began whispering his
name to one another with congratulatory murmurs. And indeed who   130
there did not know him? And from the lips of the rejoicing congregation sounded the whisper, "Victorinus, Victorinus." They were
quick to utter their exultation at seeing him and as quickly fell silent
to hear him. He uttered the true faith with glorious confidence, and
they would gladly have snatched him to their very heart. Indeed, they   135
did take him to their heart in their love and their joy: with those
hands they took him.

III

O loving God, what is it in men that makes them rejoice more for the
salvation* of a soul that was despaired of or one delivered from a
major peril, than if there had always been hope or the peril had been   140
less? Even You, O Merciful Father, rejoice more *upon one sinner doing
penance than upon ninety and nine just who need not penance*
(Lk 15:7). It is with special joy that we hear how the lost sheep is

145 brought home upon the exultant shoulders of the shepherd and how
the coin is put back into Your treasury while the neighbors rejoice
with the woman who found it. And the joy we feel at mass* in Your
church brings tears as we hear of that younger son who was dead and
made alive again, who had been lost and was found. You rejoice in us
and in Your angels who stand fast in holy charity. For You are ever the
150 same because You ever know, and in the one way of knowing, all
those things which are not always existent nor always the same.

What is it in the soul, I ask again, that makes it delight more to
have found or regained the things it loves than if it had always had
them? Creatures other than man bear the same witness, and all things
155 are filled with testimonies acclaiming that it is so. The victorious general has his triumph; but he would not have been victorious if he had
not fought; and the greater danger there was in the battle, the greater
rejoicing in the triumph. The storm tosses the sailors and threatens to
wreck the ship; all are pale with the threat of death. But the sky grows
160 clear, the sea calm, and now they are as wild with exultation as before
with fear. A friend is sick and his pulse threatens danger; all who want
him well feel as if they shared his sickness. He begins to recover,
though he cannot yet walk as strongly as of old: and there is more joy
than there was before, when he was still well and could walk properly.
165 Note too that men procure the actual pleasures of human life by way
of pain—I mean not only the pain that comes upon us unlooked for
and beyond our will, but unpleasantness planned and willingly
accepted. There is no pleasure in eating or drinking, unless the dis-
comfort of hunger and thirst come before. Drunkards eat salty things
170 to develop a thirst so great as to be painful, and pleasure arises when
the liquor quenches the pain of the thirst. And it is the custom that
promised brides do not give themselves at once lest the husband
should hold the gift cheap unless delay had set him craving.

We see this in base and dishonorable pleasure, but also in the plea-
175 sure that is licit and permitted, and again in the purest and most
honorable friendship. We have seen it in the case of him who had
been dead and was brought back to life, who had been lost and was
found. Universally the greater joy is heralded by greater pain. What

does this mean, O Lord my God, when Thou art an eternal joy to
Thyself, Thou Thyself art joy itself, and things about Thee ever   180
rejoice in Thee? What does it mean that this part of creation thus
alternates between need felt and need met, between discord and harmony? Is this their mode of being, this what Thou didst give them,
when from the heights of heaven to the lowest earth, from the beginning of time to the end, from the angel to the worm, from the first   185
movement to the last, Thou didst set all kinds of good things and all
Thy just works each in its place, each in its season? Alas for me, how
high art Thou in the highest, how deep in the deepest! And Thou dost
never depart from us, yet with difficulty do we return to Thee.

IV

Come, Lord, work upon us, call us back, set us on fire and clasp us   190
close, be fragrant to us, draw us to Thy loveliness: let us love, let us
run to Thee. Do not many from a deeper pit of blindness than Victorinus come back to Thee, enlightened by that light in which they
receive from Thee the power to be made Thy sons? But because they
are not so well-known, there is less rejoicing over them even by those   195
who do know them. For when many rejoice together, the joy of each
one is richer: they warm themselves at each other's flame. Further in
so far as they are known widely, they guide many to salvation and are
bound to be followed by many. So that even those who have gone
before rejoice much on their account, because the rejoicing is not   200
only on their account. It would be shameful if in Your tabernacle* the
persons of the rich should be welcome before the poor, or the nobly
born before the rest: since Thou has rather chosen the weak things of
the world to confound the strong, and hast chosen the base things of
the world and the things that are contemptible, and things that are   205
not, in order to bring to nought things that are. It was by Paul's
tongue that You uttered these words. Yet when Paulus the proconsul
came under the light yoke of Christ and became a simple subject of
the great King, his pride brought low by the apostle's spiritual might,
even that least of Your apostles now desired to be called Paul, in place   210
of his former name of Saul, for the glory of so great a victory. Victory

215 over the enemy is greater when we win from him a man whom he holds more strongly and through whom he holds more people. He has a firmer hold on the eminent by reason of their noble rank, and through them he holds very many people by reason of their author-

220 ity. Therefore the heart of Victorinus was all the more welcome because the devil had held it as an impregnable fortress; and the tongue of Victorinus because it was a strong sharp weapon with which the devil had slain many. It was right for Your sons to rejoice with more abounding joy because our King had bound the strong man, and they saw his vessels taken from him and cleansed and made

225 available unto Your honor and *profitable table to the Lord unto every good work.*

V

Now when this man of Yours, Simplicianus, had told me the story of Victorinus, I was on fire to imitate him: which indeed was why he had told me. He added that in the time of the emperor Julian, when

230 a law was made prohibiting Christians from teaching Literature and Rhetoric, Victorinus had obeyed the law, preferring to give up his own school of words rather than Your word, by which You make elo-quent the tongues of babes. In this he seemed to me not only courageous but actually fortunate, because it gave him the chance to

235 devote himself wholly to You. I longed for the same chance, but I was bound not with the iron of another's chains, but by my own iron will. The enemy held my will; and of it he made a chain and bound me. Because my will was perverse it changed to lust, and lust yielded to became habit, and habit not resisted became necessity. These were

240 like links hanging one on another—which is why I have called it a chain—and their hard bondage held me bound hand and foot. The new will which I now began to have, by which I willed to worship You freely and to enjoy You, O God, the only certain Joy, was not yet strong enough to overcome that earlier will rooted deep through the

245 years. My two wills, one old, one new, one carnal, one spiritual, were in conflict and in their conflict wasted my soul.

Thus, with myself as object of the experiment, I came to understand what I had read, how the *flesh lusts against the spirit and the spirit against the flesh* (*Galatians* 5:17). I indeed was in both camps, but more in that which I approved in myself than in that which I disapproved. For in a sense it was now no longer I that was in this second camp, because in large part I rather suffered it unwillingly than did it with my will. Yet habit had grown stronger against me by my own act, since I had come willingly where I did not now will to be. Who can justly complain when just punishment overtakes the sinner? I no longer had the excuse which I used to think I had for not yet forsaking the world and serving You, the excuse namely that I had no certain knowledge of the truth. By now I was quite certain; but I was still bound to earth and refused to take service in Your army; I feared to be freed of all the things that impeded me, as strongly as I ought to have feared the being impeded by them. I was held down as agreeably by this world's baggage as one often is by sleep; and indeed the thoughts with which I meditated upon You were like the efforts of a man who wants to get up but is so heavy with sleep that he simply sinks back into it again. There is no one who wants to be asleep always—for every sound judgment holds that it is best to be awake—yet a man often postpones the effort of shaking himself awake when he feels a sluggish heaviness in the limbs, and settles pleasurably into another doze though he knows he should not, because it is time to get up. Similarly I regarded it as settled that it would be better to give myself to Your love rather than go on yielding to my own lust; but the first course delighted and convinced my mind, the second delighted my body and held it in bondage. For there was nothing I could reply when You called me: *Rise, thou that sleepest and arise from the dead: and Christ shall enlighten thee* (*Ephesians* 5:14); and whereas You showed me by every evidence that Your words were true, there was simply nothing I could answer save only laggard lazy words: "Soon," "Quite soon," "Give me just a little while." But "soon" and "quite soon" did not mean any particular time; and "just a little while" went on for a long while. It was in vain that *I delighted in Thy law according to the inner man, when that other*

250

255

260

265

270

275

280

law in my members rebelled against the law of my mind and led me captive in the law of sin that was in my members (Romans 7:23). For the law of sin is the fierce force of habit, by which the mind is drawn and held even against its will, and yet deservedly because it had fallen wilfully into the habit. *Who then should deliver me from the body of this death, but Thy grace only, through Jesus Christ Our Lord (Romans 7:24)?*

VI

Now, O Lord, my Helper and my Redeemer, I shall tell and confess to Your name how You delivered me from the chain of that desire of the flesh which held me so bound, and the servitude of worldly things. I went my usual way with a mind ever more anxious, and day after day I sighed for You. I would be off to Your church as often as my business, under the weight of which I groaned, left me free. Alypius was with me, at liberty from his legal office after a third term as Assessor and waiting for private clients, to whom he might sell his legal advice—just as I sold skill in speaking, if indeed this can be bought. Nebridius had yielded to our friendship so far as to teach under Verecundus, a great friend of all of us, a citizen and elementary school teacher of Milan, who had earnestly asked and indeed by right of friendship demanded from our company the help he badly needed. Nebridius was not influenced in the matter by any desire for profit, for he could have done better had he chosen, in a more advanced school; but he was a good and gracious friend and too kindly a man to refuse our requests. But he did it all very quietly, for he did not want to draw the attention of those persons whom the world holds great; he thus avoided distraction of mind, for he wanted to have his mind free and at leisure for as many hours as possible to seek or read or hear truths concerning wisdom.

On a certain day—Nebridius was away for some reason I cannot recall—there came to Alypius and me at our house one Ponticianus, a fellow countryman of ours, being from Africa, holder of an important post in the emperor's court. There was something or other he wanted of us and we sat down to discuss the matter. As it happened he noticed a book on a gaming table by which we were sitting. He

picked it up, opened it, and found that it was the apostle Paul, which
surprised him because he had expected that it would be one of the   315
books I wore myself out teaching. Then he smiled a little and looked
at me, and expressed pleasure but surprise too at having come suddenly upon that book, and only that book, lying before me. For he
was a Christian and a devout Christian; he knelt before You in
church, O our God, in daily prayer and many times daily. I told him   320
that I had given much care to these writings. Whereupon he began to
tell the story of the Egyptian monk Antony, whose name was held in
high honor among Your servants, although Alypius and I had never
heard it before that time. When he learned this, he was the more
intent upon telling the story, anxious to introduce so great a man to   325
men ignorant of him, and very much marveling at our ignorance. But
Alypius and I stood amazed to hear of Your wonderful works, done in
the true faith and in the Catholic Church so recently, practically in
our own times, and with such numbers of witnesses. All three of us
were filled with wonder, we because the deeds we were now hearing   330
were so great, and he because we had never heard them before.

From this story he went on to the great groups in the monasteries,
and their ways all redolent of You, and the fertile deserts of the wilderness, of all of which we knew nothing. There was actually a monastery
at Milan, outside the city walls. It was full of worthy brethren and   335
under the care of Ambrose. And we had not heard of it. He continued
with his discourse and we listened in absolute silence. It chanced that
he told how on one occasion he and three of his companions—it was
at Treves, when the emperor was at the chariot races in the Circus—
had gone one afternoon to walk in the gardens close by the city walls.   340
As it happened they fell into two groups, one of the others staying with
him, and the other two likewise walking their own way. But as those
other two strolled on they came into a certain house, the dwelling of
some servants of Yours, poor in spirit, of whom is the kingdom of
God. There they found a small book in which was written the life of   345
Antony. One of them began to read it, marvelled at it, was inflamed
by it. While he was actually reading he had begun to think how he
might embrace such a life, and give up his worldly employment to

serve You alone. For the two men were both state officials. Suddenly
the man who was doing the reading was filled with a love of holiness
and angry at himself with righteous shame. He looked at his friend
and said to him: "Tell me, please, what is the goal of our ambition in
all these labours of ours? What are we aiming at? What is our motive
in being in the public service? Have we any higher hope at court than
to be friends of the emperor? And at that level, is not everything
uncertain and full of perils? And how many perils must we meet on
the way to this greater peril? And how long before we are there? But if
I should choose to be a friend of God, I can become one now." He
said this, and all troubled with the pain of the new life coming to birth
in him, he turned back his eyes to the book. He read on and was
changed inwardly, where You alone could see; and the world dropped
away from his mind, as soon appeared outwardly. For while he was
reading and his heart thus tossing on its own flood, at length he broke
out in heavy weeping, saw the better way and chose it for his own.
Being now Your servant he said to his friend, "Now I have broken
from that hope we had and have decided to serve God; and I enter
upon that service from this hour, in this place. If you have no will to
imitate me, at least do not try to dissuade me."

The other replied that he would remain his companion in so great
a service for so great a prize. So the two of them, now Your servants,
built a spiritual tower at the only cost that is adequate, the cost of
leaving all things and following You. Then Ponticianus and the man
who had gone walking with him in another part of the garden came
looking for them in the same place, and when they found them suggested that they should return home as the day was now declining.
But they told their decision and their purpose, and how that will had
arisen in them; and was now settled in them; and asked them not to
try to argue them out of their decision, even if they would not also
join them. Ponticianus and his friend, though not changed from their
former state, yet wept for themselves, as he told us, and congratulated
them in God and commended themselves to their prayers. Then with
their own heart trailing in the dust they went off to the palace, while

the other two, with their heart fixed upon heaven, remained in the hut. Both these men, as it happened, were betrothed, and when the two women heard of it they likewise dedicated their virginity to You. 385

VII

This was the story Ponticianus told. But You, Lord, while he was speaking, turned me back towards myself, taking me from behind my own back where I had put myself all the time that I preferred not to see myself. And You set me there before my own face that I might see how vile I was, how twisted and unclean and spotted and ulcerous. I saw 390 myself and was horrified; but there was no way to flee from myself. If I tried to turn my gaze from myself, there was Ponticianus telling what he was telling; and again You were setting me face to face with myself, forcing me upon my own sight, that I might see my iniquity and loathe it. I had known it, but I had pretended not to see it, had deliberately 395 looked the other way and let it go from my mind. But this time, the more ardently I approved those two as I heard of their determination to win health for their souls by giving themselves up wholly to Your healing, the more detestable did I find myself in comparison with them. For many years had flowed by—a dozen or more—from the time when I 400 was nineteen and was stirred by the reading of Cicero's Hortensius to the study of wisdom; and here was I still postponing the giving up of this world's happiness to devote myself to the search for that of which not the finding only but the mere seeking is better than to find all the treasures and kingdoms of men, better than all the body's pleasures though 405 they were to be had merely for a nod. But I in my great worthlessness— for it was greater thus early—had begged You for chastity, saying: "Grant me chastity and continence, but not yet." For I was afraid that You would hear my prayer too soon, and too soon would heal me from the disease of lust which I wanted satisfied rather than extinguished. So 410 I had gone wandering in my sacrilegious superstition through the base ways of the Manicheans: not indeed that I was sure they were right but that I preferred them to the Christians, whom I did not inquire about in the spirit of religion but simply opposed through malice.

415   I had thought that my reason for putting off from day to day the following of You alone to the contempt of earthly hopes was that I did not see any certain goal towards which to direct my course. But now the day was come when I stood naked in my own sight and my con-
420   science accused me: "Why is my voice not heard? Surely you are the man who used to say that you could not cast off vanity's baggage for an uncertain truth. Very well: now the truth is certain, yet you are still carrying the load. Here are men who have been given wings to free their shoulders from the load, though they did not wear themselves out in searching nor spend ten years or more thinking about it."

425   Thus was I inwardly gnawed at. And I was in the grip of the most horrible and confounding shame, while Ponticianus was telling his story. He finished the tale and the business for which he had come; and he went his way, and I to myself. What did I not say against myself, with what lashes of condemnation did I not scourge my soul
430   to make it follow me now that I wanted to follow You! My soul hung back. It would not follow, yet found no excuse for not following. All its arguments had already been used and refuted. There remained only trembling silence: for it feared as very death the cessation of that habit of which in truth it was dying.

VIII

435   In the midst of that great tumult of my inner dwelling place, the tumult I had stirred up against my own soul in the chamber of my heart, I turned upon Alypius, wild in look and troubled in mind, crying out: "What is wrong with us? What is this that you heard? The unlearned arise and take heaven by force, and here are we with all our
440   learning, stuck fast in flesh and blood! Is there any shame in following because they have gone before us, would it not be a worse shame not to follow at once?" These words and more of the same sort I uttered, then the violence of my feeling tore me from him while he stood staring at me thunderstruck. For I did not sound like myself.
445   My brow, cheeks, eyes, flush, the pitch of my voice, spoke my mind more powerfully than the words I uttered. There was a garden

attached to our lodging, of which we had the use, as indeed we had of the whole house: for our host, the master of the house, did not live there. To this garden the storm in my breast somehow brought me, for there no one could intervene in the fierce suit I had brought against myself, until it should reach its issue: though what the issue was to be, You knew, not I: but there I was, going mad on my way to sanity, dying on my way to life, aware how evil I was, unaware that I was to grow better in a little while. So I went off to the garden, and Alypius close on my heels: for it was still privacy for me to have him near, and how could he leave me to myself in that state? We found a seat as far as possible from the house. I was frantic in mind, in a frenzy of indignation at myself for not going over to Your law and Your covenant, O my God, where all my bones cried out that I should be, extolling it to the skies. The way was not by ship or chariot or on foot: it was not as far as I had gone when I went from the house to the place where we sat. For I had but to will to go, in order not merely to go but to arrive: I had only to will to go—but to will powerfully and wholly, not to turn and twist a will half-wounded this way and that, with the part that would rise struggling against the part that would keep to the earth.

In the torment of my irresolution, I did many bodily acts. Now men sometimes will to do bodily acts but cannot, whether because they have not the limbs, or because their limbs are bound or weakened with illness or in some other way unable to act. If I tore my hair, if I beat my forehead, if I locked my fingers and clasped my knees, I did it because I willed to. But I might have willed and yet not done it, if my limbs had not had the pliability to do what I willed. Thus I did so many things where the will to do them was not at all the same thing as the power to do them: and I did not do what would have pleased me incomparably more to do—a thing too which I could have done as soon as I willed to, given that willing means willing *wholly*. For in that matter, the power was the same thing as the will, and the willing *was* the doing. Yet it was not done, and the body more readily obeyed the slightest wish of the mind, more readily moved its

450

455

460

465

470

475

480

limbs at the mind's mere nod, than the mind obeyed itself in carrying out its own great will which could be achieved simply by willing.

IX

Why this monstrousness? And what is the root of it? Let Your mercy
enlighten me, that I may put the question: whether perhaps the
answer lies in the mysterious punishment that has come upon men
and some deeply hidden damage in the sons of Adam. Why this
monstrousness? And what is the root of it? The mind gives the body
an order, and is obeyed at once: the mind gives itself an order and is
resisted. The mind commands the hand to move and there is such
readiness that you can hardly distinguish the command from its exe-
cution. Yet the mind is mind, whereas the hand is body. The mind
commands the mind to will, the mind is itself, but it does not do it.
Why this monstrousness? And what is the root of it? The mind I say
commands itself to will: it would not give the command unless it
willed: yet it does not do what it commands. The trouble is that it
does not totally will: therefore it does not totally command. It commands in so far as it wills; and it disobeys the command in so far
as it does not will. The will is commanding itself to be a will—
commanding itself, not some other. But it does not in its fullness give
the command, so that what it commands is not done. For if the will
were so in its fullness, it would not command itself to will, for it
would already will. It is therefore no monstrousness, partly to will,
partly not to will, but a sickness of the soul to be so weighted down
by custom that it cannot wholly rise even with the support of truth.
Thus there are two wills in us, because neither of them is entire: and
what is lacking to the one is present in the other.

X

Let them perish from thy presence, O God, as perish vain talkers and
seducers of the soul, who observing that there are two wills at issue in
our coming to a decision proceed to assert [as the Manichees do] that
there are two minds in us of different natures, one good, one evil. For
they are evil themselves in holding such evil opinions; and they will

become good only if they perceive truth and come to it as your Apostle says to them: *You were heretofore darkness but now light in the Lord*
(*Ephesians* 5:9). But these men though they want to be light, want to
be light in themselves and not in the Lord, imagining the nature of   515
the soul to be the same as God. Thus they become not light but
deeper darkness, since in their abominable arrogance they have gone
further from You, *the true Light that enlightens every man that comes
into this world* (*John* 1:9). Take heed what you say and blush for
shame: *draw near unto Him and be enlightened, and your faces shall not*   520
be ashamed (*Ps* 34:5). When I was deliberating about serving the Lord
my God, as I had long meant to do, it was I who willed to do it, I
who was unwilling. It was I. I did not wholly will, I was not wholly
unwilling. Therefore I strove with myself and was distracted by
myself. This distraction happened to me though I did not want it,   525
and it showed me not the presence of some second mind, but the
punishment of my own mind. Thus it was not I who caused it but *the
sin that dwells in me* (*Romans* 7:17), the punishment of a sin freely
committed by Adam, whose son I am.

   For if there be as many contrary natures in man as there are wills   530
in conflict with one another, then there are not two natures in us but
several. Take the case of a man trying to make up his mind whether
he would go to the Manichees' meeting-house or to the theater. The
Manichees would say: "Here you have two natures, one good, bringing him to the meeting-house, the other evil, taking him away. How   535
else could you have this wavering between two wills pulling against
each other?" Now I say that both are bad, the will that would take
him to the Manichees and the will that would take him to the theater. But they hold that the will by which one comes to them is good.
Very well! Supposing one of us is trying to decide and wavering   540
between two wills in conflict, whether to go to the theater or to our
church, will not the Manichees be in some trouble about an answer?
For either they must admit, which they do not want to, that a good
will would take a man to our church as they think it is a good will
that brings those who are receivers of their sacrament* and belong to   545
them to their church; or they must hold that there are two evil natures

and two evil wills at conflict in one man, and what they are always saying will not be true—namely that there is one good will and one evil will. Otherwise, they must be converted to the truth and not deny that when a man is taking a decision there is one soul drawn this way and that by diverse wills.

Therefore, when they perceive that there are two wills in conflict in man, they must not say that there are two opposing minds in conflict, one good, one bad, from two opposing substances and two opposing principles. For you, O God of truth, refute them and disprove them and convict them of error: as in the case where both wills are bad, when, for instance, a man is deliberating whether he shall kill another man by poison or by dagger; whether he should seize this or that part of another man's property, when he cannot seize both; whether he should spend his money on lust or hoard his money through avarice; whether he should go to the games or the theater if they happen both to come on the same day. Let us add a third possibility to this last man, whether he should go and commit a theft from someone else's house, if the occasion should arise: and indeed a fourth, whether he should go and commit adultery, if the chance occurs at the same time. If all four things come together at the same point of time, and all are equally desired, yet all cannot be done, then they tear the mind by the conflicting pull of four wills—or even more, given the great mass of things which can be desired. Yet the Manichees do not hold such a multitude of different substances.

The same reasoning applies to wills that are good. For I ask them whether it is good to find delight in the reading of the Apostle, and good to find delight in the serenity of a Psalm, and good to discuss the Gospel. To each of these they answer that it is good: but, if all these things attract us at the same moment, are not different wills tugging at the heart of man while we deliberate which we should choose? Thus they are all good, yet they are all in conflict until one is chosen, and then the whole will is at rest and at one, whereas it had been divided into many. Or again, when eternity attracts the higher faculties and the pleasure of some temporal good holds the lower, it is one same soul that wills both, but not either with its whole will; and it is therefore torn both ways and deeply troubled while truth shows the one way as better but habit keeps it to the other.

XI

Thus I was sick at heart and in torment, accusing myself with a new intensity of bitterness, twisting and turning in my chain in the hope   585
that it might be utterly broken, for what held me was so small a thing! But it still held me. And You stood in the secret places of my soul, O Lord, in the harshness of Your mercy redoubling the scourges of fear and shame lest I should give way again and that small slight tie which remained should not be broken but should grow again to full strength   590
and bind me closer even than before. For I kept saying within myself: "Let it be now, let it be now," and by the mere words I had begun to move towards the resolution. I almost made it, yet I did not quite make it. But I did not fall back into my original state, but as it were stood near to get my breath. And I tried again and I was almost there,   595
and now I could all but touch it and hold it: yet I was not quite there, I did not touch it or hold it. I still shrank from dying unto death and living unto life. The lower condition which had grown habitual was more powerful than the better condition which I had not tried. The nearer the point of time came in which I was to become different, the   600
more it struck me with horror; but it did not force me utterly back nor turn me utterly away, but held me there between the two.

Those trifles of all trifles, and vanities of vanities, my one-time mistresses, held me back, plucking at my garment of flesh and mur-muring softly: "Are you sending us away?" And "From this moment   605
shall we not be with you, now or forever?" And "From this moment shall this or that not be allowed you, now or forever?" What were they suggesting to me in the phrase I have written "this or that," what were they suggesting to me, O my God? Do you in your mercy keep from the soul of Your servant the vileness and uncleanness they were sug-   610
gesting. And now I began to hear them not half so loud; they no longer stood against me face to face, but were softly muttering behind

my back and, as I tried to depart, plucking stealthily at me to make me look behind. Yet even that was enough, so hesitating was I, to keep me from snatching myself free, from shaking them off and leaping upwards on the way I was called: for the strong force of habit said to me: "Do you think you can live without them?"

But by this time its voice was growing fainter. In the direction towards which I had turned my face and was quivering in fear of going, I could see the austere beauty of Continence, serene and indeed joyous but not evilly, honorably soliciting me to come to her and not linger, stretching forth loving hands to receive and embrace me, hands full of multitudes of good examples. With her I saw such hosts of young men and maidens, a multitude of youth and of every age, gray widows and women grown old in virginity, and in them all Continence herself, not barren but the fruitful mother of children, her joys, by You, Lord, her Spouse. And she smiled upon me and her smile gave courage as if she were saying: "Can you not do what these men have done, what these women have done? Or could men or women have done such in themselves, and not in the Lord their God? The Lord their God gave me to them. Why do you stand upon yourself and so not stand at all? Cast yourself upon Him and be not afraid; He will not draw away and let you fall. Cast yourself without fear, He will receive you and heal you."

Yet I was still ashamed, for I could still hear the murmuring of those vanities, and I still hung hesitant. And again it was as if she said: "Stop your ears against your unclean members, that they may be mortified. They tell you of delights, but not of such delights as the law of the Lord your God tells." This was the controversy raging in my heart, a controversy about myself against myself. And Alypius stayed by my side and awaited in silence the issue of such agitation as he had never seen in me.

XII

When my most searching scrutiny had drawn up all my vileness from the secret depths of my soul and heaped it in my heart's sight, a mighty storm arose in me, bringing a mighty rain of tears. That I might give way to my tears and lamentations, I rose from Alypius: for it struck me that solitude was more suited to the business of weeping. I went far enough from him to prevent his presence from being an embarrassment to me. So I felt, and he realized it. I suppose I had said something and the sound of my voice was heavy with tears. I arose, but he remained where we had been sitting, still in utter amazement. I flung myself down somehow under a certain fig tree and no longer tried to check my tears, which poured forth from my eyes in a flood, *an acceptable sacrifice to Thee*. And much I said not in these words but to this effect: "*And Thou, O, Lord, how long? How long, Lord; wilt Thou be angry forever? Remember not our former iniquities (Ps 79:8)*." For I felt that I was still bound by them. And I continued my miserable complaining: "How long, how long shall I go on saying tomorrow and again tomorrow? Why not now, why not have an end to my uncleanness this very hour?"

Such things I said, weeping in the most bitter sorrow of my heart. And suddenly I heard a voice from some nearby house, a boy's voice or a girl's voice, I do not know: but it was a sort of sing-song, repeated again and again, "Take and read, take and read." I ceased weeping and immediately began to search my mind most carefully as to whether children were accustomed to chant these words in any kind of game, and I could not remember that I had ever heard any such thing. Damming back the flood of my tears I arose, interpreting the incident as quite certainly a divine command to open my book of Scripture and read the passage at which I should open. For it was part of what I had been told about Anthony, that from the Gospel which he happened to be reading he had felt that he was being admonished as though what he read was spoken directly to himself: *Go, sell what thou hast and give to the poor and thou shalt have treasure in heaven; and come follow Me (Matt 19:21)*. By this experience he had been in that instant converted to You. So I was moved to return to the place where Alypius was sitting, for I had put down the Apostle's book there when I arose. I snatched it up, opened it and in silence read the passage upon which my eyes first fell: *Not in rioting and drunkenness, not in chambering and impurities, not in contention and envy, but put ye on*

650

655

660

665

670

675

680

the Lord Jesus Christ and make not provision for the flesh in its concupiscences (Romans 13:13). I had no wish to read further, and no need. For in that instant, with the very ending of the sentence, it was as though a light of utter confidence shone in all my heart, and all the darkness of uncertainty vanished away. Then leaving my finger in the place or marking it by some other sign, I closed the book and in complete calm told the whole thing to Alypius and he similarly told me what had been going on in himself, of which I knew nothing. He asked to see what I had read. I showed him, and he looked further than I had read. I had not known what followed. And this is what followed: *"Now him that is weak in faith, take unto you."* He applied this to himself and told me so. And he was confirmed by this message, and with no troubled wavering gave himself to God's good-will and purpose—a purpose indeed most suited to his character, for in these matters he had been immeasurably better than I.

Then we went in to my mother and told her, to her great joy. We related how it had come about: she was filled with triumphant exultation, and praised You who are mighty beyond what we ask or conceive: for she saw that You had given her more than with all her pitiful weeping she had ever asked. For You converted me to Yourself so that I no longer sought a wife nor any of this world's promises, but stood upon that same rule of faith in which You had shown me to her so many years before. Thus You changed her mourning into joy, a joy far richer than she had thought to wish, a joy much dearer and purer than she had thought to find in grandchildren of my flesh.

DISCUSSION QUESTIONS

1. In chapter 2 Victorinus asks, "*Is it the walls that make Christians?*" What do you think he means by that question, and do you think his objection is justified? Why, or why not?

2. For a time Augustine was drawn to Manichaeism.* Why might someone be attracted to its dualistic teaching? In what ways might its dualism* also be less than intellectually satisfying? (Both "Manichaeism" and "dualism*" are briefly explained in the Glossary below.)

3. Why did Augustine feel so ashamed about the way that he was living? Could he have continued his former life and still be an authentic Christian? Does the way in which his heart is finally settled and he comes to peace ring true to you? Why? Or why not?

4. Why, do you think, Augustine wrote and published this very personal and possibly even embarrassing account? And why did he direct his reminiscences of the past to God personally throughout the *Confessions?*

18

Sacred Images

Against Iconoclasm

COUNCIL OF NICAEA II (787)

INTRODUCTION

Worship of Idols?

A controversy raged in the Greek church from ca. A.D. 725 to 842 on whether it is permitted according to the Christian faith to venerate sacred images or "icons" (Gk: *eikôn*) of God and the saints. The Monophysite heresy* that minimized the human side of Jesus, the Manichaean Paulicians who tended to see all matter as evil, and possibly also Islam, which condemned all images of the divine, probably contributed to a movement to remove and destroy all sacred images in Christian churches. Emperor Leo III the Isaurian (717–741) saw the use of icons as the chief obstacle to the conversion of Jews and Muslims and so to bringing peace and unity to his realm. In 726 he declared all icons idols and ordered them destroyed. Patriarch St. Germanus of Constantinople who opposed the decree was deposed and monks, the most ardent iconodules, were severely persecuted. Leo's son, Constantine V, succeeded him in 741 and continued the iconoclast policy. Constantine's Son, Leo IV (775–80) was less adamant, and after his death his wife, the Empress Irene, regent for her young son Constantine, reversed the policy.

Nicaea II Response

In 787 the Council of Nicaea II was called and issued a decree, a selection from which is included here, in which it defined the degree of veneration due to icons and demanded their restoration throughout the Empire. In spite of this, the army remained opposed to icons, causing a second period of iconoclasm that began in 814 and resulted in much destruction and bloodshed. This persecution ended only after the death of Emperor Theophilus in 842. When his widow, Theodora, regent for her young son, had Methodius elected patriarch in 843, a great feast was inaugurated on the first Sunday of Lent in honor of icons, known ever since as the "Feast of Orthodoxy."

Theology of Icons

Well before the controversy, Leontius of Neapolis (Cyprus, ca. 590–650) articulated a profound theology of creation in a work on images in which he states: "*Through heaven and earth and sea, through wood and stone, through relics and church buildings and the Cross, through angels and humans, through all creation visible and invisible, I offer veneration and honor to the Creator and the Master and Maker of all things, and to Him alone. For creation does not venerate the Maker directly and by itself, but it is through me that the heavens declare the glory of God, through me the moon worships God, through me the waters and showers of rain, the dew and all creation, venerate God and give him glory.*" During the iconoclast period, Doctor of the Church* St. John Damascene (ca. 675–749) and St. Theodore of Studios (759–826) both wrote stirringly in defense of icons, also tying them into the Christian doctrines*of creation and incarnation.* According to Damascene, "*The Word made flesh has deified the flesh,*" so there can be no unbridgeable gap between God and humanity, spiritual and material. Theodore adds, *"If merely mental contemplation [of God] were sufficient, it would have been sufficient for him to come to us in a merely mental way."*

—Rev. John D. Laurance, S.J.

TEXT

The holy, great, and Ecumenical Synod which by the grace* of God and the will of the pious and Christ-loving Emperors, Constantine and Irene, his mother, was gathered together for the second time at Nicaea, the illustrious metropolis of Bithynia, in the holy church of God which is named Sophia, having followed the tradition* of the Catholic Church, has defined as follows: 5

Christ our Lord, who has bestowed upon us the light of the knowledge of himself, and has redeemed us from the darkness of idolatrous madness, having espoused the Holy Catholic Church to himself without spot or defect, promised that he would so preserve her: and gave his word to this effect to his holy disciples when he said: 10
"Behold! I am with you always, even to the end of the world," which promise he made, not only to them, but to us also who should believe in his name through their word. But some, not appreciating this gift, and having become fickle through the temptation of the wily enemy, have fallen from the right faith. For, withdrawing from the traditions   15
of the Catholic Church, they have wandered from the truth and as the proverb says: "The husbandmen have gone astray in their own husbandry and have gathered in their hands nothingness." Certain priests, priests in name only, not in fact, had dared to speak against the God-approved ornament of the sacred monuments, of whom   20
God cries aloud through the prophet, "Many pastors have corrupted my vineyard, they have polluted my portion."

And, indeed, following profane men, led astray by their carnal sense, they have calumniated the Church of Christ, our God, which he has espoused to himself, and have failed to distinguish between   25
holy and profane, referring to the images of our Lord and of his Saints

by the same name as the statues of diabolical idols. Seeing all this, our Lord God (not willing to see his people corrupted by this kind of plague) by his good pleasure has called us together, the chief of his priests, from every quarter, moved with a divine zeal and brought here by the will of our princes, Constantine and Irene, so that the traditions of the Catholic Church might be stabilized by our common decree. Therefore, with all diligence, making a thorough examination and analysis, and following the direction of the truth, we subtract nothing, we add nothing, but we preserve unchanged everything that pertains to the Catholic Church, and following the Six Ecumenical Synods, especially that which met in this illustrious metropolis of Nicaea, as well as that which was afterwards gathered together in the God-protected Royal City (Constantinople).

We believe . . . life of the world to come. Amen *(The Creed)*.

We detest and anathematize Arius and all the sharers of his absurd opinion, also Macedonius and those who following him are well styled "Foes of the Spirit" *(Pneumatomachi)*. We confess that our Lady, St. Mary, is properly and truly the Mother of God, because she was the Mother according to the flesh of One Person of the Holy Trinity,* that is, Christ our God, as the Council of Ephesus (431) has already defined when it cast out of the Church the impious Nestorius with his colleagues, because he taught that there were two Persons [in Christ]. With the Fathers of this synod we confess that he who was incarnate of the immaculate Mother of God and Ever-Virgin Mary has two natures, recognizing him as perfect God and perfect man, as also the Council of Chalcedon (451) has promulgated, expelling from the divine Atrium as blasphemers Eutyches and Dioscorus, and placing in the same category Severus, Peter, and a number of others, blaspheming in various ways. Moreover, with these we anathematize the fables of Origen, Evagrius, and Didymus, in accordance with the decision of the Fifth Council held at Constantinople (Constantinople II, 553). We affirm that in Christ there be two wills and two operations according to the reality of each nature, as also the Sixth Synod, held at Constantinople (III, 680–81), taught, casting out

Sergius, Honorius, Cyrus, Pyrrhus, Macarius, and those who agree with them, and all those who are unwilling to be reverent.

To make our confession short, we keep unchanged all the ecclesiastical traditions handed down to us, whether in writing or verbally, one of which is the making of pictorial representations, agreeable to the history of the preaching of the gospel, a tradition useful in many respects, but especially in this, that so the incarnation* of the Word of God is shown forth as real and not merely phantastic, for these have mutual indications and without doubt have also mutual significations.

We, therefore, following the royal pathway and the divinely inspired authority of our Holy Fathers and the traditions of the Catholic Church (for, as we all know, the Holy Spirit indwells her), define with all certitude and accuracy that just as the figure of the precious and life-giving Cross, so also the venerable and holy images, as well in painting and mosaic as of other fit materials, should be set forth in the holy churches of God, and on the sacred vessels and on the vestments and on hangings and in pictures both in houses and by the wayside, that is, the figure of our Lord God and Savior Jesus Christ, of our spotless Lady, the Mother of God, of the honorable Angels, of all Saints and of all pious people. For by so much more often as they are seen in artistic representation, by so much more readily are people lifted up to the memory of their prototypes, and to a longing after them; and to these should be given due salutation and honorable reverence, not indeed that true worship of faith *(latreia)* which pertains alone to the divine nature; but to these, as to the figure of the precious and life-giving Cross and to the Book of the Gospels and to the other holy objects, incense and lights may be offered according to ancient pious custom. For the honor which is paid to the image passes on to that which the image represents, and he who reveres the image reveres in it the subject represented. For thus the teaching of our holy Fathers, that is the tradition* of the Catholic Church, which from one end of the earth to the other has received the gospel, is strengthened. Thus we follow Paul, who spoke in Christ, and the whole divine Apostolic company and the holy Fathers, holding fast to the traditions which we have received. So we

Our Lady of Vladimir, Russian Icon.
© Scala/Art Resource

sing prophetically the triumphal hymns of the Church, "*Rejoice greatly, O daughter of Sion; Shout, O daughter of Jerusalem. Rejoice and be glad with all your heart. The Lord has taken away from you the oppression of your adversaries; you are redeemed from the hand of your enemies. The Lord is a King in your midst; you will not see evil any more, and peace be to you forever.*"

Those, therefore who dare to think or teach otherwise, or as wicked heretics to spurn the traditions of the Church and to invent some novelty, or else to reject some of those things which the Church has received (e.g., the Book of the Gospels, or the image of the cross, or the pictorial icons, or the holy relics of a martyr), or evilly and sharply to devise anything subversive of the lawful traditions of the Catholic Church or to turn to common uses the sacred vessels or the venerable monasteries, if they be bishops or clerics, we command that they be deposed; if religious or laity, that they be cut off from communion.

[*After all had signed, the acclamations began.*]

The holy Synod cried out: So we all believe, we all are so minded, we all give our consent and have signed. This is the faith of the Apostles, this is the faith of the Orthodox, this is the faith which has made firm the whole world. Believing in one God, to be celebrated in Trinity, we salute the honorable images! Those who do not so hold, let them be anathema. Those who do not thus think, let them be driven far away from the Church. For we follow the most ancient legislation of the Catholic Church. We keep the laws of the Fathers. We anathematize those who add anything to or take anything away from the Catholic Church. We anathematize the introduced novelty of the revilers of Christians. We salute the venerable images. We place under anathema those who do not do this. Anathema to them who presume to apply to the venerable images the things said in Holy Scripture about idols. Anathema to those who do not salute the holy and venerable images. Anathema to those who call the sacred images idols. Anathema to those who say that Christians resort to the sacred images as to gods. Anathema to those who say that any other delivered us from idols except Christ our God. Anathema to those who dare to say that at any time the Catholic Church received idols.

130

DISCUSSION QUESTIONS

1. The Council of Nicaea II certainly uses forceful language to assert its position on the veneration of sacred images. Why do you think it felt the need for such harsh language? Was there some central Christian dogma* which it saw iconoclasm especially attacking?

2. As you read, Nicaea II solemnly declared sacred images sacramental means of God's grace. Also deep in Christian tradition is the veneration of relics, going back at least to the 2nd century. On reflection, such practices appear rooted not only in Christian faith, but also in human nature: Russians continue to file past Lenin's body in Red Square; a sign in the Alamo asks that tourists be quiet in honor of those who died there; Rock and Roll lovers make "pilgrimages" to Graceland in Memphis; and people often treasure a letter received long in the past, or an heirloom from a beloved parent or grandparent. Are there any such objects or places in your life which you regard somehow to be "sacred?"

19

Christ the Savior

Cur Deus Homo? I: 3, 14, 24; II: 7

ST. ANSELM OF CANTERBURY (CA. 1033–1109)

INTRODUCTION

Personal Background

Born in the north of Italy in the town of Aosta in 1033, Anselm's life took him from this Alpine region to Normandy and then to England, from the vocation of a monk to that of a bishop, all the while recognized for his holiness and becoming the most important theologian of his age in Western Europe. His wealthy parents ensured that he was well educated and the stirrings of his monastic calling began early during his adolescence. Initially denied entry into the Benedictine monastery in his home town because he lacked his father's permission he later crossed the Alps and eventually made his way through France to Normandy and another Benedictine monastery at Bec where he studied under the direction of its prior Lanfranc. Anselm flourished as both monk and theologian replacing Lanfranc as prior when the latter

149

became abbot of another Benedictine monastery in Caen, also in Normandy. By the year 1079 Anselm had become abbot of Bec only again to follow in the steps of his master Lanfranc, succeeding him as Archbishop of Canterbury in England in 1093. He died while still in this office in 1109 after in his case faithfully struggling with English kings over the investiture controversy, whether the crown or the Church could appoint bishops. Although he much preferred the contemplative life of a monk, he skillfully confronted the throne, enduring exiles to France, but with the support of the Pope was able to ensure the integrity of the Church in its major pastoral appointments.

Theological Writings

Despite his active life as a bishop, including being primate of England by virtue of being the Archbishop of the See of Canterbury, Anselm wrote prolifically in theology and it is due to this aspect of his life and ministry that he is best known to subsequent generations of Christian theologians. He authored many significant theological works including the *Mononlogion* and the *Proslogion,* the latter of which became famous for his definition of theology and his proof for the existence of God. The definition, following the tradition of St. Augustine, is still considered the most concise and cogent definition of the discipline, namely, faith seeking understanding (in the original Latin—*fides quaerens intellectum*). Although beginning with faith, this monk-theologian, who suffused his theology with prayer, also gave a significant place to reason. His proof for the existence of God is well known, even in the modern era, labeled by some as the "ontological proof." Based on the axiom that God is greater than anything that can be conceived, it intends by this definition of divinity to rationally demonstrate that God must exist in reality as well as in thought since existence in reality is greater than existing only in the mind. Since God by definition must always be greater than anything else, it is then self-evident that God exists. Although not all have been persuaded by this argument (including St. Thomas Aquinas), it does indeed show that Anselm took seriously both faith and reason, the logic of the proof being dependent on the recognition of what God is.

Cur Deus Homo?

Anselm's confidence in reason, which helped inaugurate the age of scholasticism*—he is known as the "Father of Scholasticism"—when theology would flourish more in the great universities of Europe rather than only in monasteries, is also seen in the present treatise by Anselm, *Cur Deus Homo?—Why Did God Become Human?* This inquiry into the central core mystery of Christian faith, the doctrine* of the Incarnation*, attempts to demonstrate the truth of this mystery of faith by following the logic of atonement as necessary for Redemption.* It has become one of the most influential theologies of atonement in the history of Christian thought by attempting to explain the "how" of the universal Christian confession that by becoming human "for us and our salvation" Christ died on the cross "for our sake" for the forgiveness of our sins. The treatise, probably written between 1094 and 1098, assumes the form of a dialogue between teacher and pupil, Anselm and his friend Boso. This genre of writing reinforces the reasonableness and necessity of the Incarnation by proceeding carefully through the argument and overcoming all objections. Most importantly its premise is that Jesus Christ, the God-Man, is the one who can atone for human sins by providing satisfaction to God as the one who alone can both represent humanity (by virtue of his assumed human nature in the Incarnation) and be worthy of God because of his own divinity. Some scholars argue that the historical context of medieval feudalism where reparation for wrongs done to restore honor in the social arena is a requirement for the peace and order of society lends legitimacy to Anselm's theory of atonement. The question then arises as to whether different cultures and times can then understand and accept his explanation. Be that as it may, Anselm raises a perennial issue for Christian faith and theology. In confessing that Christ died for our sins, how do Christians understand the relationship between mercy and justice in God's governance of creation and in the good news of his redemption of a sinful world?

—*Dr. Ralph Del Colle*

TEXT

St. Anselm, *Cur Deus Homo?*—Why did God become Human?
http://www.fordham.edu/halsall/basis/anselm-curdeus.html

Book One

Chapter 3

We do no injustice or dishonor to God, but give him thanks with all
the heart, praising and proclaiming the ineffable height of his com-
passion. For the more astonishing a thing it is and beyond
expectation, that he has restored us from so great and deserved ills in
which we were, to so great and unmerited blessings which we had for-
feited; by so much the more has he shown his more exceeding love
and tenderness towards us. For did [the unbelievers] but carefully
consider how fitly in this way human redemption* is secured, they
would not ridicule our simplicity, but would rather join with us in
praising the wise beneficence of God. For, as death came upon the
human race by the disobedience of man, it was fitting that by man's
obedience life should be restored. And, as sin, the cause of our condemnation, had its origin from a woman, so ought the author of our
righteousness and salvation to be born of a woman. And so also was
it proper that the devil, who, being man's tempter, had conquered
him in eating of the tree, should be vanquished by man in the suffering of the tree which man bore. Many other things also, if we
carefully examine them, give a certain indescribable beauty to our
redemption as thus procured.

Chapter 14

It is impossible for God to lose his honor; for either the sinner pays
his debt of his own accord, or, if he refuse, God takes it from him.
For either man renders due submission to God of his own will, by
avoiding sin or making payment, or else God subjects him to himself

by torments, even against man's will, and thus shows that he is the Lord of man, though man refuses to acknowledge it of his own accord. And here we must observe that as man in sinning takes away what belongs to God, so God in punishing gets in return what pertains to man. For not only does that belong to a man which he has in present possession, but also that which it is in his power to have. Therefore, since man was so made as to be able to attain happiness by avoiding sin; if, on account of his sin, he is deprived of happiness and every good, he repays from his own inheritance what he has stolen, though he repay it against his will. For although God does not apply what he takes away to any object of his own, as man transfers the money which he has taken from another to his own use; yet what he takes away serves the purpose of his own honor, for this very reason, that it is taken away. For by this act he shows that the sinner and all that pertains to him are under his subjection.

Chapter 24

Just so inexcusable is man, who has voluntarily brought upon himself a debt which he cannot pay, and by his own fault disabled himself, so that he can neither escape his previous obligation not to sin, nor pay the debt which he has incurred by sin. For his very inability is guilt, because he ought not to have it; nay, he ought to be free from it; for as it is a crime not to have what he ought, it is also a crime to have what he ought not. Therefore, as it is a crime in man not to have that power which he received to avoid sin, it is also a crime to have that inability by which he can neither do right and avoid sin, nor restore the debt which he owes on account of his sin. For it is by his own free action that he loses that power, and falls into this inability. For not to have the power which one ought to have, is the same thing as to have the inability which one ought not to have. Therefore man's inability to restore what he owes to God, an inability brought upon himself for that very purpose, does not excuse man from paying; for the result of sin cannot excuse the sin itself.

Book Two

Chapter 7

55 The Divine and human natures cannot alternate, so that the Divine should become human or the human Divine; nor can they be so commingled as that a third should be produced from the two which is neither wholly Divine nor wholly human. For, granting that it were possible for either to be changed into the other, it would in that case

60 be only God and not man, or man only and not God. Or, if they were so commingled that a third nature sprung from the combination of the two (as from two animals, a male and a female of different species, a third is produced, which does not preserve entire the species of either parent, but has a mixed nature derived from both), it would

65 neither be God nor man. Therefore the God-man, whom we require to be of a nature both human and Divine, cannot be produced by a change from one into the other, nor by an imperfect commingling of both in a third; since these things cannot be, or, if they could be, would avail nothing to our purpose. Moreover, if these two complete

70 natures are said to be joined somehow, in such a way that one may be Divine while the other is human, and yet that which is God not be the same with that which is man, it is impossible for both to do the work necessary to be accomplished. For God will not do it, because he has no debt to pay; and man will not do it, because he cannot.

75 Therefore, in order that the God-man may perform this, it is necessary that the same being should be perfect God and perfect man, in order to make this atonement. For he cannot and ought not to do it, unless he be very God and very man. Since, then, it is necessary that the God-man preserve the completeness of each nature, it is no less

80 necessary that these two natures be united entire in one person, just as a body and a reasonable soul exist together in every human being; for otherwise it is impossible that the same being should be very God and very man.

DISCUSSION QUESTIONS

1. Do you think it is necessary that something be done to atone for sins in order for God to forgive sins? Can there be salvation* without atonement? Explain.

2. Do you see honor and justice, dishonor and injustice, as inter-related concepts? Do you think they can still be applied to the relationship between God and humanity wounded by sin? Explain.

3. Obviously, Anselm takes sin seriously. He also believes human beings are incapable of restoring the damage caused by sin apart from the work of Christ. Does your faith take sin that seriously? Why or why not?

4. For Anselm Incarnation* and Redemption* are intimately related. In other words, without Christmas there can be no Easter. Does your understanding of the person of Jesus Christ require both affirmations also? Explain.

20

Is Theology Necessary?
Summa Theologiae I, Q. 1, art. 1

ST. THOMAS AQUINAS (1225–1274)

INTRODUCTION

Background

Thomas Aquinas (1224–1274) was a Dominican friar* and university professor, who taught courses in Scripture at the recently founded universities of Paris, Rome, and Naples. He is known as a philosopher for his commentaries on the works of Aristotle, and distinguished himself as a theologian with two major summaries of Christian thought, the *Summa contra Gentiles,* and the *Summa theologiae.* Less than fifty years after his death, he was formally recognized as a saint of the Catholic Church. His students called him the "Doctor Angelicus," for his theology of angels; others referred to him as the "Doctor Communis," or common teacher of all Christians.

Summa Theologiae

The *Summa theologiae* is a multi-volume handbook for beginning students of theology. It is composed of a series of questions, or discussion topics, further divided into articles, or mini-debates resolving questions raised by Christian doctrine.* "The first part" (I) of the *Summa* deals with the basis of theology, God, the Trinity*, providence and predestination*, and the creation of the world, angels, and human beings. The next two sections of the *Summa* are called "the first part of the second part" (I–II)," and "the second part of the second part" (II-II)." "The first part of the second part" discusses the goals of human existence in terms of human emotion, character development, virtues*, and vices, then concludes with a series of questions on sin, the law, and divine grace. "The second part of the second part" covers the seven virtues* and the vices opposed to them. Finally, "the third part" (III) covers the life of Christ and the sacraments of his Church.

Why is Theology Necessary?

When you signed up for this course, you may have asked yourself, "why do I have to take theology when we already discussed the existence of God in our philosophy course?" Doesn't philosophy give us enough information about God? In article one of question one of the *Summa theologiae,* Thomas Aquinas addresses these questions, since his students probably asked them, too.

Thomas Aquinas lets the opponents of theological studies speak first, in two opening arguments; one is from *Ecclesiasticus (Sirach)* in the Old Testament, the other from Aristotle. He then counters these arguments with a New Testament text, where Scripture is said to be divinely inspired and useful for instruction (*2 Tim* 3:16). Responding to both sides of the argument, he points out that God is beyond the reach of human reason or investigation; to be known to us, God must reveal himself to us. Theology is the study of this divine revelation, which is found in Scripture. Responding to the two opening arguments, Aquinas reiterates that what is inaccessible to reason can be known through revelation. Different sciences use different methods to study the same objects and arrive at the same conclusions. Hence, there need be no conflict between theology and philosophy when both investigate the existence of God, although theology uses revelation, and philosophy relies solely on human reason.

—Dr. Wanda Zemler-Cizewski

TEXT

Summa Theologiae, I, 1:
The Nature and Extent of Sacred Doctrine
(In Ten Articles)

To place our purpose within proper limits, we first endeavor to investigate the nature and extent of this sacred doctrine. Concerning this there are ten points of inquiry:—

(1) Whether it is necessary? (2) Whether it is a science? (3) Whether it is one or many? (4) Whether it is speculative or practical? (5) How it is compared with other sciences? (6) Whether it is the same as wisdom? (7) Whether God is its subject-matter? (8) Whether it is a matter of argument? (9) Whether it rightly employs metaphors and similes? (10) Whether the Sacred Scripture of this doctrine may be expounded in different senses?

First Article:

Whether, besides Philosophy,
Any Further Doctrine Is Required?

We proceed thus to the First Article:—

Objection 1. It seems that, besides philosophical science, we have no need of any further knowledge. For man should not seek to know what is above reason: *Seek not the things that are too high for thee* (*Ecclus.* iii. 22). But whatever is not above reason is fully treated of in philosophical science. Therefore any other knowledge besides philosophical science is superfluous.

Chartres Cathedral, France.
Photo by John D. Laurance, S.J.

Obj. 2. Further, knowledge can be concerned only with being, for nothing can be known, save what is true; and all that is, is true. But everything that is, is treated of in philosophical science—even God Himself; so that there is a part of philosophy called theology, or the divine science, as Aristotle has proved (*Metaph.* vi). Therefore, besides philosophical science, there is no need of any further knowledge.

On the contrary, It is written (*2 Tim.* iii. 16): *All Scripture inspired of God is profitable to teach, to reprove, to correct, to instruct in justice.* Now Scripture, inspired of God, is no part of philosophical science, which has been built up by human reason. Therefore it is useful that besides philosophical science there should be other knowledge—i.e., inspired of God.

I answer that, It was necessary for man's salvation* that there should be a knowledge revealed by God, besides philosophical science built up by human reason. Firstly, indeed, because man is directed to God, as to an end that surpasses the grasp of his reason: *The eye hath not seen, O God, besides Thee, what things Thou hast prepared for them that wait for Thee (Isa.* lxiv. 3). But the end must first be known by men who are to direct their thoughts and actions to the end. Hence it was necessary for the salvation of man that certain truths which exceed human reason should be made known to him by divine revelation. Even as regards those truths about God which human reason could have discovered, it was necessary that man should be taught by a divine revelation; because the truth about God such as reason could discover, would only be known by a few, and that after a long time, and with the admixture of many errors. Whereas man's whole salvation, which is in God, depends upon the knowledge of this truth. Therefore, in order that the salvation of men might be brought about more fitly and more surely, it was necessary that they should be taught divine truths by divine revelation. It was therefore necessary that, besides philosophical science built up by reason there should be a sacred science learned through revelation.

20

25

30

35

40

45

50

Reply Obj. 1. Although those things which are beyond man's knowledge may not be sought for by man through his reason, nevertheless, once they are revealed by God they must be accepted by faith. Hence the sacred text continues, *For many things are shown to thee above the understanding of man* (*Ecclus.* iii. 22). And in this the sacred science consists.

Reply Obj. 2. Sciences are differentiated according to the various means through which knowledge is obtained. For the astronomer and the physicist both may prove the same conclusion—that the earth, for instance, is round: the astronomer by means of mathematics (i.e., abstracting from matter), but the physicist by means of matter itself. Hence there is no reason why those things which may be learned from philosophical science, so far as they can be known by natural reason, may not also be taught us by another science so far as they fall within revelation. Hence theology included in sacred doctrine differs in kind from that theology which is part of philosophy.

"Doctrine" here is the translator's rendition of *doctrina*, meaning, not "doctrine*" in the strictly religious sense of that word, but "teaching," i.e., something a *doctor* (teacher) does.

"Science" here translates *scientia*, meaning "knowledge" in the sense of an organized discipline of knowing. Not restricted then just to empirical sciences such as physics, chemistry, anthropology, etc., "science" here has the larger sense of any knowledge discipline having its own formal subject matter and methods of inquiry. And so it includes philosophy and theology as well as the physical and human sciences.

DISCUSSION QUESTIONS

1. This reading provides an example of "the scholastic method" of investigation: first presenting the *status questionis*—the present "state of the question" to be addressed, then surveying varying ways others have answered the question, and finally providing one's own attempt to resolve it. Given this example, can you think of any shortcomings of this method? If so, what are they?

2. What basic presupposition does Thomas rely on to make his argument here which he evidently doesn't feel he needs to prove because his readers would share it? Is there anything about the nature of theology as a "science" which would allow him to do this?

3. The whole argument of this question appears to rest on an understanding theology as a "doctrine," that is, a teaching. Thomas also states, "*man's whole salvation, which is in God, depends upon the knowledge of this truth.*" How, then, would you say, is Thomas' understanding of salvation here essentially any different from that held by the Gnostics? Or is it any different? (See "Gnosticism*" in the Glossary below.)

21

Mystical Prayer

Revelations of Divine Love 58–60

JULIAN OF NORWICH (1342 -CA. 1420)

INTRODUCTION

Julian and Her Writings

The anonymous anchoress* who authored the first work by a woman in English is called "Julian" or "Dame Julian," probably after the church to which her monastic cell was attached, in the city of Norwich, England. Julian lived during an era of Church turmoil, the plague, the writings of Chaucer, and a flourishing of mysticism. She spent years in prayer and solitude, and was revered as a holy recluse and wise spiritual counselor.

Julian's writings in mystical theology matured over two decades of prayerful contemplation, following sixteen visions or "showings" she experienced in May, 1373, while near death from illness. The visions focus on the Triune God affirmed in the Nicene Creed, and the Christian mysteries of creation, fall, incarnation*, and redemption.*

In Julian's day, women were officially forbidden to be theological teachers. Yet, after momentarily mistaking her visions for disease-induced "ravings," Julian and others became convinced that they were of divine origin, and that she had a duty, out of love of God and her fellow-Christians, to share them. Her writing is poetic and creative, yet deeply indebted to Scripture (especially wisdom traditions and the Gospel of John) and Catholic theology and piety.

The leitmotif of Julian's revelations is the depth, breadth, and intimacy of God's love. Julian communicates this "homely," familiar, and "magnificently courteous" love through a rich variety of images. She says: "I saw that he is to us everything that is good and comfortable for us. He is our clothing that for love wraps us, clasps us, and completely encloses us for tender love, that he may never leave us, being to us all things good. . . ." God is present in every creature as "maker, lover, and keeper." Suffusing her theology is Julian's trusting and hopeful encounter with the Divine Trinity* as Goodness, whose properties are Life—"marvelous homeliness,", Love—"gentle courtesy," and Light—"endless kindness" (Revelations, Ch. 83).

The Trinity and Jesus as Mother

The author of the Revelations was a devout woman steeped in the affective spirituality of her day. Her prayer-life focused tenderly on Jesus' humanity and sufferings for our sake. She may well have been familiar with Anselm of Canterbury's imaging of Christ giving humankind new birth by his death on the cross, his sufferings like spiritual labor-pains. This late-medieval piety was a congenial context for Julian's contemplation of the motherhood of God. Echoing biblical motifs [Hosea, Paul], Julian speaks passionately of God as our true and faithful husband, and we his "loved wife and sweetheart." Originally developing Anselm's birthing imagery, she calls Jesus our mother, as well as brother and savior.

In the following excerpt, Julian speaks of the mystery of the Trinity and God's relations with humanity. God's almighty power is encompassed in the first Person, whose distinguishing attribute is fatherhood.

God's deep wisdom (recall Proverbs 8) is the second Person—Jesus Christ, whose attribute is motherhood. God's great love and goodness overflows as the third Person—the Holy Spirit, whose attribute is empowering and serving lordship. Throughout each stage of our life, God works, dynamically and wonderfully, to bestow nature, mercy, and grace. In our Father, God almighty, we have our being. In our "merciful Mother," Jesus Christ, we have reformation and renewal. In yielding to the gracious and generous impulse of the Holy Spirit we are made perfect. Why is Jesus Christ called "Mother"? Because "we owe our being to him—this is the essence of motherhood!" In creation, he gives us our sensual nature. He is also mother to us in grace, as the one through whom we are reborn to new life in God's kingdom. ". . . [H]e, All-love, bears us to joy and eternal life! . . . Thus he carries us within himself in love. . . ." Our beloved Mother, Jesus, feeds us with himself in the sacraments. And like a good mother, Jesus adjusts his methods of teaching to the stages of our growth. So, Julian reiterates, "God is as really our Mother as he is our Father." In her visions, God declares: "[I]t is I who am the strength and goodness of Fatherhood; I who am the wisdom of Motherhood; I who am the light and grace of blessed love . . . I who enable you to love; I who enable you to long. It is I, the eternal satisfaction of every genuine desire" (Compare to Augustine, Confessions, Book 8).

Mysticism's Aim: Loving Union with God

Authentic Christian mysticism is always embedded in the living religious community of the Church. It is a process or way of life whose defining note is the experience of deep union with the divine. As the gifted experience of divine mystery, it is a potential aspect of every Christian's life. In a more intense sense, mysticism is "the graced transformation of consciousness that follows upon a direct or immediate experience of the presence of God leading to deeper union with God" (R. McBrien, Catholicism, 1052). It was for this intense mystical union or "oneing" that Julian longed. By God's "magnificent courtesy" and "homely love," she experienced this union through her near-death visions, through subsequent years of prayer and reflection, in her inspiration to share her "showings" with all her beloved fellow-Christians.

As for the ultimate meaning of her revelations, Julian wrote later in life: ". . . I desired often to understand what was our Lord's meaning. And fifteen years after, and more, I was answered in spiritual understanding:

'Would you know your Lord's meaning in this thing?

Know it well: Love was his meaning.

Who showed it to you? Love.

What did he show you? Love.

For what purpose did he show it? For love. . . .' Thus was I taught that Love was our Lord's meaning" (Ch. 86).

—*Dr. Christine Firer Hinze*

TEXT

58 God the blessed Trinity* is everlasting Being. Just as he is eternal, without beginning, so has his purpose been eternal, namely to make mankind. This fine nature was prepared in the first instance for his own Son, the Second Person. And when he so willed, with
5   the concurrence of each Person of the Trinity, he made all of us at one and the same time. When he made us he joined and united us to himself. By such union we are kept as pure and noble as when we were first made. It is because of this most precious union that we can love our Maker, please him and praise him, thank him and
10 rejoice in him for ever. And this is the plan continually at work in every soul to be saved—the divine will that I have already mentioned. So when he made us God almighty was our kindly Father, and God all-wise our kindly Mother, and the Holy Spirit their love and goodness; all one God, one Lord. In this uniting together he is
15 our real, true husband, and we his loved wife and sweetheart. He is never displeased with his wife! 'I love you and you love me,' he says, 'and our love will never be broken.'

I saw the blessed Trinity working. I saw that there were these three attributes: fatherhood, motherhood, and lordship all in one God. In the almighty Father we have been sustained and blessed with regard to our created natural being from before all time. By the skill and wisdom of the Second Person we are sustained, restored, and saved with regard to our sensual nature, for he is our Mother, Brother, and Savior. In our good Lord the Holy Spirit we have, after our life and hardship is over, that reward and rest which surpasses for ever any and everything we can possibly desire—such is his abounding grace* and magnificent courtesy.

Our life too is threefold. In the first stage we have our being, in the second our growth, and in the third our perfection. The first is nature, the second mercy, and the third grace. For the first I realized that the great power of the Trinity is our Father, the deep wisdom our Mother, and the great love our Lord. All this we have by nature and in our created and essential being. Moreover I saw that the Second Person who is our Mother with regard to our essential nature, that same dear Person has become our Mother in the matter of our sensual nature. We are God's creation twice: essential being and sensual nature. Our being is that higher part which we have in our Father, God almighty, and the second Person of the Trinity is Mother of this basic nature, providing the substance in which we are rooted and grounded. But he is our Mother also in mercy, since he has taken our sensual nature upon himself. Thus 'our Mother' describes the different ways in which he works, ways which are separate to us, but held together in him. In our Mother, Christ, we grow and develop; in his mercy he reforms and restores us; through his passion, death, and resurrection he has united us to our being. So does our Mother work in mercy for all his children who respond to him and obey him.

Grace works with mercy too, and especially in two ways. The work is that of the Third Person, the Holy Spirit, who works by rewarding and giving. Rewarding is the generous gift of truth that the Lord makes to him who has suffered. Giving is a magnanimous gesture which he makes freely by his grace: perfect, and far beyond the deserts of any of his creatures.

55 Thus in our Father, God almighty, we have our being. In our merciful Mother we have reformation and renewal, and our separate parts are integrated into perfect man. In yielding to the gracious impulse of the Holy Spirit we are made perfect. Our essence is in our Father, God almighty, and in our Mother, God all-wise, and in our Lord the Holy Spirit, God all-good. Our essential nature is entire in each Person of the Trinity, who is one God. Our sensual nature is in the Second Per-

60 son alone, Jesus Christ. In him is the Father too, and the Holy Spirit. In and by him have we been taken out of hell with a strong arm; and out of earth's wretchedness have been wonderfully raised to heaven, and united, most blessedly, to him who is our true being. And we have developed in spiritual wealth and character through all Christ's

65 virtues,* and by the gracious work of the Holy Spirit.

59 All this blessedness is ours through mercy and grace. We would never have had it or known it if goodness (that is, God) had not been opposed. It is because of this that we enjoy this bliss. Wickedness was allowed to rise up against goodness, and the goodness of mercy and

70 grace rose up against wickedness and then turned it all into goodness and honour, at least as far as those who are to be saved are concerned. For it is the way of God to set good against evil. So Jesus Christ who sets good against evil is our real Mother. We owe our being to him— and this is the essence of motherhood!—and all the delightful, loving

75 protection which ever follows. God is as really our Mother as he is our Father. He showed this throughout, and particularly when he said that sweet word, 'It is I.' In other words, 'It is I who am the strength and goodness of Fatherhood; I who am the wisdom of Motherhood; I who am light and grace and blessed love; I who am

80 Trinity; I who am Unity; I who am the sovereign goodness of every single thing; I who enable you to love; I who enable you to long. It is I the eternal satisfaction of every genuine desire.'

For the soul is at its best, its most noble and honorable, when it is most lowly, and humble, and gentle. Springing from this fundamen-

85 tal source and as part of our natural endowment, are all the virtues of our sensual nature, aided and abetted as they are by mercy and grace. Without such assistance we should be in a poor way!

Our great Father, God almighty, who is Being, knew and loved us from eternity. Through his knowledge, and in the marvelous depths of his charity, together with the foresight and wisdom of the whole blessed Trinity, he willed that the Second Person should become our Mother, Brother, and Savior. Hence it follows that God is as truly our Mother as he is our Father. Our Father decides, our Mother works, our good Lord, the Holy Spirit, strengthens. So we ought to love our God in whom we have our own being, reverently thanking him, and praising him for creating us, earnestly beseeching our Mother for mercy and pity, and our Lord, the Spirit, for help and grace. For in these three is contained our life: nature, mercy, grace. From these we get our humility, gentleness, patience and pity. From them too we get our hatred of sin and wickedness—it is the function of virtue* to hate these.

So we see that Jesus is the true Mother of our nature, for he made us. He is our Mother, too, by grace, because he took our created nature upon himself. All the lovely deeds and tender services that beloved motherhood implies are appropriate to the Second Person. In him the godly will is always safe and sound, both in nature and grace*, because of his own fundamental goodness. I came to realize that there were three ways of looking at God's motherhood: the first is based on the fact that our nature is made; the second is found in the assumption of that nature—there begins the motherhood of grace; the third is the motherhood of work which flows out over all by that same grace—the length and breadth and height and depth of it is everlasting. And so is his love.

60 But now I must say a little more about this 'over-flowing' as I understand its meaning: how we have been brought back again by the motherhood of mercy and grace to that natural condition which was ours originally when we were made through the motherhood of natural love which love, indeed, has never left us.

Our Mother by nature and grace—for he would become our Mother in everything—laid the foundation of his work in the Virgin's womb with great and gentle condescension. (This was shown in the first revelation when I received a mental picture of the Virgin's genuine simplicity at the time she conceived.) In other words, it was in

90

95

100

105

110

115

120

this lowly place that God most high, the supreme wisdom of all, adorned and arrayed himself with our poor flesh, ready to function and serve as Mother in all things.

A mother's is the most intimate, willing, and dependable of all services, because it is the truest of all. None has been able to fulfil it properly but Christ, and he alone can. We know that our own mother's bearing of us was a bearing to pain and death, but what does Jesus, our true Mother, do? Why, he, All-love, bears us to joy and eternal life! Blessings on him! Thus he carries us within himself in love. And he is in labor until the time has fully come for him to suffer the sharpest pangs and most appalling pain possible—and in the end he dies. And not even when this is over, and we ourselves have been born to eternal bliss, is his marvelous love completely satisfied. This he shows in that overwhelming word of love, 'If I could possibly have suffered more, indeed I would have done so.'

He might die no more, but that does not stop him working, for he needs to feed us . . . it is an obligation of his dear, motherly, love. The human mother will suckle her child with her own milk, but our beloved Mother, Jesus feeds us with himself, and, with the most tender courtesy, does it by means of the Blessed Sacrament*, the precious food of all true life. And he keeps us going through his mercy and grace by all the sacraments. This is what he meant when he said, 'It is I whom Holy Church preaches and teaches.' In other words, 'All the health and life of sacraments, all the virtue and grace of my word, all the goodness laid up for you in Holy Church—it is I.' The human mother may put her child tenderly to her breast, but our tender Mother Jesus simply leads us into his blessed breast through his open side, and there gives us a glimpse of the Godhead and heavenly joy— the inner certainty of eternal bliss. The tenth revelation showed this, and said as much with that word, 'See how I love you,' as looking into his side he rejoiced.

This fine and lovely word Mother is so sweet and so much its own that it cannot properly be used of any but him, and of her who is his own true Mother—and ours. In essence motherhood means love and kindness, wisdom, knowledge, goodness. Though in comparison with our spiritual birth our physical birth is a small, unimportant, straightforward sort of thing, it still remains that it is only through his working that it can be done at all by his creatures. A kind, loving mother who understands and knows the needs of her child will look after it tenderly just because it is the nature of a mother to do so. As the child grows older she changes her methods—but not her love. Older still, she allows the child to be punished so that its faults are corrected and its virtues and graces developed. This way of doing things, with much else that is right and good, is our Lord at work in those who are doing them. Thus he is our Mother in nature, working by his grace in our lower part, for the sake of the higher. It is his will that we should know this, for he wants all our love to be fastened on himself. Like this I could see that our indebtedness, under God, to fatherhood and motherhood—whether it be human or divine—is fully met in truly loving God. And this blessed love Christ himself produces in us. This was shown in all the revelations, and especially in those splendid words that he uttered, 'It is I whom you love.'

160

165

170

DISCUSSION QUESTION

1. Two holy women, St. Teresa of Avila and St. Therese of Lisieux, are listed among those whom the Catholic Church has singled out as "Doctors of the Church"* because of how their lives and writings in unique and important ways help reveal the truth of the Gospel. In reading through this passage from the mystic Julian of Norwich, what do you think she has to teach both the Church and the world about God and our relationship to God?

22

Authentic Faith

*Preface to the Epistle of St. Paul
to the Romans (1522)*

MARTIN LUTHER (1483–1546)

INTRODUCTION

Luther's Life

Born in 1483, Martin Luther was named for St. Martin of Tours and raised in a pious German Catholic home. A promising student, he earned the Bachelor's and Master's degrees at the University of Erfurt in 1502 and 1505, respectively. On his way back to Erfurt after a visit home in July 1505, Luther was caught in a thunderstorm and, fearing for his life, cried out: "Help me St. Anne, and I'll become a monk." Thus, against his father's wishes, he abandoned plans to study law and chose the religious life instead. He took vows as an Augustinian friar* in 1505, was ordained a priest in 1507, and received the Doctor's degree in 1512. He then assumed the chair in Bible at the newly founded university in the city of Wittenberg, residence of the

Christ as Savior El Greco (1541–1614).
© Bridgeman-Giraudon/Art Resource

Prince-Elector of Saxony. As a result of his attack on indulgences (see below), he was excommunicated. Eventually, Luther became the leading theologian for a group of German princes who, at his urging, had begun the reform of the churches in their territories. Luther abandoned his monastic habit in 1524, and in 1525 was married to a former nun, Katharina von Bora. They had six children and their home became the model for the married Protestant ministry. Until his death in 1546, Luther continued to teach in the university, where he trained most of the first generation of "Lutheran" pastors.

Background to the "Preface to Romans"

In October 1517, Luther was suddenly thrust into the international spotlight. In a series of propositions drawn up for academic debate (the *95 Theses*), he challenged the western church's practice of offering "indulgences" to remit the temporal punishments that remained after penance. Enterprising printers soon made Luther's strongly worded attack widely available not only in the original Latin, but in German as well, and a heated controversy erupted. After an intense period of theological debate and political maneuvering, Luther was first excommunicated and then summoned to the German city of Worms to appear before an international congress of the Holy Roman Empire. On 8 May 1521, after Luther had refused to recant his theological views, the congress issued the so-called "Edict of Worms." He was judged an outlaw and condemned to death. The Edict, however, came too late. On 4 May, following a staged "attack" on the small group with which he was traveling home, Luther had been spirited away to the remote Wartburg castle—"my Patmos," as he put it—where he remained in hiding under the protection of his prince, Frederick the Wise, until February 1522.

Taken out of the fight unwillingly, Luther was lonely and bored at the Wartburg. Pen and ink became the outlet of choice for his pent up energies. He wrote dozens of letters to friends and supporters, and a series of model sermons ("postils") for the seasons of Advent and Christmas. Most importantly, he began translating the New Testament (later, the whole Bible) into German. Working from the 1519 Greek edition published by the Dutch humanist, Desiderius Erasmus, Luther completed the work with amazing speed. In September 1522 the first edition rolled off the presses and became an instant bestseller. For each of the biblical books, Luther provided not only a felicitous German translation, but also a brief preface to guide readers into the teaching of Holy Scripture. The prefaces also introduced Luther's new theology of Word and faith. Thus, the Bible itself became one of the most important means by which Luther's message was spread.

A New Language of Faith

Probably the most famous of Luther's prefaces is the one written for Paul's letter to the Romans. The evangelist John Wesley, for example, was listening to a reading of this preface in 1738 when he felt his heart "strangely warmed" and experienced an evangelical conversion. Romans, Luther claims, is the "chief part" of the New Testament, a work whose teaching, rightly understood, can illumine the Scriptures as a whole. The challenge for the reader, he insists, is rightly to understand Paul's distinctive theological vocabulary. One must distinguish, for example, between human law, which demands only external obedience, and the divine *Law*, which requires internal obedience from the heart. Apart from God's gracious intervention, sinners find themselves able to *keep* the Law externally, but completely unable to *fulfill* it internally. The preaching of the *Gospel*, which sets forth Christ's person and work, changes all that. The Gospel offers both the *grace* and the *gift* of God (Rom. 5:15). Grace means the unmerited favor of God given for Christ's sake alone; gift, on the other hand, means both the Holy Spirit and the Spirit's gifts. Chief among these gifts is faith. *Faith,* in Luther's understanding, is "a divine work in us," the root virtue* that sets the believer right with God. Through faith alone, grace brings the sinner into God's favor in such a way that she is "accounted completely righteous before God." This is justification* by grace through faith alone. *Unbelief,* on the other hand, means the refusal of the grace and gifts of the Gospel. This is the root vice at work in all those who live in opposition to God.

Saints, and Sinners at the Same Time

As a divine work, authentic faith is a "living, busy, active, mighty thing." Whoever has faith inevitably does good works. Who works not, has not faith. Luther's remarkable confidence that believers will spontaneously busy themselves with good works did not result, as one might have guessed, in an unwillingness to apply the consolation of the Gospel to the struggling Christian. As an experienced pastor—indeed, as an experienced Christian—he knew that struggle all too well. His explanation for the experiential gap between fact and theory was as simple as it was ingenious. In her whole person, the believer is *flesh* insofar as she produces "works of the flesh." She is wholly *spirit,* on the other hand, insofar as she produces works of the Spirit. Her justification* before God by grace is an accomplished fact because God deals with her according to her faith and does not count sin against her. She has the Spirit and is therefore holy, a saint. But the gifts of God have only begun their work. Sin—i.e., "the flesh"—is not yet "slain," and the believer therefore remains a sinner. She is a saint and a sinner at the same time, and the struggle for faithfulness in this life is in part a struggle of the self against the self.

—*Dr. Mickey L. Mattox*

TEXT

Translation by Charles M. Jacobs, revised by E. Theodore Bachmann, in *Word and Sacrament I,* Luther's Works: American Edition: Vol. 35, (Philadelphia: Fortress Press, 1960), 365–371.

This epistle is really the chief part of the New Testament, and is truly the purest gospel. It is worthy not only that every Christian should know it word for word, by heart, but also that he should occupy himself with it every day, as the daily bread of the soul. We can never read it or ponder over it too much; for the more we deal with it, the more precious it becomes and the better it tastes. 5

Therefore I too will do my best, so far as God has given me power, to open the way into it through this preface, so that it may be the better understood by everyone. Heretofore it has been badly obscured by glosses and all kinds of idle talk, though in itself it is a bright light, almost sufficient to illuminate the entire holy Scriptures.

To begin with we must have knowledge of its language and know what St. Paul means by the words: "law," "sin," "grace," "faith," "righteousness*," "flesh," "spirit," and the like. Otherwise no reading of the book has any value.

The little word "law" you must here not take in human fashion as a teaching about what works are to be done or not done. That is the way with human laws; a law is fulfilled by works, even though there is no heart in the doing of them. But God judges according to what is in the depths of the heart. For this reason, his law too makes its demands on the inmost heart; it cannot be satisfied with works, but rather punishes as hypocrisy and lies the works not done from the bottom of the heart. Hence all men are called liars in Psalm 116[:11], because no one keeps or can keep God's law from the bottom of the heart. For everyone finds in himself displeasure in what is good and pleasure in what is bad. If, now, there is no willing pleasure in the good, then the inmost heart is not set on the law of God. Then, too, there is surely sin, and God's wrath is deserved, even though outwardly there seem to be many good deeds and an honorable life.

Hence St. Paul concludes, in chapter 2[:13], that the Jews are all sinners, saying that only the doers of the law are righteous before God. He means by this that no one, in terms of his works, is a doer of the law. Rather, he speaks to them thus, "You teach one must not commit adultery, but you yourself commit adultery" [2:22]; and again, "In passing judgment upon another you condemn yourself, because you, the judge, are doing the very same things" [2:1]. This is as if to say, "You live a fine outward life in the works of the law, and you pass judgment on those who do not so live. You know how to teach everyone; you see the speck that is in the eye of another, but do not notice the log that is in your own eye" [Matt. 7:3].

For even though you keep the law outwardly, with works, from fear of punishment or love of reward, nevertheless you do all this unwillingly, without pleasure in and love for the law, but with reluctance and under compulsion. For if the law were not there, you would prefer to act otherwise. The conclusion is that from the bottom of your heart you hate the law. What point is there then in your teaching others not to steal, if you yourself are a thief at heart, and would gladly be one outwardly if you dared? Though, to be sure, the outward work does not lag far behind among such hypocrites! So you teach others, but not yourself; nor do you yourself know what you are teaching—you have never yet understood the law correctly. Moreover the law increases sin, as St. Paul says in chapter 5[:20], because the more the law demands of men what they cannot do, the more they hate the law.

For this reason he says, in chapter 7[:14], "The law is spiritual." What does that mean? If the law were for the body, it could be satisfied with works; but since it is spiritual, no one can satisfy it—unless all that you do is done from the bottom of your heart. But such a heart is given only by God's Spirit, who fashions a man after the law, so that he acquires a desire for the law in his heart, doing nothing henceforth out of fear and compulsion but out of a willing heart. The law is thus spiritual in that it will be loved and fulfilled with such a spiritual heart, and requires such a spirit. Where that spirit is not in the heart, there sin remains, also displeasure with the law and hostility toward it even though the law itself is good and just and holy.

Accustom yourself, then, to this language, that doing the works of the law and fulfilling the law are two very different things. The work of the law is everything that one does, or can do, toward keeping the law of his own free will or by his own powers. But since in the midst of all these works and along with them there remains in the heart a dislike of the law and compulsion with respect to it, these works are all wasted and have no value. That is what St. Paul means in chapter 3[:20], when he says, "By works of the law will no man be justified in God's sight." Hence you see that the wranglers and sophists practice deception when they teach men to prepare themselves for grace by means of works. How can a man prepare himself for good by means of works, if he does good works only with aversion and unwillingness in his heart? How shall a work please God if it proceeds from a reluctant and resisting heart?

To fulfill the law, however, is to do its works with pleasure and love, to live a godly and good life of one's own accord, without the compulsion of the law. This pleasure and love for the law is put into the heart by the Holy Spirit, as St. Paul says in chapter 5[:5]. But the Holy Spirit is not given except in, with, and by faith in Jesus Christ, as St. Paul says in the introduction. Faith, moreover, comes only through God's Word or gospel, which preaches Christ, saying that he is God's Son and a man, and has died and risen again for our sakes, as he says in chapters 3[:25], 4[:25], and 10[:9].

So it happens that faith alone makes a person righteous and fulfils the law. For out of the merit of Christ it brings forth the Spirit. And the Spirit makes the heart glad and free, as the law requires that it shall be. Thus good works emerge from faith itself. That is what St. Paul means in chapter 3[:31]; after he has rejected the works of the law, it sounds as if he would overthrow the law by this faith. "No," he says, "we uphold the law by faith"; that is, we fulfill it by faith.

Sin, in the Scripture, means not only the outward works of the body but also all the activities that move men to do these works, namely, the inmost heart, with all its powers. Thus the little word "do" ought to mean that a man falls all the way and lives in sin. Even outward works of sin do not take place, unless a man plunges into it completely with body and soul. And the Scriptures look especially into the heart and single out the root and source of all sin, which is unbelief in the inmost heart. As, therefore, faith alone makes a person righteous, and brings the Spirit and pleasure in good outward works, so unbelief alone commits sin, and brings forth the flesh and pleasure in bad outward works, as happened to Adam and Eve in paradise, Genesis 3.

Hence Christ calls unbelief the only sin, when he says in John 16[:8–9], "The Spirit will convince the world of sin . . . because they do not believe in me." For this reason too, before good or bad works take place, as the good or bad fruits, there must first be in the heart faith or unbelief. Unbelief is the root, the sap, and the chief power of all sin. For this reason, in the Scriptures it is called the serpent's head and the head of the old dragon, which the seed of the woman, Christ, must tread under foot, as was promised to Adam, Genesis 3[:15].

Between grace and gift there is this difference. Grace actually means God's favor, or the good will which in himself he bears toward us, by which he is disposed to give us Christ and to pour into us the Holy Spirit with his gifts. This is clear from chapter 5[:15], where St. Paul speaks of "the grace and gift in Christ," etc. The gifts and the Spirit increase in us every day, but they are not yet perfect since there remain in us the evil desires and sins that war against the Spirit, as he says in Romans 7[:5ff.] and Galatians 5[:17], and the conflict between the seed of the woman and the seed of the serpent, as foretold in Genesis 3[:15]. Nevertheless grace does so much that we are accounted completely righteous before God. For his grace is not divided or parceled out, as are the gifts, but takes us completely into favor for the sake of Christ our Intercessor and Mediator. And because of this, the gifts are begun in us.

In this sense, then, you can understand chapter 7. There St. Paul still calls himself a sinner; and yet he can say, in chapter 8[:1], that there is no condemnation for those who are in Christ, simply because of the incompleteness of the gifts and of the Spirit. Because the flesh is not yet slain, we are still sinners. But because we believe in Christ and have a beginning of the Spirit, God is so favorable and gracious to us that he will not count the sin against us or judge us because of it. Rather he deals with us according to our faith in Christ, until sin is slain.

Faith is not the human notion and dream that some people call faith. When they see that no improvement of life and no good works follow—although they can hear and say much about faith—they fall into the error of saying, "Faith is not enough; one must do works in order to be righteous and be saved." This is due to the fact that when they hear the gospel, they get busy and by their own powers create an idea in their heart which says, "I believe"; they take this then to be a true faith. But, as it is a human figment and idea that never reaches the depths of the heart, nothing comes of it either, and no improvement follows.

Faith, however, is a divine work in us which changes us and makes us to be born anew of God, John 1[:12–13]. It kills the old Adam and makes us altogether different men, in heart and spirit and mind and powers; and it brings with it the Holy Spirit. O it is a living, busy, active, mighty thing, this faith. It is impossible for it not to be doing good works incessantly. It does not ask whether good works are to be done, but before the question is asked, it has already done them, and is constantly doing them. Whoever does not do such works, however, is an unbeliever. He gropes and looks around for faith and good works, but knows neither what faith is nor what good works are. Yet he talks and talks, with many words, about faith and good works.

Faith is a living, daring confidence in God's grace, so sure and certain that the believer would stake his life on it a thousand times. This knowledge of and confidence in God's grace makes men glad and bold and happy in dealing with God and with all creatures. And this is the work which the Holy Spirit performs in faith. Because of it, without compulsion, a person is ready and glad to do good to everyone, to serve everyone, to suffer everything, out of love and praise to God who has shown him this grace. Thus it is impossible to separate works from faith, quite as impossible as to separate heat and light from fire. Beware, therefore, of your own false notions and of the idle talkers who imagine themselves wise enough to make decisions about faith and good works, and yet are the greatest fools. Pray God that he may work faith in you. Otherwise you will surely remain forever without faith, regardless of what you may think or do.

Righteousness*, then, is such a faith. It is called "the righteousness of God" because God gives it, and counts it as righteousness for the sake of Christ our Mediator, and makes a man to fulfill his obligation to everybody. For through faith a man becomes free from sin and comes to take pleasure in God's commandments, thereby he gives God the honor due him, and pays him what he owes him. Likewise he serves his fellow-men willingly, by whatever means he can, and

thus pays his debt to everyone. Nature, free will, and our own powers cannot bring this righteousness into being. For as no one can give
himself faith, neither can he take away his own unbelief. How, then,
will he take away a single sin, even the very smallest? Therefore all
that is done apart from faith, or in unbelief, is false; it is hypocrisy and
sin, Romans 14[:23], no matter how good a showing it makes.

Flesh and spirit you must not understand as though flesh is only
that which has to do with unchastity and spirit is only that which has
to do with what is inwardly in the heart. Rather, like Christ in John
3[:6], Paul calls everything "flesh" that is born of the flesh—the whole
man, with body and soul, mind and senses—because everything about
him longs for the flesh. Thus you should learn to call him "fleshly" too
who thinks, teaches, and talks a great deal about lofty spiritual matters,
yet does so without grace. From the "works of the flesh" in Galatians
5[:19–21], you can learn that Paul calls heresy* and hatred "works of
the flesh." And in Romans 8[:3] he says that "the law is weakened by
the flesh"; yet this is said not of unchastity, but of all sins, and above
all of unbelief, which is the most spiritual of all vices.

On the contrary, you should call him "spiritual" who is occupied
with the most external kind of works, as Christ was when he washed
the disciples' feet [John 13:1–14], and Peter when he steered his boat
and fished. Thus "the flesh" is a man who lives and works, inwardly
and outwardly, in the service of the flesh's gain and of this temporal
life. "The spirit" is the man who lives and works, inwardly and outwardly, in the service of the Spirit and of the future life.

Without such a grasp of these words, you will never understand
this letter of St. Paul, nor any other book of Holy Scripture. Therefore beware of all teachers who use these words in a different sense,
no matter who they are, even Origen, Ambrose, Augustine, Jerome,
and others like them or even above them. And now we will take up
the epistle. . . .

180

185

190

195

200

205

DISCUSSION QUESTIONS

1. Why is it insufficient, on Luther's account, to keep the Law of God out of "fear of punishment" or "love of reward?"

2. What relationship do you see here between the Law of God, the person of the Holy Spirit, and the fulfillment of the Law?

3. Luther says that it is false and deceitful to teach sinners that they can "prepare for grace by means of works." Why should not sinners do everything they can in the hope that God will reward them with grace?

4. What difference does Luther see between what we might imagine faith to be, and what it is in fact? What decisive elements differentiate the two?

23

God's Greater Glory
Autobiography & The Spiritual Exercises (Selections)

ST. IGNATIUS OF LOYOLA (1491–1556)

INTRODUCTION TO THE *AUTOBIOGRAPHY*

Literary Genre

In an autobiography (Gr. *autos*=self; *bios*=life; *graphe*=writing) someone tells the story of his or her own life, often because the author has done something conspicuous. Although others may know something of his or her public deeds and words, an autobiography allows the person to relate interior motives and personal perspectives behind visible deeds.

Background

St. Ignatius Loyola (1491–1556) is a canonized saint in the Catholic Church. The term *saint* refers to a holy man or woman whom the Church officially holds as a model of Christian life and as one who can intercede with God for all of us. The term derives from the same Latin root (*sacer*=sacred, holy, set apart) as *sanctify*, which means "to make holy." Jesus the Christ teaches, governs, and sanctifies the faithful in and through the preaching of the gospel, the celebration of the Church's liturgy, and the invisible work of grace. Saints are those in whom this ministry of Christ has come to its fullest effect.

The Autobiography

Chapter One of the *Autobiography* makes it plain that the young Ignatius was a fiery leader, but otherwise an ordinary, sinful human being until something happened in 1521. This event had an external and public aspect of a soldier wounded in battle and then recuperating at home. It had an internal aspect as well.

Chapter One gives us a detailed description of how day-dreams, stimulated by books supplied to him during the healing of his leg, began Ignatius' journey to God. He read, now from love-stories involving gallant deeds—a kind of the soap-opera of the time—,now from books on the lives of Christ and the saints. Fantasizing alternately on both types of stories, he noticed the difference in moods generated by each type of reading. He was drawn by deep peace to imitate the sacrifices of the heroes of the faith rather than the chivalrous feats of medieval knights. From that awakening to his own interior life there gradually resulted a new consciousness and life in the Spirit, marked by a particular way of helping other people hear and live the gospel.

In 1522 Ignatius began a pilgrimage to the Holy Land but delayed for ten months of prayer, living in a cave at Manresa, some miles west of Barcelona. When he returned from his journey to the holy sites, he devoted himself to academic studies: three years in Spain and seven more at the University of Paris. In Spain he was detained and questioned by the Inquisition because, until he eventually finished studying theology at Paris, he was teaching others about God's ways as a layman without the solid benefit of theology, though he had divine guidance.

The Effects of His Life

Ignatius is widely known through history as the founder of the Society of Jesus, the "Jesuits." During his student days in Paris he attracted student-companions who also wanted to devote themselves to God. He guided them, one at a time, through a month-long prayer experience according to notes he took during his own ten months of prayer in Manresa, notes which came to be known as the *Spiritual Exercises.* Out of that nucleus of men, formed by those exercises, there emerged a new religious congregation. "Religious" here is a term referring to that kind of *imitatio Christi* (imitation of Christ) in the Church organized by vows of poverty, chastity, and obedience for the purpose of promoting personal union with God in oneself and in others. In the perspective of faith, marriage and religious life are complementary, not opposing, routes toward the same goal of loving God above all things and one's neighbor as oneself—sharing in Christ's mission to the world.

—Rev. D. Thomas Hughson, S.J.

TEXT[1]

The Life of Father Ignatius
as first written by Father Luis González
who received it from the lips of
the Father himself.

Author's Preface

1 One Friday morning of the year 1553, it being August 4th and the eve of Our Lady of the Snows, . . . while Master Polanco[2] and I were eating, our Father told me that Master Nadal[3] and others of the Society had often made a request of him, but that he had never made up his mind about it; but that after he had spoken with me, thinking the matter over in his room, he felt a great inclination and devotion to do so. He spoke in such a way as to show that God had greatly enlightened him about his duty so to do, and that he had for once and all made up his mind. That request was to make known all that had taken place in his soul up to that moment. He had also decided that it was I to whom he was going to make these things known.

2 At that time, the Father was in very bad health, and was not accustomed to promise himself life from one day to the next. In fact, when he heard anyone saying, "I will do this two weeks from now, or a week from now," the Father was always a bit amazed: "How's that? Do you count on living that long?" And yet, on this occasion, he said that he hoped to live three or four months so as to bring this matter to an end. . . . It was in September (I don't recall the day), that the Father called me and began the narrative of his whole life, recounting his youthful excesses clearly and distinctly with all their circum-

---

[1] Translated by William J. Young, S.J.

[2] A Spanish Jesuit, probably from a family of Jewish converts to Christianity, Fr. Juan Alfonso de Polanco was secretary to Ignatius in the saint's capacity as General superior of the Society of Jesus.

[3] Fr. Jerónimo Nadal, a native of Majorca and another assistant to Ignatius, was a brilliant theologian and the finest interpreter of Ignatius' mind to the rest of the Society of Jesus.

stances. Later in the same month he called me three or four times, and carried his story up to within a few days of his stay at Manresa, as will be seen in the part written by a different hand.

3 The Father's way of telling his story is what he uses in all things. It is done with such clearness that it makes the whole past present to the beholder. There was no need, therefore, of putting any questions, for the Father remembered and told whatever was worth knowing. I went at once to write it out, without a word to the Father, first in notes in my own hand, and later at greater length as it now stands. I have taken pains not to insert any word that I did not hear from our Father, and if there is anything in which I am afraid of having failed, it is that by not wishing to depart from the words of the Father, I have not been able to explain clearly the meaning of some of them. I kept writing in this way until September of 1553, as I have said. But from then on, after the arrival of Father Nadal, October 18, 1554, the Father constantly kept excusing himself because of some illness or the various engagements which turned up, saying, "When this matter is finished, remind me"; and when that was finished, he kept saying, "Now we are busy with this. When it is finished, remind me."

4 When Father Nadal arrived, he was delighted to find that we had begun, and bade me importune the Father, often telling me that the Father could in nothing do more good to the Society [of Jesus] than in this, that this was really to found the Society. He too, therefore, frequently spoke to the Father, and the Father told me that I should remind him when they finished the business of the endowment of the college. But when that was finished, he had to go on with the affair of Prester John,[4] and the mail was ready to leave. On the ninth of March we began to take up the history. But at once, Pope Julius became dangerously ill and died the 25th. Then the Father kept putting it off until we had a new pope who, as soon as he was named, also fell ill and died

25

30

35

40

45

50

---

[4] This refers to the plans for a mission to Ethiopia, the emperor of which the Portuguese and others at the time thought was the famous Prester John.

(Marcellus).[5] The Father delayed until the creation of Paul IV,[6] and then, what with the great heat and his numerous occupations, he kept holding off until the 21st of September, when arrangements began to be made for my transfer to Spain. For these reasons I urged the Father to make good his promise, and so he arranged for a meeting on the morning of the 22nd in the Red Tower. When I finished Mass I went to him to ask whether it was time.

He answered me to go and wait for him in the Red Tower,[7] so that I should be there when he came. . . . At length he returned, so that in that same Tower he finished dictating what has been written. But as I was on the point of beginning my journey, the preceding day being the last on which the Father spoke to me about this matter, I did not have time to write out everything at length at Rome. And because I did not have a Spanish secretary at Genoa, I dictated in Italian the points I had jotted down and brought with me from Rome. This writing I finished at Genoa in December 1555.

Chapter 1

1 Up to his twenty-sixth year he was a man given over to the vanities of the world, and took a special delight in the exercise of arms, with a great and vain desire of winning glory. He was in a fortress[8] which the French were attacking, and although the others were of the opinion that they should surrender on terms of having their lives spared, as they clearly saw there was no possibility of a defense, he gave so many reasons to the governor that he persuaded him to carry on the defense against the judgment of the officers, who found some strength in his spirit and courage. On the day on which they expected the attack to take place, he made his confession to one of his com-

---

[5] Marcellus II (Cervini) was elected pope April 9, 1555 and died the 30th of the same month.

[6] Paul IV (Pietro Carafa), elected May 23, 1555.

[7] A small dwelling adjoining the professed house at Rome, frequently used as an infirmary.

[8] The castle of Pamplona.

panions in arms. After the assault had been going on for some time, a cannon ball struck him in the leg, crushing its bones, and because it passed between his legs it also seriously wounded the other.

2 With his fall, the others in the fortress surrendered to the French, 80 who took possession, and treated the wounded man with great kindliness and courtesy. After twelve or fifteen days in Pamplona they bore him in a litter to his own country. Here he found himself in a very serious condition. The doctors and surgeons whom he had called from all parts were of the opinion that the leg should be operated on 85 again and the bones reset, either because they had been poorly set in the first place, or because the jarring of the journey had displaced them so that they would not heal. Again he went through this butchery, in which as in all the others that he had suffered he uttered no word, nor gave any sign of pain other than clenching his fists. 90

3 His condition grew worse. Besides being unable to eat he showed other symptoms which are usually a sign of approaching death. The feast of St. John[9] drew near, and as the doctors had very little hope of his recovery, they advised him to make his confession. He received the last sacraments*[10] on the eve of the feast of Sts. Peter and Paul,[11] and 95 the doctors told him that if he showed no improvement by midnight, he could consider himself as good as dead. The patient had some devotion to St. Peter, and so our Lord wished that his improvement should begin that very midnight. So rapid was his recovery that within a few days he was thought to be out of danger of death. 100

4 When the bones knit, one below the knee remained astride another, which caused a shortening of the leg. The bones so raised caused a protuberance that was not pleasant to the sight. The sick man was not able to put up with this, because he had made up his mind to seek his fortune in the world. He thought the protuberance 105

---

[9] June 24th, the feast of the Birth of St. John the Baptist.

[10] The "Last Sacraments" are the reception together of Reconciliation, Holy Communion, and Anointing of the Sick.

[11] The feast day itself is June 29th.

was going to be unsightly and asked the surgeons whether it could not be cut away. They told him that it could be cut away, but that the pain would be greater than all he had already suffered, because it was now healed and it would take some time to cut if off. He determined, nevertheless, to undergo this martyrdom to gratify his own inclinations. His elder brother was quite alarmed and declared that he would not have the courage to undergo such pain. But the wounded man put up with it with his usual patience.

5 After the superfluous flesh and the bone were cut away, means were employed for preventing the one leg from remaining shorter than the other. Many ointments were applied and devices employed for keeping the leg continually stretched which caused him many days of martyrdom. But it was our Lord Who restored his health. In everything else he was quite well, but he was not able to stand upon that leg, and so had to remain in bed. He had been much given to reading worldly books of fiction and knight errantry, and feeling well enough to read he asked for some of these books to help while away the time. In that house, however, they could find none of those he was accustomed to read, and so they gave him a Life of Christ[12] and a book of the Lives of the Saints in Spanish.

6 By the frequent reading of these books he conceived some affection for what he found there narrated. Pausing in his reading, he gave himself up to thinking over what he had read. At other times he dwelt on the things of the world which formerly had occupied his thoughts. Of the many vain things that presented themselves to him, one took such possession of his heart that without realizing it he could spend two, three, or even four hours on end thinking of it, fancying what he would have to do in the service of a certain lady, of the means he would take to reach the country where she was living, of the verses, the promises he would make her, the deeds of gallantry he would do

---

[12] By Ludolf of Saxony.

in her service. He was so enamored with all this that he did not see how impossible it would all be, because the lady was of no ordinary rank; neither countess, nor duchess, but of a nobility much higher than any of these.[13]

7 Nevertheless, our Lord came to his assistance, for He saw to it that   140
these thoughts were succeeded by others which sprang from the things he was reading. In reading the Life of the Lord and the Lives of the Saints, he paused to think and reason with himself. "Suppose that I should do what St. Francis did, what St. Dominic did?" He thus let his thoughts run over many things that seemed good to him, always   145
putting before himself things that were difficult and important which seemed to him easy to accomplish when he proposed them. But all this thought was to tell himself, "St. Dominic did this, therefore I must do it. St. Francis did this; therefore, I must do it." These thoughts also lasted a good while. And then other things taking their place, the   150
worldly thoughts above mentioned came upon him and remained a long time with him. This succession of diverse thoughts was of long duration, and they were either of worldly achievements which he desired to accomplish, or those of God which took hold of his imagination to such an extent, that worn out with the struggle, he turned   155
them all aside and gave his attention to other things.

8 There was, however, this difference. When he was thinking of the things of the world he was filled with delight, but when afterwards he dismissed them from weariness, he was dry and dissatisfied. And when he thought of going barefoot to Jerusalem and of eating nothing but   160
herbs and performing the other rigors he saw that the saints had performed, he was consoled, not only when he entertained these thoughts, but even after dismissing them he remained cheerful and satisfied. But he paid no attention to this, nor did he stop to weigh the difference until one day his eyes were opened a little and he began to wonder at   165

---

[13] Who this lady was is not clearly known. From the wording of the Spanish text her station was higher than that of countess or duchess. Some have suggested Queen Germaine, widow of Ferdinand; others, the Princess Catherine, sister of Charles V.

the difference and to reflect on it, learning from experience that one kind of thoughts left him sad and the other cheerful. Thus, step by step, he came to recognize the difference between the two spirits that moved him, the one being from the evil spirit, the other from God.

9 He acquired no little light from this reading and began to think more seriously of his past life and the great need he had of doing penance for it. It was during this reading that these desires of imitating the saints came to him, but with no further thought of circumstances than of promising to do with God's grace what they had done. What he desired most of all to do, as soon as he was restored to health, was to go to Jerusalem, as above stated, undertaking all the disciplines and abstinences which a generous soul on fire with the love of God is wont to desire.

10 The thoughts of the past were soon forgotten in the presence of these holy desires, which were confirmed by the following vision. One night, as he lay awake, he saw clearly the likeness of our Lady with the holy Child Jesus, at the sight of which he received most abundant consolation for a considerable interval of time. He felt so great a disgust with his past life, especially with its offenses of the flesh, that he thought all such images which had formerly occupied his mind were wiped out. And from that hour until August of 1553, when this is being written, he never again consented to the least suggestion of the flesh. This effect would seem to indicate that the vision was from God, although he never ventured to affirm it positively, or claim that it was anything more than he had said it was. But his brother and other members of the family easily recognized the change that had taken place in the interior of his soul from what they saw in his outward manner.

11 Without a care in the world he went on with his reading and his good resolutions. All the time he spent with the members of the household he devoted to the things of God, and in this way brought profit to their souls. He took great delight in the books he was reading, and the thought came to him to select some short but important passages from the Life of Christ and the Lives of the Saints. And so he

St. Ignatius glorifying God, St. Peter's Basilica, Rome.

200 began to write very carefully in a book, as he had already begun to move a little about the house. The words of Christ he wrote in red ink and those of Our Lady in blue, on polished and lined paper in a good hand, for he was an excellent penman. Part of his time he spent in writing, part in prayer. It was his greatest consolation to gaze upon the

205 heavens and the stars, which he often did, and for long stretches at a time, because when doing so he felt within himself a powerful urge to be serving our Lord. He gave much time to thinking about his resolve, desiring to be entirely well so that he could begin his journey.

12 As he was going over in his mind what he should do on his

210 return from Jerusalem, so as to live in perpetual penance, the thought occurred to him of joining the Carthusians[14] of Seville. He could there conceal his identity so as to be held in less esteem, and live there on a strictly vegetable diet. But as the thought returned of a life of penance which he wanted to lead by going about the world, the desire of the

215 Carthusian life grew cool, since he felt that there he would not be able to indulge the hatred he had conceived against himself. And yet, he instructed a servant of the house who was going to Burgos to bring back information about the Carthusian Rule,[15] and the information brought to him seemed good. But for the reason given above, and

220 because his attention was entirely occupied with the journey he was thinking of making at once, he gave up thinking about the Carthusians as it was a matter that could await his return. Indeed, feeling that he was pretty well restored, he thought it was time to be up and going and told his brother so. "You know, my lord, the Duke of Nájera is

225 aware that I have recovered. It will be good for me to go to Navarrete." The Duke was there at the time. His brother led him from one room to another, and with a great show of affection, begged him not to make a fool of himself. He wanted him to see what hopes the people

---

[14] A strictly contemplative religious order, combining Benedictine monachism with eremitical asceticism,* founded by St. Bruno in 1084 at the Grande Chartreuse, France.

[15] A monastery of the Carthusians was near Burgos and is still standing.

placed in him and what influence he might have, along with other like suggestions, all with the intention of turning him from the good desire   230
he had conceived. But, without departing from the truth, for he was very scrupulous about that, he reassured him in a way that allowed him to slip away from his brother.[16]

INTRODUCTION TO THE "SPIRITUAL EXERCISES"

A Retreat* Manual

The *Spiritual Exercises* is a retreat* manual, a guide-book for prayer and for prayerful decision-making based on Ignatius of Loyola's (1491–1556) own experiences of conversion and of growth in the love of God. He directed his earliest companions through these exercises; they subsequently became a fundamental basis for the religious community of priests and brothers which he founded, the Society of Jesus, popularly known as the Jesuits.

A "How To" Book

The text of the *Spiritual Exercises* is intended principally as instructions for the person who directs an individual retreatant (or a group of retreatants) in their use. Going through the full course of these exercises takes approximately one month. During that time, the retreatant withdraws from the ordinary activities of everyday life in order to concentrate on prayer and the reflective evaluation of that prayer. Five hour-long exercises of prayer are normally scheduled for each day and the retreatant also meets with the director on a daily basis; during this meeting the director reviews with the retreatant what spiritual movements have taken place in the course of that day's prayer exercises, and then proposes a focus for the exercises of the next day, based on the "points" for prayerful consideration which Ignatius provides as part of each exercise.

---

[16] The date of his departure from home is not certain.

Four "Weeks"

The pace at which a retreatant moves through the four main divisions (or "weeks") of the *Spiritual Exercises* is left to the judgment of the director. Ignatius indicates that some persons will be ready to make only the First Week of the Exercises, which focuses on a conversion from sin to God through a growing awareness in prayer of God's love and forgiveness. The Second, Third and Fourth Weeks of the *Spiritual Exercises* focus on particular aspects of the Gospel narratives of Jesus: the Second Week on his incarnation*, birth and public ministry; the Third Week on his passion and death; and the Fourth Week on his resurrection and post-resurrectional appearances.

The Purposes of the Spiritual Exercises

One principal purpose of these "weeks" is to prepare the retreatant for a God-centered decision concerning any major choice the person may be faced with, especially which "state of life" to enter, so that one's choice will accord with God's plan of salvation. Another reason for doing the *Exercises* is simply to enter more deeply into the mystery of Christ, in the spirit of St. Paul: "*All I want is to know Christ and the power of his resurrection and to share his sufferings by reproducing the pattern of this death*" (*Philippians* 3:10). In fact, many people return each year to Jesuit retreat* houses throughout the world precisely for this purpose.

The Selections

At a number of key places in the course of these exercises, Ignatius proposes subject matter which is not part of the gospel narrative. The selections presented here are of this kind.

The first selection ("Principle and Foundation") is taken from the beginning of the *Spiritual Exercises,* where it precedes the start of the First Week. A major purpose of this exercise is to dispose the retreatant to seeing his or her life and activity in the context of God's plan of salvation.

The second selection, the Meditation on the Two Standards, is from the Second Week. It is placed between the exercises which focus on Jesus' incarnation and birth and those which follow the course of Jesus' public ministry. It is the first exercise with an explicit focus on the choice of a state of life.

The third selection, the Contemplation to Attain Love, comes at the conclusion of the Fourth Week. It returns the retreatant to a consideration of the larger context of God's plan of salvation with a focus on the active presence of God's love in all of creation and in all human activities.

—*Rev. Philip J. Rossi, S. J.*

TEXT[17]

Spiritual Exercises

TO CONQUER ONESELF AND REGULATE ONE'S LIFE WITHOUT DETERMINING ONESELF THROUGH ANY TENDENCY THAT IS DISORDERED

Presupposition

In order that both the one giving the Spiritual Exercises, and the one receiving them, may more help and benefit themselves, let it be presupposed that every good Christian is to be more ready to save his neighbor's proposition than to condemn it. If he cannot save it, let him inquire how the other means it; and if he means it badly, let him correct him with charity. If that is not enough, let him seek all the suitable means to bring him to mean it well, and save himself.

5

---

[17] This 1909 translation by Elder Mullan, S. J., has been slightly adjusted to be more gender inclusive, except for the First Principle and Foundation, which defied all modification short of a complete paraphrasing that would have destroyed its original simplicity and directness.

[The First Week]

FIRST PRINCIPLE AND FOUNDATION

Man is created to praise, reverence, and serve God our Lord, and by this means to save his soul.

And the other things on the face of the earth are created for man and that they may help him in prosecuting the end for which he is created.

From this it follows that man is to use them as much as they help him on to his end, and ought to rid himself of them so far as they hinder him as to it.

For this it is necessary to make ourselves indifferent to all created things in all that is allowed to the choice of our free will and is not prohibited to it; so that, on our part, we want not health rather than sickness, riches rather than poverty, honor rather than dishonor, long rather than short life, and so in all the rest; desiring and choosing only what is most conducive for us to the end for which we are created.

[The Second Week: The Fourth Day]

"THE TWO STANDARDS"

Meditation on the Two Standards

The one of Christ, our Commander-in-chief and Lord; The other of Lucifer, mortal enemy of our human nature.

Prayer. The usual Preparatory Prayer.

First Prelude. The First Prelude is the narrative. It will be here how Christ calls and wants all under His standard; and Lucifer, on the contrary, under his.

Second Prelude. The second, a composition, seeing the place. It will be here to see a great field of all that region of Jerusalem, where the supreme Commander-in-chief of the good is Christ our Lord; another field in the region of Babylon, where the chief of the enemy is Lucifer.

Third Prelude. The third, to ask for what I want: and it will be here to ask for knowledge of the deceits of the bad chief and help to guard myself against them, and for knowledge of the true life which the supreme and true Captain shows and grace to imitate Him.

First Point. The first Point is to imagine as if the chief of all the enemy seated himself in that great field of Babylon, as in a great[18] chair of fire and smoke, in shape horrible and terrifying.

Second Point. The second, to consider how he issues a summons to innumerable demons and how he scatters them, some to one city and others to another, and so through all the world, not omitting any provinces, places, states, nor any persons in particular.

Third Point. The third, to consider the discourse which he makes them, and how he tells them to cast out nets, and chains; that they have first to tempt with a longing for riches—as he is accustomed to do in most cases[19]—that men may more easily come to vain honor of the world, and then to vast pride. So that the first step shall be that of riches; the second, that of honor; the third, that of pride; and from these three steps he draws on to all the other vices.

So, on the contrary, one has to imagine as to the supreme and true Captain, Who is Christ our Lord.

First Point. The first Point is to consider how Christ our Lord puts Himself in a great field of that region of Jerusalem, in lowly place, beautiful and attractive.

Second Point. The second, to consider how the Lord of all the world chooses so many persons—Apostles, Disciples, etc.,—and sends them through all the world spreading His sacred doctrine* through all states and conditions of persons.

Third Point. The third, to consider the discourse which Christ our Lord makes to all His servants and friends whom He sends on this expedition, recommending them to want to help all, by bringing them first to the highest spiritual poverty, and—if His Divine Majesty would be served and would want to choose them—no less to actual poverty; the second is to be of contumely and contempt; because

---

[18] "great" *is inserted, perhaps in the hand of St. Ignatius.*

[19] "as he is accustomed to do in most cases" *is inserted in the Saint's handwriting.*

from these two things humility follows. So that there are to be three steps; the first, poverty against riches; the second, contumely or contempt against worldly honor; the third, humility against pride. And from these three steps let them induce to all the other virtues*.

First Colloquy. One Colloquy to Our Lady, that she may get me grace from Her Son and Lord that I may be received under His standard; and first in the highest spiritual poverty, and—if His Divine Majesty would be served and would want to choose and receive me—not less in actual poverty; second, in suffering contumely and injuries, to imitate Him more in them, if only I can suffer them without the sin of any person, or displeasure of His Divine Majesty; and with that a HAIL MARY.

Second Colloquy. I will ask the same of the Son that He may get it for me of the Father; and with that say the SOUL OF CHRIST.

Third Colloquy. I will ask the same of the Father, that He may grant it to me; and say an OUR FATHER.

"SOUL OF CHRIST"

(Anima Christi)

Soul of Christ, sanctify me.
Body of Christ, save me.
Blood of Christ, inebriate me.
Water from the side of Christ, wash me.
Passion of Christ, strengthen me.
O good Jesus, hear me:
Within your wounds, hide me;
Suffer me not to be separated from thee;
From the malicious enemy defend me;
In the hour of death call me,
And bid me to come to thee,
That with thy saints I may praise thee,
Forever and ever. Amen

[The Fourth Week]

"THE CONTEMPLATION FOR OBTAINING LOVE"

Note. First, it is well to remark two things: the first is that love ought to be put more in deeds than in words.

The second, love consists in interchange between the two parties; that is to say in the lover's giving and communicating to the beloved what he has or out of what he has or can; and so, on the contrary, the beloved to the lover. So that if the one has knowledge, he give to the one who has it not. The same of honors, of riches; and so the one to the other.

Prayer. The usual Prayer.

First Prelude. The first Prelude is a composition, which is here to see how I am standing before God our Lord, and of the Angels and of the Saints interceding for me.

Second Prelude. The second, to ask for what I want. It will be here to ask for interior knowledge of so great good received, in order that being entirely grateful, I may be able in all to love and serve His Divine Majesty.

First Point. The First Point is, to bring to memory the benefits received, of Creation, Redemption and particular gifts, pondering with much feeling how much God our Lord has done for me, and how much He has given me of what He has, and then the same Lord desires to give me Himself as much as He can, according to His Divine ordination. And with this to reflect on myself, considering with much reason and justice, what I ought on my side to offer and give to His Divine Majesty, that is to say, everything that is mine, and myself with it, as one who makes an offering with much feeling:

Take, Lord, and receive all my liberty, my memory, my intellect, and all my will—all that I have and possess. Thou gavest it to me: to Thee, Lord, I return it! All is Thine, dispose of it according to all Thy will. Give me Thy love and grace, for this is enough for me.

Second Point. The second, to look how God dwells in creatures, in the elements, giving them being, in the plants vegetating, in the animals feeding in them, in men giving them to understand:[20] and so in me, giving me being, animating me, giving me sensation and making me to understand;[21] likewise making a temple of me, being created to the likeness and image of His Divine Majesty; reflecting as much on myself in the way which is said in the first Point, or in another which I feel to be better. In the same manner will be done on each Point which follows.

Third Point. The third, to consider how God works and labors for me in all things created on the face of the earth—that is, behaves like one who labors—as in the heavens, elements, plants, fruits, cattle, etc., giving them being, preserving them, giving them vegetation and sensation, etc.

Then to reflect on myself.

Fourth Point. The fourth, to look how all the good things and gifts descend from above, as my poor power from the supreme and infinite power from above; and so justice, goodness, pity, mercy, etc.; as from the sun descend the rays, from the fountain the waters, etc.

Then to finish reflecting on myself, as has been said.

I will end with a Colloquy and an OUR FATHER.

---

[20] "giving them to understand" *is an addition, very probably in St. Ignatius' hand.*

[21] "making me to understand; likewise" *is in the Saint's handwriting, correcting a word erased, probably* "understanding."

DISCUSSION QUESTIONS

1. What similarities can you find between the conversion stories of St. Ignatius of Loyola and that of St. Augustine of Hippo? Do you think there might be a common pattern in how God deals with all human beings? Why or why not?

2. In the "First Principle and Foundation" of the *Spiritual Exercises* St. Ignatius writes that "*it is necessary to make ourselves indifferent to all created things.*" What do you think St. Ignatius means by this, and why does he think it so necessary? Do you agree? Why or why not? To what did St. Augustine become "indifferent" in this way, and to what did St. Ignatius in his life become "indifferent?"

3. Jesuit spirituality, based on the *Exercises,* is famous for the practice of the "Discernment of Spirits," detecting God's will in one's life, and how the evil spirit works to draw one away from God's will, as "The Two Standards" meditation indicates. Do you believe that God has a particular will for each and every person in the world to discern and follow? If so, why, and do you have any evidence of it? If not, why not?

4. Compare the first point of "The Contemplation for Obtaining Love" with *Deuteronomy* 26 presented earlier in this book. What similarities do you find? If *Deuteronomy* 26 is content to have the worshiper simply return signs of gratitude for how God acted in the past, why do you think St. Ignatius felt the need to include points 2, 3, and 4 in this contemplation? What do you think he is trying to achieve by them?

24
The Church's Social Teaching
"Rerum Novarum" (Selections)
POPE LEO XIII (1810–1903)

INTRODUCTION

Pope Leo XIII

Leo XIII, pope from February 1878, to July 10, 1903, was born Gioacchino Vicenzo Pecci on March 2, 1810, at Carpineto, Italy. Although chosen at age 68 as an interim pope, he lived to guide the Catholic Church throughout the world for almost 25 more years. During that time he fought socialism, communism and nihilism, and he encouraged the study of Thomism (the theology of St. Thomas Aquinas), the objective writing of history, and use of critical methods in biblical scholarship. Most importantly, Pope Leo fostered a much needed *rapprochement* between Catholicism and modern society, although in his declining years especially he continued to centralize church power in Rome. Not always successful in diplomatic efforts, he managed to enhance the stature of the papacy beyond what it had

been for centuries. A man of deep piety, he wrote eleven encyclicals*
on the Blessed Virgin and the Rosary and in 1900 consecrated the
human race to the Sacred Heart of Jesus.

"Rerum Novarum"

Leo's most famous legacy to the Church and the world, and probably
the most influential of all papal encyclicals*, is his social manifesto,
Rerum Novarum (May 15, 1891). Leo is the first pope to show a grasp
in his writings of the intolerable suffering of the urban proletariat
because of the Industrial Revolution and laissez-faire capitalism, and
to act on this by making the natural rights of the worker official
church doctrine*. The encyclical, justly earning Leo the title, "the
workers' pope," upholds private property, the just wage, workers'
rights, and trade unions. Its social teaching is based on a gospel understanding of the sacredness of the human person and the family, the
moral purpose of the state, and the dignity and religious significance
of work. The reader will notice how the encyclical echoes other themes
that appear earlier in this volume: (a) the Markan understanding of
Christ based on Isaiah 53, how Christian discipleship involves willingness to suffer out of love for God and neighbor, a theme seen also
in St. Ignatius' "Two Standards" meditation; (b) how St. Paul's
1 Corinthians 12 "body of Christ" underlies Pope Leo's teaching that
humanity is an organic unity wherein individuals are part of, contribute in unique ways to, a common reality; and (c) Pope Leo's
remark that "the only important thing is to use [creatures] aright"
(par. 21), reprising St. Ignatius' "First Principle and Foundation."

Rerum Novarum is rightly called the "Magna Carta" of Catholic
social teaching (Pius XI), but because of Leo's nineteenth-century
European, aristocratic background, the encyclical also suffers from a
paternalism and an uncritical legitimation of social stratification
among human beings according to their differing capacity, skill, health
and fortune, and gender. Consequently, although later papal writings
strongly reiterate the noble social principles of Rerum Novarum, in
adding their own insights within the changing conditions in society

St. Peter on his teaching chair by Arnolfo di Cambio (1245–1310).
St. Peter's Basilica, Rome.
© Scala/Firenze

over this 100 year period, they also attempt to avoid its limitations. In spite of its nineteenth-century characteristics, *Rerum Novarum* continues powerfully to teach basic principles of true Christian living in human community.

Influence on Later Papal Teaching

Through the course of the twentieth century *Rerum Novarum* has inspired the issuance of four other social encyclicals on four of its decile anniversaries: Pope Pius XI's *Quadragesimo Anno* ("On the Fortieth Year," May 15, 1931), Pope John XXIII's *Mater et Magistra* ("Mother and Teacher," May 15, 1961), and Pope John Paul II's *Laborem Exercens* ("Engaging in Labor," September 14, 1981) and *Centesiumus Annus* ("The Centenary Year," May 1, 1991).

—*(Rev.) John D. Laurance, S.J.*

TEXT

To Our Venerable Brethren the Patriarchs, Primates, Archbishops, Bishops, and other Ordinaries of Places having Peace and Communion with the See.

1. That the spirit of revolutionary change *(Rerum novarum),* which has long been disturbing the nations of the world, should have passed beyond the sphere of politics and made its influence felt in the cognate sphere of practical economics is not surprising. The elements of the conflict now raging are unmistakable, in the vast expansion of industrial pursuits and the marvelous discoveries of science; in the changed relations between employers and workers; in the enormous fortunes of some few individuals, and the utter poverty of the masses; in the increased self-reliance and closer mutual combination of the working classes; as also, finally, in the prevailing moral degeneracy. The momentous gravity of the state of things now obtaining fills every mind with painful apprehension; wise people are discussing it; practical people are proposing schemes; popular meetings, legislatures, and rulers of nations are all busied with it—actually there is no question which has taken a deeper hold on the public mind.

2. Therefore, venerable brethren, as on former occasions when it seemed opportune to refute false teaching, We have addressed you in the interests of the Church and of the common good, and have issued letters bearing on political power, human liberty, the Christian constitution of the State, and like matters, so have We thought it expedient now to speak on the condition of the working classes.[22] . . . .

3. . . . . we clearly see, and on this there is general agreement, that some opportune remedy must be found quickly for the misery and wretchedness pressing so unjustly on the majority of the working class: for the ancient workingmen's guilds were abolished in the last century, and no other protective organization took their place. Public institutions and the laws set aside the ancient religion. Hence, by degrees it has come to pass that working people have been surrendered, isolated and helpless, to the hardheartedness of employers and the greed of unchecked competition. The mischief has been increased by rapacious usury, which, although more than once condemned by the Church, is nevertheless, under a different guise, but with like injustice, still practiced by covetous and grasping men. To this must be added that the hiring of labor and the conduct of trade are concentrated in the hands of comparatively few; so that a small number of very rich men have been able to lay upon the teeming masses of the laboring poor a yoke little better than that of slavery itself.

Private Property vs. Socialism:

4. To remedy these wrongs the socialists, working on the poor man [and woman's] envy of the rich, are striving to do away with private property, and contend that individual possessions should become the common property of all, to be administered by the State or by municipal bodies. They hold that by thus transferring property from private

---

[22] The title sometimes given to this encyclical, "On the Condition of the Working Classes," is therefore perfectly justified. A few lines after this sentence the Pope gives a more comprehensive definition of the subject of "*Rerum Novarum.*"

individuals to the community, the present mischievous state of things will be set to rights, inasmuch as each citizen will then get his fair share of whatever there is to enjoy. But their contentions are so clearly powerless to end the controversy that were they carried into effect the working person himself would be among the first to suffer. They are, moreover, emphatically unjust, for they would rob the lawful possessor, distort the functions of the State, and create utter confusion in the community.

5. It is surely undeniable that, when a person engages in remunerative labor, the impelling reason and motive of his work is to obtain property, and thereafter to hold it as his very own. If one person hires out to another his strength or skill, he does so for the purpose of receiving in return what is necessary for the satisfaction of his needs; he therefore expressly intends to acquire a right full and real, not only to the remuneration, but also to the disposal of such remuneration, just as he pleases. Thus, if he lives sparingly, saves money, and, for greater security, invests his savings in land, the land, in such case, is only his wages under another form; and, consequently, a working person's little estate thus purchased should be as completely at his full disposal as are the wages he receives for his labor. But it is precisely in such power of disposal that ownership obtains, whether the property consist of land or chattels (personal property). Socialists, therefore, by endeavoring to transfer the possessions of individuals to the community at large, strike at the interests of every wage-earner, since they would deprive him of the liberty of disposing of his wages, and thereby of all hope and possibility of increasing his resources and of bettering his condition in life.

6. What is of far greater moment, however, is the fact that the remedy they propose is manifestly against justice. For, every person has by nature the right to possess property as his own. This is one of the chief points of distinction between human beings and the animal creation, for the brute has no power of self-direction, but is governed by two main instincts, which keep his powers on the alert, impel him to develop them in a fitting manner, and stimulate and determine him to action without any power of choice. One of these instincts is self-preservation, the other the propagation of the species. Both can attain their purpose by means of things which lie within range; beyond their verge the brute creation cannot go, for they are moved to action by their senses only, and in the special direction which these suggest. But with a human being it is wholly different. He possesses, on the one hand, the full perfection of the animal being, and hence enjoys at least as much as the rest of the animal kind, the fruition of things material. But animal nature, however perfect, is far from representing the human being in its completeness, and is in truth but humanity's humble handmaid, made to serve and to obey. It is the mind, or reason, which is the predominant element in us who are human creatures; it is this which renders a human being human, and distinguishes him essentially from the brute. And on this very account—that man alone among the animal creation is endowed with reason—it must be within his right to possess things not merely for temporary and momentary use, as other living things do, but to have and to hold them in stable and permanent possession; he must have not only things that perish in the use, but those also which, though they have been reduced into use, continue for further use in after time.

7. This becomes still more clearly evident if human nature be considered a little more deeply. For a human being, fathoming by his faculty of reason matters without number, linking the future with the present, and being master of his own acts, guides his ways under the eternal law and the power of God, whose providence governs all things. Wherefore, it is in his power to exercise his choice not only as to matters that regard his present welfare, but also about those which he deems may be for his advantage in time yet to come. Hence, man not only should possess the fruits of the earth, but also the very soil, inasmuch as from the produce of the earth he has to lay by provision for the future. His needs do not die out, but forever recur; although satisfied today, they demand fresh supplies for tomorrow. Nature accordingly must have given to man a source that is stable and remaining always with him, from which he might look to draw continual

115 supplies. And this stable condition of things he finds solely in the earth and its fruits. There is no need to bring in the State. Man precedes the State, and possesses, prior to the formation of any State, the right of providing for the substance of his body.

8. The fact that God has given the earth for the use and enjoyment
120 of the whole human race can in no way be a bar to the owning of private property. For God has granted the earth to humankind in general, not in the sense that all without distinction can deal with it as they like, but rather that no part of it was assigned to any one in particular, and that the limits of private possession have been left to
125 be fixed by a person's own industry, and by the laws of individual [cultures]. Moreover, the earth, even though apportioned among private owners, ceases not thereby to minister to the needs of all, inasmuch as there is not one who does not sustain life from what the land produces. Those who do not possess the soil contribute their
130 labor; hence, it may truly be said that all human subsistence is derived either from labor on one's own land, or from some toil, some calling, which is paid for either in the produce of the land itself, or in that which is exchanged for what the land brings forth. . . .

11. With reason, then, the common opinion of humankind, little
135 affected by the few dissentients who have contended for the opposite view, has found in the careful study of nature, and in the laws of nature, the foundations of the division of property, and the practice of all ages has consecrated the principle of private ownership, as being pre-eminently in conformity with human nature, and as leading in
140 the most unmistakable manner to the peace and tranquillity of human existence. The same principle is confirmed and enforced by the civil laws—laws which, so long as they are just, derive from the law of nature their binding force. The authority of the divine law adds its sanction, forbidding us in severest terms even to covet that
145 which is another's: "*Thou shalt not covet thy neighbor's wife; nor his house, nor his field, nor his man-servant, nor his maid-servant, nor his ox, nor his ass, nor anything that is his.*" (*Deuteronomy* 5:21). . . . . .

Human Unity vs. Class Struggle of Communism:

19. The great mistake made in regard to the matter now under consideration is to take up with the notion that class is naturally hostile to class, and that the wealthy and the working men are intended by nature to live in mutual conflict. So irrational and so false is this view that the direct contrary is the truth. Just as the symmetry of the human frame is the result of the suitable arrangement of the different parts of the body, so in a State is it ordained by nature that these two classes should dwell in harmony and agreement, so as to maintain the balance of the body politic. Each needs the other: capital cannot do without labor, nor labor without capital. Mutual agreement results in the beauty of good order, while perpetual conflict necessarily produces confusion and savage barbarity. Now, in preventing such strife as this, and in uprooting it, the efficacy of Christian institutions is marvelous and manifold. First of all, there is no intermediary more powerful than religion (whereof the Church is the interpreter and guardian) in drawing the rich and the working class together, by reminding each of its duties to the other, and especially of the obligations of justice.

20. Of these duties, the following bind the proletarian and the worker: fully and faithfully to perform the work which has been freely and equitably agreed upon; never to injure the property, nor to outrage the person, of an employer; never to resort to violence in defending their own cause, nor to engage in riot or disorder; and to have nothing to do with men of evil principles, who work upon the people with artful promises of great results, and excite foolish hopes which usually end in useless regrets and grievous loss. The following duties bind the wealthy owner and the employer: not to look upon their work people as their bondsmen, but to respect in every man [and woman their] dignity as a person ennobled by Christian character. They are reminded that, according to natural reason and Christian philosophy, working for gain is creditable, not shameful, to a person, since it enables him to earn an honorable livelihood; but to

115

120

125

130

135

140

145   misuse people as though they were things in the pursuit of gain, or to value them solely for their physical powers—that is truly shameful and inhuman. Again justice demands that, in dealing with the working person, religion and the good of his soul must be kept in mind. Hence, the employer is bound to see that the worker has time for his

150   religious duties; that he be not exposed to corrupting influences and dangerous occasions; and that he be not led away to neglect his home and family, or to squander his earnings. Furthermore, the employer must never tax his work people beyond their strength, or employ them in work unsuited to their sex and age. His great and principal

155   duty is to give every one what is just. Doubtless, before deciding whether wages are fair, many things have to be considered; but wealthy owners and all masters of labor should be mindful of this— that to exercise pressure upon the indigent and the destitute for the sake of gain, and to gather one's profit out of the need of another, is

160   condemned by all laws, human and divine. To defraud any one of wages that are his due is a great crime which cries to the avenging anger of Heaven. *"Behold, the hire of the laborers . . . which by fraud has been kept back by you, crieth; and the cry of them hath entered into the ears of the Lord of Sabaoth"* (*James* 5:4). Lastly, the rich must reli-

165   giously refrain from cutting down the workers' earnings, whether by force, by fraud, or by usurious dealing; and with all the greater reason because the laboring person is, as a rule, weak and unprotected, and because his slender means should in proportion to their scantiness be accounted sacred. Were these precepts carefully obeyed and

170   followed out, would they not be sufficient of themselves to keep under all strife and all its causes?

        21. But the Church, with Jesus Christ as her Master and Guide, aims higher still. She lays down precepts yet more perfect, and tries to bind class to class in friendliness and good feeling. The things of earth cannot

175   be understood or valued aright without taking into consideration the life to come, the life that will know no death. Exclude the idea of futurity, and forthwith the very notion of what is good and right would perish; nay, the whole scheme of the universe would become a dark and

unfathomable mystery. The great truth which we learn from nature her-self is also the grand Christian dogma* on which religion rests as on its 180
foundation—that, when we have given up this present life, then shall we really begin to live. God has not created us for the perishable and tran-sitory things of earth, but for things heavenly and everlasting; God has given us this world as a place of exile, and not as our abiding place. As for riches and the other things which people call good and desirable, 185
whether we have them in abundance, or are lacking in them—so far as eternal happiness is concerned—it makes no difference; the only impor-tant thing is to use them aright. Jesus Christ, when He redeemed us with plentiful redemption, took not away the pains and sorrows which in such large proportion are woven together in the web of our mortal life. 190
He transformed them into motives of virtue and occasions of merit; and no person can hope for eternal reward unless he follow in the blood-stained footprints of his Savior. "*If we suffer with Him, we shall also reign with Him*"(*2 Timothy* 2:12). Christ's labors and sufferings, accepted of His own free will, have marvelously sweetened all suffering and all labor. 195
And not only by His example, but by His grace and by the hope held forth of everlasting recompense, has He made pain and grief more easy to endure; "*for that which is at present momentary and light of our tribu-lation, worketh for us above measure exceedingly an eternal weight of glory*" (*2 Corinthians* 4:17). . . . 200

Worker Unions vs. Laissez-Faire Capitalism:

48. In the last place, employers and workers may of themselves effect much, in the matter We are treating, by means of such associations and organizations as afford opportune aid to those who are in distress, and which draw the two classes more closely together. Among these may be enumerated societies for mutual help; various benevolent 205
foundations established by private persons to provide for the work-man, and for his widow or his orphans, in case of sudden calamity, in sickness, and in the event of death; and institutions for the welfare of boys and girls, young people, and those more advanced in years.

49. The most important of all are workers' unions, for these virtually include all the rest. History attests what excellent results were brought about by the artificers' guilds of olden times. They were the means of affording not only many advantages to the workmen, but in no small degree of promoting the advancement of art, as numerous monuments remain to bear witness. Such unions should be suited to the requirements of this our age—an age of wider education, of different habits, and of far more numerous requirements in daily life. It is gratifying to know that there are actually in existence not a few associations of this nature, consisting either of workers alone, or of workers and employers together, but it were greatly to be desired that they should become more numerous and more efficient. . . .

50. The consciousness of his own weakness urges a person to call in aid from without. We read in the pages of holy Writ: "*It is better that two should be together than one; for they have the advantage of their society. If one fall he shall be supported by the other. Woe to him that is alone, for when he falleth he hath none to lift him up*" (*Ecclesiastes* 4:9–10). And further: "*A brother that is helped by his brother is like a strong city*" (*Proverbs* 18:19). It is this natural impulse which binds people together in civil society; and it is likewise this which leads them to join together in associations which are, it is true, lesser and not independent societies, but, nevertheless, real societies. . . . .

64. On each of you, venerable brethren, and on your clergy and people, as an earnest of God's mercy and a mark of Our affection, we lovingly in the Lord bestow the apostolic benediction.

Given at St. Peter's in Rome, the fifteenth day of May, 1891, the fourteenth year of Our pontificate.

DISCUSSION QUESTIONS

1. Why, according to Pope Leo, is the Socialist solution to the unjust distribution of wealth itself unjust? In their scheme for the distribution of wealth what is it about human nature that he believes they completely overlook?

2. Is there anything like *absolutely* private property according to Leo? Remembering the very first reading in this book, do you think the authors of *Genesis* would agree with the Pope's position here? Why or why not? Do you agree with it? Why or why not?

3. According to Leo, does the Church have any business entering into the relationship between capital and labor? Why or why not? Do you agree? Why or why not?

4. Given the fact that Pope Leo believes the employer's duties toward employees extend beyond merely paying a just wage, how far do you think his principles would take him in the direction of a full welfare state where all the needs of citizens, from womb to tomb, are fully met?

25

The Church & Racial Injustice

"Letter From a Birmingham Jail"

DR. MARTIN LUTHER KING, JR. (1929–1968)

INTRODUCTION

Civil Rights Background

The movement to guarantee the civil rights of African Americans did not begin with the activism of the late 1950s.[23] Nearly a century earlier, during the Reconstruction era (1866 to 1875), Congress passed seven Civil Rights Acts to confirm the newly freed people as citizens,

---

[23] For a good general history, see John Hope Franklin and Alfred A. Moss, Jr., *From Slavery to Freedom: A History of African Americans* 7th ed. (New York: Alfred A. Knopf, 1994); David J. Garrow, *Protest at Selma: Martin Luther King, Jr., and the Voting Rights Act of 1965* (New Haven, CT: Yale University Press, 1978) and idem, *Bearing the Cross: Martin Luther King, Jr., and the Southern Christian Leadership Conference* (New York: William Morrow, 1986), idem, ed., *Birmingham, Alabama: 1956–1963* (Brooklyn, NY: Carlson Publishing, 1989). In addition, the University's Instructional Media Center has the PBS Documentary Series on the Civil Rights Movement, "Eyes on the Prize."

to safeguard their civil rights, and to ensure that they were accorded full and equal benefit of all laws.[24] The very feebleness of this legislation is insinuated by the Voting Rights Act of 1965. This is the wider historical context in which Martin Luther King's impact upon the country as well as the religious and theological, ethical and moral significance of the "Letter from a Birmingham Jail" may, perhaps, be more fully appreciated.

Dr. King's Life

Martin Luther King, Jr., was born January 15, 1929, in Atlanta, Georgia, into a middle-class family, the second child and first son of Alberta Christine Williams and Martin Luther King, Sr. Both his father and paternal grandfather Alfred Daniel Williams were Baptist ministers. The South in which King was born and grew to adulthood was shaped by 'Jim Crow' restrictions or segregation. This meant that African Americans were excluded by law and by custom from or segregated in parks, swimming pools, lunch counters, department stores, and theaters—simply on the basis of race.[25]

King graduated from Atlanta's Morehouse College at nineteen-years of age, then he attended Crozer Seminary in Chester, Pennsylvania. There he was exposed to Mahatma Gandhi's nonviolent activism for social change and Reinhold Niebuhr's critique of pacifism. Theologian James Cone writes that despite some "bitter

---

[24] See Albert P. Blaustein and Robert L. Zangrando, ed., *Civil Rights and the Black American: A Documentary History* (New York: Washington Square Press, 1968): On May 21, 1866, Congress passed a statute making it a criminal offense to "kidnap or carry away any other person, whether [N]egro, mulatto, or otherwise, with the intent that such person should be sold or carried into involuntary servitude, or held as a slave." Also, this statute made it a crime to "transport any [Negro] to a foreign country to be held or sold as a slave." On March 2, 1867, Congress passed "An Act to abolish and forever prohibit the System of Peonage in the Territory of New Mexico and other Parts of the United States" (227–228).

[25] Martin Luther King, Jr., *Strive Toward Freedom* (New York: Harper, 1959), 37.

experiences" with racist whites, "the social and intellectual environment at Crozer and in the surrounding area reinforced King's optimism that justice could and would be achieved with intelligent blacks and whites working together to eliminate racism."[26]

On completion of the degree from Crozer, King then enrolled in the doctoral program in systematic theology at Boston University. After completing courses and examinations, in 1953 King married Coretta Scott. The couple moved to Montgomery, Alabama, where he began duties as the full-time pastor of Dexter Avenue Baptist Church. During the first year of his pastorate, King not only distinguished himself each Sunday in the pulpit and initiated several new ministries, but he completed his dissertation and became involved in the political life of the Montgomery community.[27]

The Montgomery Bus Boycott

When Rosa Parks, a seamstress at a downtown Montgomery department store, refused to surrender her bus seat to a white person on December 1, 1955, she inaugurated a new era in the black struggle for civil rights.[28] Although her arrest galvanized the community, African American leadership was "divided, contentious and apprehensive."[29] They chose King, the twenty-five-year-old newcomer, to lead the Montgomery Improvement Association.

---

[26] Ibid., 28.

[27] The topic of King's dissertation was "A Comparison of the Conceptions of God in the Thinking of Paul Tillich and Henry Wieman."

[28] There were several 'bus incidents' in Montgomery before 1955. One of the best-known involved a fifteen-year-old high school student, Claudette Colvin, who was arrested for refusing to give up her seat to a white passenger. The Colvin incident did not result in a bus boycott, rather a committee of black citizens approached the manager of the bus company and the City Commission to request more courteous treatment and clarification of the seating policy.

[29] David Levering Lewis, "Martin Luther King, Jr., and the Promise of Nonviolent Populism," 278, in *Black Leaders of the Twentieth Century*, ed. John Hope Franklin and August Meier (Urbana: University of Illinois Press, 1982).

The Montgomery boycott is legendary: For 381 days in heat and cold, in sun and rain, despite harassment by the police, intimidation by the Ku Klux Klan, jeopardized jobs, city ordinances to prohibit organized taxi transportation of the boycotters, even bombings, black people of all ages in Montgomery refused to ride buses—mostly they walked. On November 13, 1956, the U. S. Supreme Court ruled Alabama's state and local laws enforcing segregation on buses to be unconstitutional. This success made King a national, even international, figure. For the next twelve years, he devoted his life to ending racial segregation in the United States on moral and religious grounds.

Provocation for "Letter from a Birmingham Jail"

Despite numerous U.S. Supreme Court rulings and federal directives, racial desegregation moved forward throughout most of the South at a snail's pace, if at all. In 1963, King and the staff of the Southern Christian Leadership Conference (SCLC), working in conjunction with local black civil rights leaders and pastors, selected Birmingham, Alabama, as a test site to push the federal government to implement with speed the Supreme Court's decision. The objectives were to desegregate Birmingham's schools, public facilities, and commercial institutions, to initiate hiring and promotion of African American personnel in downtown retail stores, and to establish a biracial committee to monitor racial progress.[30]

Because of mayoral elections in early March and a runoff between Albert Boutwell and Sheriff Eugene "Bull" Connor in early April, the first nonviolent demonstrations in Birmingham began on April 3,

---

[30] Ibid., 285; see also, Cone, *Martin and Malcolm and America,* 120–150.

1963.[31] Led by Sheriff Connor, the city responded with mass arrests, the use of police dogs, night sticks, tear gas, and high-pressure fire hoses. On April 12, Dr. King defied a judicial injunction to bar the protest marches and was arrested and jailed.

Eight leading white clergymen of Birmingham—Catholic, Protestant, and Jewish—in open letter denounced King as an agitator from outside the community. They condemned his conduct as unworthy of a man of God and urged the blacks of Birmingham to withdraw their support from his crusade.[32] Held in solitary confinement and deprived of adequate writing materials, King composed his response on the margins of newspapers and scraps of paper.

—Dr. M. Shawn Copeland

---

[31] Volunteers in the Birmingham campaign signed a "Commitment Card" that read in part: "1. MEDITATE daily on the teachings and life of Jesus. 2. REMEMBER always that the nonviolent movement in Birmingham seeks justice and reconciliation—not victory. 3. WALK and TALK in the manner of love, for God is love. 4. PRAY daily to be used by God in order that all men [sic] might be free. 5. SACRIFICE personal wishes in order that all men [sic] might be free. 6. OBSERVE with both friend and foe the ordinary rules of courtesy. 7. SEEK to perform regular service for others and for the world. 8. REFRAIN from the violence of fist, tongue, or heart. 9. STRIVE to be in good spiritual and bodily health. 10. FOLLOW the directions of the movement and of the captain on a demonstration," cited in John J. Ansbro, *Martin Luther King, Jr., The Making of a Mind* (1982; Maryknoll, NY: Orbis Books, 1984), vi.

[32] These men were Bishop C. C. J. Carpenter, Bishop Joseph A. Durick, Rabbi Hilton L. Grafman, Bishop Paul Hardin, Bishop Holan B. Harmon, the Reverend George M. Murray, the Reverend Edward V. Ramage, and the Reverend Earl Stallings.

TEXT

My dear Fellow Clergymen,

While confined here in the Birmingham city jail, I came across your recent statement calling our present activities "unwise and untimely." Seldom, if ever, do I pause to answer criticism of my work and ideas. If I sought to answer all of the criticisms that cross my desk, my secretaries would be engaged in little else in the course of the day, and I would have no time for constructive work. But since I feel that you are men of genuine good will and your criticisms are sincerely set forth, I would like to answer your statement in what I hope will be patient and reasonable terms.

I think I should give the reason for my being in Birmingham, since you have been influenced by the argument of "outsiders coming in." I have the honor of serving as president of the Southern Christian Leadership Conference, an organization operating in every southern state, with headquarters in Atlanta, Georgia. We have some eighty-five affiliate organizations all across the South—one being the Alabama Christian Movement for Human Rights. Whenever necessary and possible we share staff, educational and financial resources with our affiliates. Several months ago our local affiliate here in Birmingham invited us to be on call to engage in a nonviolent direct-action program if such were deemed necessary. We readily consented and when the hour came we lived up to our promises. So I am here, along with several members of my staff, because we were invited here. I am here because I have basic organizational ties here.

Beyond this, I am in Birmingham because injustice is here. Just as the eighth century prophets left their little villages and carried their "thus saith the Lord" far beyond the boundaries of their hometowns; and just as the Apostle Paul left his little village of Tarsus and carried the gospel of Jesus Christ to practically every hamlet and city of the Graeco-Roman world, I too am compelled to carry the gospel of freedom beyond my particular hometown. Like Paul, I must constantly respond to the Macedonian call for aid.

Moreover, I am cognizant of the interrelatedness of all communities and states. I cannot sit idly by in Atlanta and not be concerned

about what happens in Birmingham. Injustice anywhere is a threat to   35
justice everywhere. We are caught in an inescapable network of mutu-
ality, tied in a single garment of destiny. Whatever affects one directly
affects all indirectly. Never again can we afford to live with the narrow,
provincial "outside agitator" idea. Anyone who lives in the United
States can never be considered an outsider anywhere in this country.   40

You deplore the demonstrations that are presently taking place in
Birmingham. But I am sorry that your statement did not express a
similar concern for the conditions that brought the demonstrations
into being. I am sure that each of you would want to go beyond the
superficial social analyst who looks merely at effects, and does not   45
grapple with underlying causes. I would not hesitate to say that it is
unfortunate that so-called demonstrations are taking place in Birmingham at this time, but I would say in more emphatic terms that it
is even more unfortunate that the white power structure of this city
left the Negro community with no other alternative.   50

In any nonviolent campaign there are four basic steps: (1) collection of the facts to determine whether injustices are alive,
(2) negotiation, (3) self-purification, and (4) direct action. We have
gone through all of these steps in Birmingham. There can be no gain-
saying of the fact that racial injustice engulfs this community.   55

Birmingham is probably the most thoroughly segregated city in the
United States. Its ugly record of police brutality is known in every section of this country. Its unjust treatment of Negroes in the courts is a
notorious reality. There have been more unsolved bombings of Negro
homes and churches in Birmingham than any city in this nation.   60
These are the hard, brutal and unbelievable facts. On the basis of
these conditions Negro leaders sought to negotiate with the city
fathers. But the political leaders consistently refused to engage in
good faith negotiation.

Then came the opportunity last September to talk with some of   65
the leaders of the economic community. In these negotiating sessions
certain promises were made by the merchants—such as the promise
to remove the humiliating racial signs from the stores. On the basis
of these promises Rev. Shuttlesworth and the leaders of the Alabama

70 Christian Movement for Human Rights agreed to call a moratorium on any type of demonstrations. As the weeks and months unfolded we realized that we were the victims of a broken promise. The signs remained. Like so many experiences of the past we were confronted with blasted hopes, and the dark shadow of a deep disappointment

75 settled upon us. So we had no alternative except that of preparing for direct action, whereby we would present our very bodies as a means of laying our case before the conscience of the local and national community. We were not unmindful the difficulties involved. So we decided to go through a process of self-purification. We started hav-

80 ing workshops on nonviolence and repeatedly asked ourselves the questions, "Are you able to accept blows without retaliating?" "Are you able to endure the ordeals of jail?" We decided to set our direct-action program around the Easter season, realizing that with the exception of Christmas, this was the largest shopping period of the

85 year. Knowing that a strong economic withdrawal program would be the by-product of direct action, we felt that this was the best time to bring pressure on the merchants for the needed changes. Then it occurred to us that the March election was ahead and so we speedily decided to postpone action until after election day. When we discov-

90 ered that Mr. Connor was in the run-off, we decided again to postpone action so that the demonstrations could not be used to cloud the issues. At this time we agreed to begin our nonviolent witness the day after the run-off.

This reveals that we did not move irresponsibly into direct action.

95 We too wanted to see Mr. Connor defeated; so we went through postponement after postponement to aid in this community need. After this we felt that direct action could be delayed no longer.

You may well ask, "Why direct action? Why sit-ins, marches, etc.? Isn't negotiation a better path?" You are exactly right in your call for

100 negotiation. Indeed, this is the purpose of direct action. Nonviolent direct action seeks to create such a crisis and establish such creative tension that a community that has constantly refused to negotiate is forced to confront the issue. It seeks so to dramatize the issue that it can no longer be ignored. I just referred to the creation of tension as

a part of the work of the nonviolent resister. This may sound rather shocking. But I must confess that I am not afraid of the word tension. I have earnestly worked and preached against violent tension, but there is a type of constructive nonviolent tension that is necessary for growth. Just as Socrates felt that it was necessary to create a tension in the mind so that individuals could rise from the bondage of myths and half-truths to the unfettered realm of creative analysis and objective appraisal, we must see the need of having nonviolent gadflies to create the kind of tension in society that will help men to rise from the dark depths of prejudice and racism to the majestic heights of understanding and brotherhood. So the purpose of the direct action is to create a situation so crisis packed that it will inevitably open the door to negotiation. We, therefore, concur with you in your call for negotiation. Too long has our beloved Southland been bogged down in the tragic attempt to live in monologue rather than dialogue.

One of the basic points in your statement is that our acts are untimely. Some have asked, "Why didn't you give the new administration time to act?" The only answer that I can give to this inquiry is that the new administration must be prodded about as much as the outgoing one before it acts. We will be sadly mistaken if we feel that the election of Mr. Boutwell will bring the millennium to Birmingham. While Mr. Boutwell is much more articulate and gentle than Mr. Connor, they are both segregationists, dedicated to the task of maintaining the status quo. The hope I see in Mr. Boutwell is that he will be reasonable enough to see the futility of massive resistance to desegregation. But he will not see this without pressure from the devotees of civil rights. My friends, I must say to you that we have not made a single gain in civil rights without determined legal and nonviolent pressure. History is the long and tragic story of the fact that privileged groups seldom give up their privileges voluntarily. Individuals may see the moral light and voluntarily give up their unjust posture; but as Reinhold Niebuhr has reminded us, groups are more immoral than individuals.

We know through painful experience that freedom is never voluntarily given by the oppressor; it must be demanded by the oppressed.

140 Frankly, I have never yet engaged in a direct action movement that was "well-timed," according to the timetable of those who have not suffered unduly from the disease of segregation. For years now I have heard the words "Wait!" It rings in the ear of every Negro with a piercing familiarity. This "Wait" has almost always meant "Never." It
145 has been a tranquilizing thalidomide, relieving the emotional stress for a moment, only to give birth to an ill-formed infant of frustration. We must come to see with the distinguished jurist of yesterday that "justice too long delayed is justice denied." We have waited for more than 340 years for our constitutional and God-given rights.
150 The nations of Asia and Africa are moving with jetlike speed toward the goal of political independence, and we still creep at horse and buggy pace toward the gaining of a cup of coffee at a lunch counter. I guess it is easy for those who have never felt the stinging darts of segregation to say, "Wait." But when you have seen vicious mobs
155 lynch your mothers and fathers at will and drown your sisters and brothers at whim; when you have seen hate-filled policemen curse, kick, brutalize and even kill your black brothers and sisters with impunity; when you see the vast majority of your twenty million Negro brothers smothering in an airtight cage of poverty in the midst
160 of an affluent society; when you suddenly find your tongue twisted and your speech stammering as you seek to explain to your six-year-old daughter why she can't go to the public amusement park that has just been advertised on television, and see tears welling up in her little eyes when she is told that Funtown is closed to colored children,
165 and see the depressing clouds of inferiority begin to form in her little mental sky, and see her begin to distort her little personality by unconsciously developing a bitterness toward white people; when you have to concoct an answer for a five-year-old son asking in agonizing pathos: "Daddy, why do white people treat colored people so
170 mean?"; when you take a cross-country drive and find it necessary to sleep night after night in the uncomfortable corners of your automobile because no motel will accept you; when you are humiliated day in and day out by nagging signs reading "white" and "colored"; when your first name becomes "nigger" and your middle name becomes

"boy" (however old you are) and your last name becomes "John," and   175
when your wife and mother are never given the respected title "Mrs.";
when you are harried by day and haunted by night by the fact that
you are a Negro, living constantly at tiptoe stance never quite knowing what to expect next, and plagued with inner fears and outer
resentments; when you are forever fighting a degenerating sense of   180
"nobodiness"; then you will understand why we find it difficult to
wait. There comes a time when the cup of endurance runs over, and
men are no longer willing to be plunged into an abyss of injustice
where they experience the blackness of corroding despair. I hope, sirs,
you can understand our legitimate and unavoidable impatience.   185

You express a great deal of anxiety over our willingness to break
laws. This is certainly a legitimate concern. Since we so diligently urge
people to obey the Supreme Court's decision of 1954 outlawing segregation in the public schools, it is rather strange and paradoxical to
find us consciously breaking laws. One may well ask, "How can you   190
advocate breaking some laws and obeying others?" The answer is
found in the fact that there are two types of laws: there are just and
there are unjust laws. I would agree with Saint Augustine that "An
unjust law is no law at all."

Now what is the difference between the two? How does one deter-   195
mine when a law is just or unjust? A just law is a man-made code that
squares with the moral law or the law of God. An unjust law is a code
that is out of harmony with the moral law. To put it in the terms of
Saint Thomas Aquinas, an unjust law is a human law that is not
rooted in eternal and natural law. Any law that uplifts human per-   200
sonality is just. Any law that degrades human personality is unjust.
All segregation statutes are unjust because segregation distorts the
soul and damages the personality. It gives the segregator a false sense
of superiority, and the segregated a false sense of inferiority. To use the
words of Martin Buber, the great Jewish philosopher, segregation sub-   205
stitutes an "I-it" relationship for the "I-thou" relationship, and ends
up relegating persons to the status of things. So segregation is not
only politically, economically and sociologically unsound, but it is
morally wrong and sinful. Paul Tillich has said that sin is separation.

210   Isn't segregation an existential expression of man's tragic separation, an expression of his awful estrangement, his terrible sinfulness? So I can urge men to disobey segregation ordinances because they are morally wrong.

Let us turn to a more concrete example of just and unjust laws. An
215   unjust law is a code that a majority inflicts on a minority that is not binding on itself. This is difference made legal. On the other hand a just law is a code that a majority compels a minority to follow that it is willing to follow itself. This is sameness made legal.

Let me give another explanation. An unjust law is a code inflicted
220   upon a minority which that minority had no part in enacting or creating because they did not have the unhampered right to vote. Who can say that the legislature of Alabama which set up the segregation laws was democratically elected? Throughout the state of Alabama all types of conniving methods are used to prevent Negroes from becom-
225   ing registered voters and there are some counties without a single Negro registered to vote despite the fact that the Negro constitutes a majority of the population. Can any law set up in such a state be considered democratically structured?

These are just a few examples of unjust and just laws. There are some
230   instances when a law is just on its face and unjust in its application. For instance, I was arrested Friday on a change of parading without a permit. Now there is nothing wrong with an ordinance which requires a permit for a parade, but when the ordinance is used to preserve segregation and to deny citizens the First Amendment privilege of peaceful
235   assembly and peaceful protest, then it becomes unjust.

I hope you can see the distinction I am trying to point out. In no sense do I advocate evading or defying the law as the rabid segregationist would do. This would lead to anarchy. One who breaks an unjust law must do it *openly, lovingly* (not hatefully as the white
240   mothers did in New Orleans when they were seen on television screaming, "nigger, nigger, nigger"), and with a willingness to accept the penalty. I submit that an individual who breaks a law that conscience tells him is unjust, and willingly accepts the penalty by

staying in jail to arouse the conscience of the community over its injustice, is in reality expressing the very highest respect for law.   245

Of course, there is nothing new about this kind of civil disobedience. It was seen sublimely in the refusal of Shadrach, Meshach and Abednego to obey the laws of Nebuchadnezzar because a higher moral law was involved. It was practiced superbly by the early Christians who were willing to face hungry lions and the excruciating pain   250
of chopping blocks, before submitting to certain unjust laws of the Roman Empire. To a degree academic freedom is a reality today because Socrates practiced civil disobedience.

We can never forget that everything Hitler did in Germany was "legal" and everything the Hungarian freedom fighters did in Hungary was "illegal." It was "illegal" to aid and comfort a Jew in Hitler's   255
Germany. But I am sure that if I had lived in Germany during that time I would have aided and comforted my Jewish brothers even though it was illegal. If I lived in a Communist country today where certain principles dear to the Christian faith are suppressed, I believe   260
I would openly advocate disobeying these anti-religious laws. I must make two honest confessions to you, my Christian and Jewish brothers. First, I must confess that over the last few years I have been gravely disappointed with the white moderate. I have almost reached the regrettable conclusion that the Negro's great stumbling block in   265
the stride toward freedom is not the White Citizen's Counciler or the Ku Klux Klanner, but the white moderate who is more devoted to "order" than to justice; who prefers a negative peace which is the absence of tension to a positive peace which is the presence of justice; who constantly says, "I agree with you in the goal you seek, but I can't   270
agree with your methods of direct action"; who paternalistically feels that he can set the timetable for another man's freedom; who lives by the myth of time and who constantly advised the Negro to wait until a "more convenient season." Shallow understanding from people of good will is more frustrating than absolute misunderstanding from   275
people of ill will. Lukewarm acceptance is much more bewildering than outright rejection.

280   I had hoped that the white moderate would understand that law and order exist for the purpose of establishing justice, and that when they fail to do this they become dangerously structured dams that block the flow of social progress. I had hoped that the white moderate would understand that the present tension of the South is merely a necessary phase of the transition from an obnoxious negative peace, where the Negro passively accepted his unjust plight, to a substance-
285 filled positive peace, where all men will respect the dignity and worth of human personality. Actually, we who engage in nonviolent direct action are not the creators of tension. We merely bring to the surface the hidden tension that is already alive. We bring it out in the open where it can be seen and dealt with. Like a boil that can never be
290 cured as long as it is covered up but must be opened with all its pus-flowing ugliness to the natural medicines of air and light, injustice must likewise be exposed, with all of the tension its exposing creates, to the light of human conscience and the air of national opinion before it can be cured.

295   In your statement you asserted that our actions, even though peaceful, must be condemned because they precipitate violence. But can this assertion be logically made? Isn't this like condemning the robbed man because his possession of money precipitated the evil act of robbery? Isn't this like condemning Socrates because his unswerving
300 commitment to truth and his philosophical delvings precipitated the misguided popular mind to make him drink the hemlock? Isn't this like condemning Jesus because His unique God-consciousness and never-ceasing devotion to his will precipitated the evil act of crucifixion? We must come to see, as federal courts have consistently affirmed,
305 that it is immoral to urge an individual to withdraw his efforts to gain his basic constitutional rights because the quest precipitates violence. Society must protect the robbed and punish the robber.

      I had also hoped that the white moderate would reject the myth of time. I received a letter this morning from a white brother in Texas
310 which said: "All Christians know that the colored people will receive equal rights eventually, but it is possible that you are in too great of a

religious hurry. It has taken Christianity almost two thousand years to accomplish what it has. The teachings of Christ take time to come to earth." All that is said here grows out of a tragic misconception of time. It is the strangely irrational notion that there is something in the very flow of time that will inevitably cure all ills. Actually time is neutral. It can be used either destructively or constructively. I am coming to feel that the people of ill will have used time much more effectively than the people of good will. We will have to repent in this generation not merely for the vitriolic words and actions of the bad people, but for the appalling silence of the good people. We must come to see that human progress never rolls in on wheels of inevitability. It comes through the tireless efforts and persistent work of men willing to be co-workers with God, and without this hard word time itself becomes an ally of the forces of social stagnation. We must use time creatively, and forever realize that the time is always ripe to do right. Now is the time to make real the promise of democracy, and transform our pending national elegy into a creative psalm of brotherhood. Now is the time to lift our national policy from the quicksand of racial injustice to the solid rock of human dignity.

You spoke of our activity in Birmingham as extreme. At first I was rather disappointed that fellow clergymen would see my nonviolent efforts as those of the extremist. I started thinking about the fact that I stand in the middle of two opposing forces in the Negro community. One is a force of complacency made up of Negroes who, as a result of long years of oppression, have been so completely drained of self-respect and a sense of "somebodiness" that they have adjusted to segregation, and, of a few Negroes in the middle class who, because of a degree of academic and economic security, and because at points they profit by segregation, have unconsciously become insensitive to the problems of the masses. The other force is one of bitterness and hatred, and comes perilously close to advocating violence. It is expressed in the various black nationalist groups that are springing up over the nation, the largest and best known being Elijah Muhammad's Muslim movement. This movement is nourished by the contemporary frustration over the continued existence of racial discrimination. It is made up of people who have lost faith in America, who have absolutely repudiated Christianity, and who have concluded that the white man is an incurable "devil." I have tried to stand between these two forces, saying that we need not follow the "do-nothingism" of the complacent or the hatred and despair of the black nationalist. There is the more excellent way of love and nonviolent protest. I'm grateful to God that, through the Negro church, the dimension of nonviolence entered our struggle. If this philosophy had not emerged, I am convinced that by now many streets of the South would be flowing with floods of blood. And I am further convinced that if our white brothers dismiss us as "rabble-rousers" and "outside agitators" those of us who are working through the channels of nonviolent direct action and refuse to support our nonviolent efforts, millions of Negroes, out of frustration and despair, will seek solace and security in black nationalist ideologies, a development that will lead inevitably to a frightening racial nightmare.

Oppressed people cannot remain oppressed forever. The urge for freedom will eventually come. This is what happened to the American Negro. Something within has reminded him of his birthright of freedom; something without has reminded him that he can gain it. Consciously and unconsciously, he has been swept in by what the Germans call the *Zeitgeist,* and with his black brothers of Africa, and his brown and yellow brothers of Asia, South America and the Caribbean, he is moving with a sense of cosmic urgency toward the promised land of racial justice. Recognizing this vital urge that has engulfed the Negro community, one should readily understand public demonstrations. The Negro has many pent-up resentments and latent frustrations. He has to get them out. So let him march sometime; let him have his prayer pilgrimages to the city hall; understand why he must have sit-ins and freedom rides. If his repressed emotions do not come out in these nonviolent ways, they will come out in ominous expressions of violence. This is not a threat; it is a fact of history. So I have not said to my people "get rid of your discontent." But I have tried to say that this normal and healthy discontent can be channelized through the creative outlet of nonviolent direct action. Now this approach is being dismissed as extremist. I must admit that I was initially disappointed in being so categorized.

But as I continued to think about the matter I gradually gained a bit of satisfaction from being considered an extremist. Was not Jesus an extremist in love—"Love your enemies, bless them that curse you, pray for them that despitefully use you." Was not Amos an extremist for justice—"Let justice roll down like waters and righteousness like a mighty stream." Was not Paul an extremist for the gospel of Jesus Christ—"I bear in my body the marks of the Lord Jesus." Was not Martin Luther an extremist—"Here I stand; I can do none other so help me God." Was not John Bunyan an extremist—"I will stay in jail to the end of my days before I make a butchery of my conscience." Was not Abraham Lincoln an extremist—"This nation cannot survive half slave and half free." Was not Thomas Jefferson an extremist—"We hold these truths to be self-evident, that all men are created equal." So the question is not whether we will be extremist but what kind of extremist will we be. Will we be extremists for hate or will we be extremists for love? Will we be extremists for the preservation of injustice—or will we be extremists for the cause of justice? In that dramatic scene on Calvary's hill, three men were crucified. We must not forget that all three were crucified for the same crime—the crime of extremism. Two were extremists for immorality, and thusly fell below their environment. The other, Jesus Christ, was an extremist for love, truth and goodness, and thereby rose above his environment. So, after all, maybe the South, the nation and the world are in dire need of creative extremists.

I had hoped that the white moderate would see this. Maybe I was too optimistic. Maybe I expected too much. I guess I should have realized that few members of a race that has oppressed another race can understand or appreciate the deep groans and passionate yearnings of those that have been oppressed and still fewer have the vision to see that injustice must be rooted out by strong, persistent and determined action. I am thankful, however, that some of our white brothers have grasped the meaning of this social revolution and committed themselves to it. They are still all too small in quantity, but

385

390

395

400

405

410

415

they are big in quality. Some like Ralph McGill, Lillian Smith, Harry Golden and James Dabbs have written about our struggle in eloquent, prophetic and understanding terms. Others have marched with us down nameless streets of the South. They have languished in filthy roach-infested jails, suffering the abuse and brutality of angry policemen who see them as "dirty nigger-lovers." They, unlike so many of their moderate brothers and sisters, have recognized the urgency of the moment and sensed the need for powerful "action" antidotes to combat the disease of segregation.

Let me rush on to mention my other disappointment. I have been so greatly disappointed with the white church and its leadership. Of course, there are some notable exceptions. I am not unmindful of the fact that each of you has taken some significant stands on this issue. I commend you, Rev. Stallings, for your Christian stance on this past Sunday, in welcoming Negroes to your worship service on a non-segregated basis. I commend the Catholic leaders of this state for integrating Spring Hill College[33] several years ago.

But despite these notable exceptions I must honestly reiterate that I have been disappointed with the church. I do not say that as one of the negative critics who can always find something wrong with the church. I say it as a minister of the gospel, who loves the church; who was nurtured in its bosom; who has been sustained by its spiritual blessings and who will remain true to it as long as the cord of life shall lengthen.

I had the strange feeling when I was suddenly catapulted into the leadership of the bus protest in Montgomery several years ago that we would have the support of the white church. I felt that the white ministers, priests and rabbis of the South would be some of our strongest allies. Instead, some have been outright opponents, refusing to understand the freedom movement and misrepresenting its leaders; all too many others have been more cautious than courageous and have remained silent behind the anesthetizing security of the stained-glass windows.

---

[33] A small Jesuit liberal arts college in Mobile, Alabama.

In spite of my shattered dreams of the past, I came to Birmingham with the hope that the white religious leadership of this community would see the justice of our cause, and with deep moral concern, serve as the channel through which our just grievances would get to the power structure. I had hoped that each of you would understand. But again I have been disappointed. I have heard numerous religious leaders of the South call upon their worshippers to comply with a desegregation decision because it is the *law,* but I have longed to hear white ministers say, "Follow this decree because integration is morally *right* and the Negro is your brother." In the midst of blatant injustices inflicted upon the Negro, I have watched white churches stand on the sideline and merely mouth pious irrelevancies and sanctimonious trivialities. In the midst of a mighty struggle to rid our nation of racial and economic injustice, I have heard so many ministers say, "Those are social issues with which the gospel has no real concern," and I have watched so many churches commit themselves to a completely otherworldly religion which made a strange distinction between body and soul, the sacred and the secular.

So here we are moving toward the exit of the twentieth century with a religious community largely adjusted to the status quo, standing as a taillight behind other community agencies rather than a headlight leading men to higher levels of justice.

I have traveled the length and breadth of Alabama, Mississippi and all the other southern states. On sweltering summer days and crisp autumn mornings I have looked at her beautiful churches with their lofty spires pointing heavenward. I have beheld the impressive outlay of her massive religious education buildings. Over and over again I have found myself asking: "What kind of people worship here? Who is their God? Where were their voices when the lips of Governor Barnett dripped with words of interposition and nullification? Where were they when Governor Wallace gave the clarion call for defiance and hatred? Where were their voices of support when tired, bruised and weary Negro men and women decided to rise from the dark dungeons of complacency to the bright hills of creative protest?"

450

455

460

465

470

475

480

Yes, these questions are still in my mind. In deep disappointment, I have wept over the laxity of the church. But be assured that my tears have been tears of love. There can be no deep disappointment where there is not deep love. Yes, I love the church; I love her sacred walls. How could I do otherwise? I am in the rather unique position of being the son, the grandson and the great-grandson of preachers. Yes, I see the church as the body of Christ. But, oh! How we have blemished and scarred that body through social neglect and fear of being nonconformists.

There was a time when the church was very powerful. It was during that period when the early Christians rejoiced when they were deemed worthy to suffer for what they believed. In those days the church was not merely a thermometer that recorded the ideas and principles of popular opinion; it was a thermostat that transformed the mores of society. Wherever the early Christians entered a town the power structure got disturbed and immediately sought to convict them for being "disturbers of the peace" and "outside agitators." But they went on with the conviction that they were "a colony of heaven," and had to obey God rather than man. They were small in number but big in commitment. They were too God-intoxicated to be "astronomically intimidated." They brought an end to such ancient evils as infanticide and gladiatorial contest.

Things are different now. The contemporary church is often a weak, ineffectual voice with an uncertain sound. It is so often the arch-supporter of the status quo. Far from being disturbed by the presence of the church, the power structure of the average community is consoled by the church's silent and often vocal sanction of things as they are.

But the judgment of God is upon the church as never before. If the church of today does not recapture the sacrificial spirit of the early church, it will lose its authentic ring, forfeit the loyalty of millions, and be dismissed as an irrelevant social club with no meaning for the twentieth century. I am meeting young people every day whose disappointment with the church has risen to outright disgust.

Maybe again, I have been too optimistic. Is organized religion too   515
inextricably bound to the status quo to save our nation and the
world? Maybe I must turn my faith to the inner spiritual church, the
church within the church, as the true *ecclesia* and the hope of the
world. But again I am thankful to God that some noble souls from
the ranks of organized religion have broken loose from the paralyzing   520
chains of conformity and joined us as active partners in the struggle
for freedom. They have left their secure congregations and walked the
streets of Albany, Georgia, with us. They have gone through the high-
ways of the South on tortuous rides for freedom. Yes, they have gone
to jail with us. Some have been kicked out of their churches, and lost   525
support of their bishops and fellow ministers. But they have gone
with the faith that right defeated is stronger than evil triumphant.
These men have been the leaven in the lump of the race. Their witness has been the spiritual salt that has preserved the true meaning of
the gospel in these troubled times. They have carved a tunnel of hope   530
through the dark mountain of disappointment.

I hope the church as a whole will meet the challenge of this decisive hour. But even if the church does not come to the aid of justice,
I have no despair about the future. I have no fear about the outcome
of our struggle in Birmingham, even if our motives are presently mis-   535
understood. We will reach the goal of freedom in Birmingham and all
over the nation, because the goal of America is freedom. Abused and
scorned though we may be, our destiny is tied up with the destiny of
America. Before the Pilgrims landed at Plymouth we were here.
Before the pen of Jefferson etched across the pages of history the   540
majestic words of the Declaration of Independence, we were here. For
more than two centuries our foreparents labored in this country without wages; they made cotton king; and they built the homes of their
masters in the midst of brutal injustice and shameful humiliation—
and yet out of a bottomless vitality they continued to thrive and   545
develop. If the inexpressible cruelties of slavery could not stop us, the
opposition we now face will surely fail. We will win our freedom

because the sacred heritage of our nation and the eternal will of God are embodied in our echoing demands.

I must close now. But before closing I am impelled to mention one other point in your statement that troubled me profoundly. You warmly commended the Birmingham police force for keeping "order" and "preventing violence." I don't believe you would have so warmly commended the police force if you had seen its angry violent dogs literally biting six unarmed, nonviolent Negroes. I don't believe you would so quickly commend the policemen if you would observe their ugly and inhuman treatment of Negroes here in the city jail; if you would watch them push and curse old Negro women and young Negro girls; if you would see them slap and kick old Negro men and young boys; if you will observe them, as they did on two occasions, refuse to give us food because we wanted to sing our grace together. I'm sorry that I can't join you in your praise for the police department.

It is true that they have been rather disciplined in their public handling of the demonstrators. In this sense they have been rather publicly "nonviolent." But for what purpose? To preserve the evil system of segregation. Over the last few years I have consistently preached that nonviolence demands that the means we use must be as pure as the ends we seek. So I have tried to make it clear that it is wrong to use immoral means to attain moral ends. But now I must affirm that it is just as wrong, or even more so, to use moral means to preserve immoral ends. Maybe Mr. Connor and his policemen have been rather publicly nonviolent, as Chief Pritchett was in Albany, Georgia, but they have used the moral means of nonviolence to maintain the immoral end of flagrant racial injustice. T. S. Eliot has said that there is no greater treason than to do the right deed for the wrong reason.

I wish you had commended the Negro sit-inners and demonstrators of Birmingham for their sublime courage, their willingness to suffer and their amazing discipline in the midst of the most inhuman provocation. One day the South will recognize its real heroes. They will be

the James Merediths, courageously and with a majestic sense of purpose   580
facing jeering and hostile mobs and the agonizing loneliness that char-
acterizes the life of the pioneer. They will be old, oppressed, battered
Negro women, symbolized in a seventy-two-year-old woman of Montgomery, Alabama, who rose up with a sense of dignity and with her
people decided not to ride the segregated buses, and responded to one   585
who inquired about her tiredness with ungrammatical profundity: "My
feet is tired, but my soul is rested." They will be the young high school
and college students, young ministers of the gospel and a host of their
elders courageously and nonviolently sitting-in at lunch counters and
willingly going to jail for conscience's sake. One day the South will   \590
know that when these disinherited children of God sat down at lunch
counters they were in reality standing up for the best in the American
dream and the most sacred values in our Judeo-Christian heritage, and
thusly, carrying our whole nation back to those great wells of democracy which were dug deep by the Founding Fathers in the formulation   595
of the Constitution and the Declaration of Independence.

Never before have I written a letter this long (or should I say a
book?). I'm afraid that it is much too long to take your precious time.
I can assure you that it would have been much shorter if I had been
writing from a comfortable desk, but what else is there to do when   600
you are alone for days in the dull monotony of a narrow jail cell other
than write long letters, think strange thoughts, and pray long prayers?

If I have said anything in this letter that is an overstatement of the
truth and is indicative of an unreasonable impatience, I beg you to forgive me. If I have said anything in this letter that is an understatement   605
of the truth and is indicative of my having a patience that makes me
patient with anything less than brotherhood, I beg God to forgive me.

I hope this letter finds you strong in the faith. I also hope that circumstances will soon make it possible for me to meet each of you, not
as an integrationist or a civil rights leader, but as a fellow clergyman   610
and a Christian brother. Let us all hope that the dark clouds of racial

615

prejudice will soon pass away and the deep fog of misunderstanding will be lifted from our fear-drenched communities and in some not too distant tomorrow the radiant stars of love and brotherhood will shine over our great nation with all or their scintillating beauty.

Yours for the cause of Peace and Brotherhood,

Martin Luther King, Jr.[34]

DISCUSSION QUESTIONS

1. Dr. King was accused of being an "outsider" coming in and creating civil unrest. What is his response to this complaint? What theological basis, if any, can you point to in any of this book's previous readings for what King calls the *"interrelatedness of all communities"*?

2. According to King, what is the purpose of non-violent direct action, such as sit-ins, marches, and economic boycotts? Would it be effective in any historical situation? Why or why not? If not, what, if anything, do you think must be present first in order for it to work?

3. Why, according to King, does he break the law in his attempts to eliminate the practice of racial segregation? In what larger sense is he actually not *breaking* the law, but *fulfilling* it?

4. How, according to King, did most white religious communities make a *"strange distinction between the body and the soul, the sacred and the secular?"* What dogma* (s) of Christian faith in particular are they denying by their "strange distinction"?

---

[34] Martin Luther King, Jr., *Why We Can't Wait* (New York: Harper & Row, 1963, 1964). The American Friends Committee first published this essay as a pamphlet. It has probably been reprinted more than anything else Dr. King wrote.

26

The Sacred Liturgy

Sacrosanctum Concilium 1–14

THE SECOND VATICAN COUNCIL (1962–1965)

INTRODUCTION

An Ecumenical Council and Its Documents

An "ecumenical council" is in principle a gathering of all the bishops of the world in union with the Pope as bishop of Rome, who according to present legislation is to act as presider and confirmer of its decisions. Pope John XXIII called for a council to renew the spiritual life of the Church, modernize church institutions, and foster ecumenism*. Vatican II opened on October 11, 1962, and, after Pope John died in 1963, was presided over by Pope Paul VI who closed it on December 8, 1965. About 3,000 bishops altogether participated in the Council's different sessions and it produced 16 official documents:

2 Dogmatic Constitutions: "On the Church" *(Lumen Gentium),* and "On Divine Revelation" *(Dei Verbum);*

1 Constitution: "On the Sacred Liturgy" *(Sacrosanctum Concilium);*

1 Pastoral Constitution: "The Church in the Modern World" *(Gaudium et Spes);*

9 Decrees: "On the Instruments of Social Communication" *(Inter Mirifica),* "On Ecumenism" *(Unitatis Redintegratio),* "On Eastern Catholic Churches" *(Orientalium Ecclesiarum),* "On the Bishops' Pastoral Office in the Church" *(Christus Dominus),* "On Priestly Formation" *(Optatum Totius),* "On the Appropriate Renewal of Religious Life" *(Perfectae Caritatis),* "On the Laity" *(Apostolicam Actuositatem),* "On the Ministry and Life of Priests" *(Presbyterorum Ordinis),* and "On the Missions" *(Ad Gentes);* and:

3 Declarations: "On Christian Education" *(Gravissimum Educationis),* "On the Relationship of the Church to Non-Christian Religions" *(Nostra Aetate),* and "On Religious Freedom" *(Dignitatis Humanae).*

A Basic Theology of Christian Liturgy

The first of the council's documents, *"Sacrosanctum Concilium"* (SC), promulgated on December 4, 1963, presents in 130 paragraphs the Catholic Church's faith-understanding of the nature and role of the liturgy in Christian life, and sets down principles and norms for the renewal of the liturgy to foster that life. Consolidating the major insights of 19th and 20th century theologians, from Johann Adam Möhler (+1838) through Dom Odo Casel (+1948), the Council taught that Christ is present in the liturgy, not only in the consecrated bread and wine of the Eucharist as his body and blood, but also in his Paschal Mystery, that is, in the saving events of his life, death, and resurrection. Paragraph 5, in which is set forth a fundamental theology of Christian liturgy, begins with an allusion to *Hebrews* 1:1 (*"In times past, God spoke . . ."*) and then goes on to state, *"Thus in Christ 'there came forth the perfect satisfaction needed for our reconciliation and we received the means for giving worthy worship to God.' "* In light of the teaching of *Hebrews,* this *"worthy worship"* given to the Church is its participation in Christ's own self-offering in faith to the Father. And so the paragraph ends with a marvelous scriptural image encapsulating this theology of Christian liturgy: "*For it was from the side of Christ as he slept the sleep of death upon the cross that there came forth the wondrous sacrament* which is the whole Church.*" Thus, as Eve is depicted in *Genesis* as formed from Adam's rib sharing his nature, the Church in its essential nature is that true community of the human race both resulting from and *offering itself in* the once-for-all self-offering of Christ on the cross, through which God speaks himself out completely to the world of all ages.

Summit and Source of Christian Life

The Church, then, acts as and becomes Christ's sacrament in the world, not only through (a) witness *(martyria)* and (b) service to others *(diakonia)* (par. 9), but most fully through participation already in Christ's heavenly worship of the Father (par. 8) by means of the traditional forms of her (c) sacred liturgy *(leitourgia)*. The Council therefore describes the liturgy as "*the summit toward which the activity of the Church is directed [as well as] the fountain from which all her power flows*" (par. 10), because in the liturgy especially can Christ be seen to save and sanctify the Church through the Church's own *symbolic* self-offering in faith. SC, 14 therefore concludes, "*the faithful [should] be led to that full, conscious, and active participation in liturgical celebrations which is demanded by the very nature of the liturgy.*"

The Liturgy is Reformable

In the century prior to Vatican II, historical studies revealed the extent to which the Church's liturgy changed and grew over the centuries. Although it is precisely the traditional forms handed down from apostolic times that witness how the Church's liturgy is a participation in Christ's historical saving events, the Council teaches that the Church can and should make those liturgical adaptations which are necessary in order to communicate within changing human cultures its fundamental unchanging faith. And so, in its remaining paragraphs the Constitution proceeds to address particular areas of the Church's liturgy, setting down principles for their promotion and reform.

—*Rev. John D. Laurance, S.J.*

TEXT[35]

PAUL, BISHOP SERVANT OF THE SERVANTS OF GOD TOGETHER WITH THE FATHERS OF THE SACRED COUNCIL FOR EVERLASTING MEMORY

1. It is the goal of this most sacred Council *(Sacrosanctum concilium)* to intensify the daily growth of Catholics in Christian living; to make more responsive to the requirements of our times those Church observances which are open to adaptation; to nurture whatever can contribute to the unity of all who believe in Christ; and to strengthen those aspects of the Church which can help summon all of mankind into her embrace. Hence the Council has special reasons for judging it a duty to provide for the renewal and fostering of the liturgy.

2. For it is through the liturgy, especially the divine Eucharistic Sacrifice, that *"the work of our redemption is exercised."*[36] The liturgy is thus the outstanding means by which the faithful can express in their lives, and manifest to others, the mystery of Christ and the real nature of the true Church.[37] It is of the essence of the Church that she be both human and divine, visible and yet invisibly endowed, eager to act and yet devoted to contemplation, present in this world and yet not at home in it. She is all these things in such a way that in her the human is directed and subordinated to the divine, the visible likewise to the invisible, action to contemplation, and this present world to that city yet to come, which we seek (cf. Heb.13:14). Day by day the liturgy builds up those within the Church into the Lord's

---

[35] The original translation has been changed slightly to make the text more gender inclusive.—*Ed., Introduction to Theology.*

[36] *Secret* (prayer in the Mass now called Prayer over the Offerings) for the ninth Sunday after Pentecost.

[37] Liturgy is seen as something profound rather than merely external. In many ways this Constitution is the germ of the Constitution on the Church, promulgated on Nov. 21, 1964.

holy temple, into a spiritual dwelling for God (cf. Eph. 2:21–22)—
an enterprise which will continue until Christ's full stature is achieved
(cf. Eph. 4:13). At the same time the liturgy marvelously fortifies the
faithful in their capacity to preach Christ. To outsiders the liturgy
thereby reveals the Church as a sign raised above the nations (cf. Is.   25
11:12). Under this sign the scattered sons and daughters of God are
being gathered into one (cf. Jn. 11:52) until there is one fold and one
shepherd (cf. Jn. 10:16).

3. Therefore this most sacred Council judges that the following
principles concerning the promotion and reform of the liturgy should   30
be called to mind, and that practical norms should be established . . .

4. Finally, in faithful obedience to tradition*, this most sacred
Council declares that holy Mother Church holds all lawfully acknowl-
edged rites to be of equal authority and dignity; that she wishes to
preserve them in the future and to foster them in every way. The   35
Council also desires that, where necessary, the rites be carefully and
thoroughly revised in the light of sound tradition, and that they be
given new vigor to meet the circumstances and needs of modern times.

Chapter I

General Principles for the Restoration and Promotion of the Sacred Liturgy

I. The Nature of the Sacred Liturgy and Its Importance in the Church's Life

5. God, who *"wishes all people to be saved and come to the knowledge
of the truth"* (1 Tim. 2:4), "in many and various ways . . . spoke of old   40
to our fathers by the prophets"[38]* (Heb. 1:1). When the fullness of
time had come He sent His Son, the Word made flesh, anointed by
the Holy Spirit, to preach the gospel to the poor, to heal the contrite

---

[38] *Revised Standard Version (Confraternity: "at sundry times and in divers
manners").—Ed.

of heart (cf. Is. 61:1; Lk. 4:18), to be a *"bodily and spiritual medicine,"*[39] the Mediator between God and man (cf. 1 Tim. 2:5).[40] For His humanity, united with the person of the Word, was the instrument of our salvation. Thus in Christ *"there came forth the perfect satisfaction needed for our reconciliation, and we received the means for giving worthy worship to God."*[41]

The wonders wrought by God among the people of the Old Testament were but a prelude to the work of Christ the Lord in redeeming mankind and giving perfect glory to God. He achieved His task principally by the paschal mystery of His blessed passion, resurrection from the dead, and glorious ascension, whereby *"dying, he destroyed our death and, rising, he restored our life."*[42] For it was from the side of Christ as He slept the sleep of death upon the cross that there came forth the wondrous sacrament which is the whole Church.[43]

6. Just as Christ was sent by the Father, so also He sent the apostles, filled with the Holy Spirit. This He did so that, by preaching the gospel to every creature (cf. Mk. 16:15), they might proclaim that the Son of God, by His death and resurrection, had freed us from the power of Satan (cf. Acts 26: 18) and from death, and brought us into the kingdom of His Father. His purpose was also that they might

---

[39] St. Ignatius of Antioch, "To the Ephesians," 7, 2; ed. F. X. Funk, Patres Apostolici I, Tübingen, 1901, p. 218.

[40] The central position of Christ as our Mediator is the theme of Pius XII's important encyclical, *Mediator Dei,* which was the Magna Carta of the liturgical renewal (1947). The present Constitution, however, goes far beyond its development.

[41] Sacramentarium Veronense (Leonianum); ed. C. Mohlberg, Rome, 1956 n. 1265.

[42] Easter Preface in the Roman Missal.

[43] Cf. St. Augustine, "Enarr. in Ps. 138" 2, Corpus Chritianorum XL, Tournai, 1956, p. 1991, and prayer after the second lesson for Holy Saturday, as it was in the Roman Missal before the restoration of Holy Week.

Outside View of St. Peter's Basilica, Rome.
Photo by John D. Laurance, S.J.

exercise the work of salvation which they were proclaiming, by means   65
of sacrifice and sacraments*, around which the entire liturgical life
revolves. Thus, by baptism, human beings are plunged into the
paschal mystery of Christ: they die with Him, are buried with Him,
and rise with Him (cf. Rom. 6:4; Eph. 2:6; Col. 3:1; 2 Tim. 2:11);
they receive the spirit of adoption as sons *"by virtue of which we cry:*   70

Abba, Father" (Rom. 8:15), and thus become those true adorers whom the Father seeks (cf. Jn. 4:23). In like manner, as often as they eat the supper of the Lord they proclaim the death of the Lord until He comes (cf. 1 Cor. 11:26). For that reason, on the very day of Pentecost, when the Church appeared before the world, "*those who received the word*" of Peter "*were baptized.*" And "*they continued steadfastly in the teaching of the apostles and in the communion of the breaking of the bread and in the prayers . . . praising God and being in favor with all the people*" (Acts 2:41–47). From that time onward the Church has never failed to come together to celebrate the paschal mystery: reading "*in all the scriptures the things referring to himself*" (Lk. 24:27), celebrating the Eucharist in which "*the victory and triumph of his death are again made present,*"[44] and at the same time giving thanks "*to God for his unspeakable gift*" (2 Cor. 9:15) in Christ Jesus, "*to the praise of his glory*" (Eph. 1:12), through the power of the Holy Spirit.

7. To accomplish so great a work, Christ is always present in His Church, especially in her liturgical celebrations. He is present in the sacrifice of the Mass, not only in the person of His minister, "*the same one now offering, through the ministry of priests, who formerly offered himself on the cross,*"[45] but especially under the Eucharistic species. By His power He is present in the sacraments, so that when a person baptizes it is really Christ Himself who baptizes.[46] He is present in His word, since it is He Himself who speaks when the holy Scriptures are read in the church. He is present, finally, when the Church prays

---

[44] Council of Trent, Session 13, Oct. 11, 1551, Decree on the Holy Eucharist c. 5: Concilium Tridentinum, Diariorum, Actorum, Epistolarum, Tractatuum nova collectio, ed. Soc. Goerresiana, VII, Actorum pars IV, Freiburg im Breisgau, 1961, p. 202.

[45] Council of Trent, Session 22, Sept. 17, 1562, Doctrine* on the Holy Sacrifice of the Mass, c. 2: Concilium Tridentinum, ed. cit., VIII, Actorum pars V, Freiburg im Breisgau, 1919, p. 960.

[46] Cf. St. Augustine, "In Ioannis Evangelium tractatus VI," c. 1, n. 7; PL 35, 1428.

and sings, for He promised: "*Where two or three are gathered together for my sake, there am I in the midst of them*" (Mt. 18:20).

Christ indeed always associates the Church with Himself in the truly great work of giving perfect praise to God and making men holy. The Church is His dearly beloved Bride who calls to her Lord, and through Him offers worship to the Eternal Father.

Rightly, then, the liturgy is considered as an exercise of the priestly office of Jesus Christ. In the liturgy the sanctification of people is manifested by signs perceptible to the senses, and is effected in a way which is proper to each of these signs; in the liturgy full public worship is performed by the Mystical Body of Jesus Christ, that is, by the Head and His members.[47]

From this it follows that every liturgical celebration, because it is an action of Christ the priest and of His Body the Church, is a sacred action surpassing all others. No other action of the Church can match its claim to efficacy, nor equal the degree of it.

8. In the earthly liturgy, by way of foretaste, we share in that heavenly liturgy which is celebrated in the holy city of Jerusalem toward which we journey as pilgrims, and in which Christ is sitting at the right hand of God, a minister of the sanctuary and of the true tabernacle (cf. Apoc. 21: 2; Col. 3:1; Heb. 8:2); we sing a hymn to the Lord's glory with all the warriors of the heavenly army; venerating the memory of the saints, we hope for some part and fellowship with them; we eagerly await the Savior, our Lord Jesus Christ, until He, our life, shall appear and we too will appear with Him in glory (cf. Phil. 3:20; Col. 3:4).

9. The sacred liturgy does not exhaust the entire activity of the Church. Before people can come to the liturgy they must be called to faith and to conversion: "*How then are they to call upon him in whom they have not believed? But how are they to believe him whom they have*

100

105

110

115

120

125

---

[47] Another important encyclical of Pius XII, *Mystici Corporis* (1943), stressed the fact of the Church as Christ's Mystical Body. This has been incorporated (and in some ways greatly surpassed) by the present Constitution and the Constitution on the Church.

not heard? And how are they to hear, if no one preaches? And how are men to preach unless they be sent?" (Rom. 10: 14–15).

Therefore the Church announces the good tidings of salvation to those who do not believe, so that all human beings may know the true God and Jesus Christ whom He has sent, and may repent and mend their ways (cf. Jn. 17:3; Lk. 24:27; Acts 2:38). To believers also the Church must ever preach faith and repentance. She must prepare them for the sacraments, teach them to observe all that Christ has commanded (cf. Mt. 28:20), and win them to all the works of charity, piety, and the apostolate. For all these activities make it clear that Christ's faithful, though not of this world, are the light of the world and give glory to the Father in the sight of people.

10. Nevertheless the liturgy is the summit toward which the activity of the Church is directed; at the same time it is the fountain from which all her power flows.[48] For the goal of apostolic works is that all who are made sons and daughters of God by faith and baptism should come together to praise God in the midst of His Church, to take part in her sacrifice, and to eat the Lord's supper.

The liturgy in its turn inspires the faithful to become *"of one heart in love"*[49] when they have tasted to their full of the paschal mysteries; it prays that *"they may grasp by deed what they hold by creed."*[50] The renewal in the Eucharist of the covenant between the Lord and humanity draws the faithful into the compelling love of Christ and sets them afire. From the liturgy, therefore, and especially from the Eucharist, as from a fountain, grace is channeled into us; and the sanctification of people in Christ and the glorification of God, to which all other activities of the Church are directed as toward their goal, are most powerfully achieved.

---

[48] This solemn paragraph represents the sum of the Church's official teaching on the Liturgy. It is thus something central, by no means secondary or peripheral.

[49] *Postcommunion in the Easter Vigil Mass and the Mass of Easter Sunday.*

[50] *Collect* (prayer) *of the Mass for Tuesday of Easter Week.*

11. But in order that the sacred liturgy may produce its full effect, it is necessary that the faithful come to it with proper dispositions, that their thoughts match their words, and that they cooperate with divine grace lest they receive it in vain (cf. 2 Cor. 6:1). Pastors of souls must therefore realize that, when the liturgy is celebrated, more is required than the mere observance of the laws governing valid and licit celebration. It is their duty also to ensure that the faithful take part knowingly, actively, and fruitfully.[51]

12. The spiritual life, however, is not confined to participation in the liturgy. The Christian is assuredly called to pray with his brethren, but he must also enter into his chamber to pray to the Father in secret (cf. Mt. 6:6); indeed, according to the teaching of the Apostle Paul, he should pray without ceasing (cf. 1 Th. 5:17). We learn from the same Apostle that we must always carry about in our body the dying of Jesus, so that the life of Jesus too may be made manifest in our bodily frame (cf. 2 Cor. 4:10–11). This is why we ask the Lord in the sacrifice of the Mass that, *"receiving the offering of the spiritual victim,"* He may fashion us for Himself *"as an eternal gift."*[52]

13. Popular devotions of the Christian people are warmly commended, provided they accord with the laws and norms of the Church. Such is especially the case with devotions called for by the Apostolic See.

Devotions proper to individual churches also have a special dignity if they are conducted by mandate of the bishops in accord with customs or books lawfully approved.

Nevertheless these devotions should be so drawn up that they harmonize with the liturgical seasons, accord with the sacred liturgy, are

155

160

165

170

175

180

---

[51] This theme of awareness and active participation by the faithful is another basic theme of the Constitution. It reinforces recent papal teaching on the meaning of liturgy.

[52] *Secret* (prayer of the Mass) *for Monday of Pentecost Week.*

in some fashion derived from it, and lead the people to it, since the liturgy by its very nature far surpasses any of them.[53]

II. The Promotion of Liturgical Instruction and Active Participation

185

14. Mother Church earnestly desires that all the faithful be led to that full, conscious, and active participation in liturgical celebrations which is demanded by the very nature of the liturgy. Such participation by the Christian people as *"a chosen race, a royal priesthood, a holy nation, a purchased people"* (1 Pet. 2:9; cf. 2:4–5), is their right and duty by reason of their baptism.

190

In the restoration and promotion of the sacred liturgy, this full and active participation by all the people is the aim to be considered before all else; for it is the primary and indispensable source from which the faithful are to derive the true Christian spirit. . . .

---

[53] While liturgy is not the whole of the Christian life and does not supplant personal prayer, all devotions must harmonize with its spirit.

DISCUSSION QUESTIONS

1. What is the relationship, according to paragraph 6, of the Church's preaching to its sacraments?

2. Paragraph 7 states that Christ is present in the liturgy in a variety of ways. From your reading of the text does it seem that any one of those ways is the source of all the others? Are they all simply aspects of one basic mode of presence? Or is each theologically independent of others? If one is *not* the source of the others, are they all equally significant and important? Explain.

3. In paragraph 8 we are told that, "*In the earthly liturgy, by way of foretaste, we share in [the] heavenly liturgy.*" What do you think this statement means? Has the document previously provided any theological grounds on which to make such a statement?

4. Paragraph 11 notes that for the liturgy to have its full effect, it is important that "*the faithful come to it with the proper dispositions.*" Why do you suppose this is so? What "effect" does the Council have in mind here? And how, according to the text, is one to gain those "proper dispositions?"

27

"The Church of Christ"

Lumen gentium, 1, 8, 13–17

SECOND VATICAN COUNCIL (1962–1965)

INTRODUCTION

The Event of the Second Vatican Council

A church council is a gathering of bishops and other church members from a given geographical area. This gathering, usually named for the city in which it is celebrated, assembles in order to make decisions on issues affecting the various regional churches represented by the people in attendance. A council that makes decisions that are valid or binding for the whole Catholic Church throughout the world is called an ecumenical council. By most counts 21 ecumenical councils have been celebrated over the centuries. The formal public sessions of the last of these took place in Saint Peter's Basilica in Vatican City. Blessed Pope John XXIII surprised the world when he convoked this Second Vatican Council (the First was held in 1869–1870) on 25 January 1959, just three months after his election. He solemnly opened the proceedings on 11 October 1962, after having

261

ordered a world-wide consultation of church leaders concerning the Council's agenda. After his death the next year, his successor, Pope Paul VI, decided to continue the Council, which celebrated its solemn conclusion on 8 December 1965. The Council accepted three main goals from these popes: renewing the Catholic Church through a return to its deepest sources, updating that Church in order to engage it in a dialogue with the contemporary world so it could better serve that world, and committing the Catholic Church to search for the unity of all Christian churches separated from each other. The Council made history because it seated by far the most participants of any ecumenical council ever (3,058) and because for the first time participants in an ecumenical council came from cultures outside of Europe and the Mediterranean world. Since the end of the Council, the Catholic Church and other Christian communities have not ceased finding its documents an important reference point for every sort of thing they believe and do.

Background to Lumen gentium

Since the eleventh century, various individuals and groups had called for Church reform. Differences over the urgency and direction of such reform had splintered the Church since the sixteenth century. The nineteenth and twentieth centuries saw the rise of three interconnected movements that made it ever more necessary for an ecumenical council to take as its theme, for the first time in history, what the Church believed about itself. First, the critical historical study of the Bible, of ancient and medieval Christian authors, and of the Christian liturgical tradition led to a new emphasis on the invisible, divinely given aspects of Church life as the heart and soul of its visible institutions and rituals. Second, the opposition that grew between the Church and modern democratic, industrial, and scientific culture after the French Revolution contributed to a decline in Church membership and to deep questions on the Church's role in society. And third, the movement toward a renewed unity of Christian churches was leading all Christians to reconsider just what were the Church, its essential structures, and its unity. In this context, the tragedies and disruptions occasioned by the Second World War convinced many in the Catholic Church that it needed to find a whole new way of being itself that was truer to its original inspiration and better adapted to a world ever more in need of the Gospel. Thus, the nature and renewal of the Church became central to the Second Vatican Council's agenda, and the debates concerning the Dogmatic Constitution on the Church came to affect all that the Council did.

The Church as a Sacrament*

Emphasis on the Church's invisible, divinely given aspects poses the question of their relationship to the visible institutional aspects of its life. Following the teaching of John XXIII's immediate predecessor, Pope Pius XII, *Lumen gentium* teaches that the invisible and the visible, the divinely given and the humanly invented, do not form two distinct churches, but a single complex reality that is the Church. To express this unity of distinct aspects in the one Church, *Lumen gentium* resorts to three traditional concepts among others: mystery, sacrament*, and the model of Jesus' incarnation*. As you read the excerpts below, watch especially how the latter two of these concepts function to express the differentiated unity of the Church.

Where is the Church?

Christianity has been divided into separate churches on a continuous basis since the fifth century. All of them more or less claim the right to exist separately from the others as the one true Church. Frequently these churches and communities differ significantly—even contradict each other—in their faith and practice. So which is the true Church, or in which community can one find it? Is there only one true Church? Emphasis on the invisible, spiritual, and divinely given aspects of the Church might lead one to wonder if any concrete church can claim this title. In addressing this question, *Lumen gentium* stepped back from Pius XII's simple identification of the true Church of Christ with the Roman Catholic Church. Instead, the Dogmatic Constitution claims that the true Church of Christ *subsists in* the Roman Catholic Church. The word *subsists* here means four things at once: continues to exist concretely, exists in a self-revealing manner, exists fully, and exists not exclusively. This fourth meaning allowed the Dogmatic Constitution to recognize that the true Church of Christ does exist in many ways in separate Christian churches and communities other than the Roman Catholic Church. Note how the excerpts you will read describe and enumerate those ways.

Relations of Others to the Catholic Church and to the Saving God

By confessing the Church to be "catholic" in their Creed, Christians are asserting that the Church is in a certain sense universal and thus related to all people. Thus, how the Church is related to various categories of people depends on what the word "catholic" means in the Creed. Ultimately, the Church's relation to others and its catholicity depend on God's initiative to save all people. How does God reach those outside the Catholic Church, even outside any Christian church or community? And since he can save people untouched by the Church and its Gospel, why accept the Gospel, join the Church, and preach its Gospel to those who have not yet heard it? As you read the excerpts from *Lumen gentium* given below, pay attention to how the Second Vatican Council addresses these issues about the place of the Church in the world and in God's saving plan.

—*Rev. Joseph G. Mueller, S.J.*

TEXT

DOGMATIC CONSTITUTION ON THE CHURCH
LUMEN GENTIUM
SOLEMNLY PROMULGATED BY HOLINESS
POPE PAUL VI
ON NOVEMBER 21, 1964

Chapter I

The Mystery of the Church

1. Christ is the Light of nations. Because this is so, this Sacred Synod gathered together in the Holy Spirit eagerly desires, by proclaiming the Gospel to every creature,[54] to bring the light of Christ to all men, a light brightly visible on the countenance of the Church. Since the Church is in Christ like a sacrament* or as a sign and instrument both of a very   5 closely knit union with God and of the unity of the whole human race, it desires now to unfold more fully to the faithful of the Church and to the whole world its own inner nature and universal mission. This it intends to do following faithfully the teaching of previous councils. The present- day conditions of the world add greater urgency to this work of   10 the Church so that all men, joined more closely today by various social, technical and cultural ties, might also attain fuller unity in Christ. . . .

8. Christ, the one Mediator, established and continually sustains here on earth His holy Church, the community of faith, hope and charity, as an entity with visible delineation[55] through which He com-   15 municated truth and grace to all. But, the society structured with hierarchical organs and the Mystical Body of Christ, are not to be considered as two realities, nor are the visible assembly and the spiritual community, nor the earthly Church and the Church enriched with heavenly things; rather they form one complex reality which   20 coalesces from a divine and a human element.[56] For this reason, by no

---

[54] See *Mark* 16:15.

[55] Leo XIII, Litt. Encycl. Sapientiae christianae, 10 ian. 1890 AAS 22 (1889–90) p. 392. Id., Epist. Encycl. Satis cognitum, 29 iun. 1896; AAS 28 (1895–96) pp. 710 ct 724 ss. Pius XII, Litt. Encycl. Mystici Corporis, 1. c., pp. 199–200.

[56] See Pius XII, Litt. Encycl. Mystici Corporis, 1. c., p. 221 ss. Id., Lin. Encycl. Humani genesis, 12 Aug. 1950: AAS 42 (1950) p. 571.

weak analogy, it is compared to the mystery of the incarnate Word. As the assumed nature inseparably united to Him, serves the divine Word as a living organ of salvation, so, in a similar way, does the visible social structure of the Church serve the Spirit of Christ, who vivifies it, in the building up of the body.[57]

This is the one Church of Christ which in the Creed is professed as one, holy, catholic and apostolic,[58] which our Savior, after His Resurrection, commissioned Peter to shepherd,[59] and him and the other apostles to extend and direct with authority,[60] which He erected for all ages as "the pillar and mainstay of the truth."[61] This Church constituted and organized in the world as a society, subsists in the Catholic Church, which is governed by the successor of Peter and by the Bishops in communion with him, although many elements of sanctification and of truth are found outside of its visible structure. These elements, as gifts belonging to the Church of Christ, are forces impelling toward catholic unity.

Just as Christ carried out the work of redemption in poverty and persecution, so the Church is called to follow the same route that it might communicate the fruits of salvation to men. Christ Jesus, "though He was by nature God . . . emptied Himself, taking the nature of a slave,"[62] and "being rich, became poor"[63] for our sakes. Thus, the Church, although it needs human resources to carry out its mission, is not set up to seek earthly glory, but to proclaim, even by its own example, humility and self sacrifice. Christ was sent by the Father "to bring good news to the poor, to heal the contrite of

---

[57] See *Ephesians* 4, 16.; Leo XIII, Epist. Encycl. Satis cognitum, 1. c., p. 713.

[58] See Symbolum Apostolicum: Denz. 6–9 (10–13); Symb. Nic.-Const.: Denz. 86 (150), coll. Prof. fidei Trid.: Denz. 994 et 999 (1862 et 1868).

[59] See *John* 21:17.

[60] See *Matthew* 28:18ff.

[61] *1 Timothy* 3:15.

[62] *Philippians* 2:6.

[63] *2 Corinthians* 8:9.

heart,"[64] "to seek and to save what was lost."[65] Similarly, the Church encompasses with love all who are afflicted with human suffering and in the poor and afflicted sees the image of its poor and suffering Founder. It does all it can to relieve their need and in them it strives to serve Christ. While Christ, holy, innocent and undefiled[66] knew nothing of sin,[67] but came to expiate only the sins of the people,[68] the Church, embracing in its bosom sinners, at the same time holy and always in need of being purified, always follows the way of penance and renewal. The Church, "like a stranger in a foreign land, presses forward amid the persecutions of the world and the consolations of God"(14*), announcing the cross and death of the Lord until He comes.[69] By the power of the risen Lord it is given strength that it might, in patience and in love, overcome its sorrows and its challenges, both within itself and from without, and that it might reveal to the world, faithfully though darkly, the mystery of its Lord until, in the end, it will be manifested in full light.

Chapter II

On the People of God

. . . .

13. All men are called to belong to the new people of God. Wherefore this people, while remaining one and only one, is to be spread throughout the whole world and must exist in all ages, so that the decree of God's will may be fulfilled. In the beginning God made human nature one and decreed that all His children, scattered as they

---

[64] *Luke* 4:18.

[65] *Luke* 19:10.

[66] *Hebrews* 7:26.

[67] *2 Corinthians* 5:21.

[68] See *Hebrews* 2:17.

[69] See *1 Corinthians* 11:26.

were, would finally be gathered together as one. It was for this purpose that God sent His Son, whom He appointed heir of all things,[70] that be might be teacher, king and priest of all, the head of the new and universal people of the sons of God. For this too God sent the Spirit of His Son as Lord and Life-giver. He it is who brings together the whole Church and each and every one of those who believe, and who is the well-spring of their unity in the teaching of the apostles and in fellowship, in the breaking of bread and in prayers.[71]

It follows that though there are many nations there is but one people of God, which takes its citizens from every race, making them citizens of a kingdom which is of a heavenly rather than of an earthly nature. All the faithful, scattered though they be throughout the world, are in communion with each other in the Holy Spirit, and so, he who dwells in Rome knows that the people of India are his members."[72] Since the kingdom of Christ is not of this world,[73] the Church or people of God in establishing that kingdom takes nothing away from the temporal welfare of any people. On the contrary it fosters and takes to itself, insofar as they are good, the ability, riches and customs in which the genius of each people expresses itself. Taking them to itself it purifies, strengthens, elevates and ennobles them. The Church in this is mindful that she must bring together the nations for that king to whom they were given as an inheritance,[74] and to whose city they bring gifts and offerings.[75] This characteristic of universality which adorns the people of God is a gift from the Lord Himself. By reason of it, the Catholic Church strives constantly and

---

[70] *Hebrews* 1:2.

[71] See *Acts* 2:42.

[72] Cfr. S. Io. Chrysostomus, In Io. Hom. 65, 1: PG 59, 361.

[73] See *John* 18:26.

[74] See *Psalm* 2:8.

[75] See *Psalm* 71 (72):10; *Isaiah* 60:4–7; *Revelation* 21:24.

with due effect to bring all humanity and all its possessions back to its source in Christ, with Him as its head and united in His Spirit.[76]

In virtue of this catholicity each individual part contributes 95
through its special gifts to the good of the other parts and of the whole Church. Through the common sharing of gifts and through the common effort to attain fullness in unity, the whole and each of the parts receive increase. Not only, then, is the people of God made up of different peoples but in its inner structure also it is composed 100
of various ranks. This diversity among its members arises either by reason of their duties, as is the case with those who exercise the sacred ministry for the good of their brethren, or by reason of their condition and state of life, as is the case with those many who enter the religious state and, tending toward holiness by a narrower path, stim- 105
ulate their brethren by their example. Moreover, within the Church particular Churches hold a rightful place; these Churches retain their own traditions, without in any way opposing the primacy of the Chair of Peter, which presides over the whole assembly of charity[77] and protects legitimate differences, while at the same time assuring 110
that such differences do not hinder unity but rather contribute toward it. Between all the parts of the Church there remains a bond of close communion whereby they share spiritual riches, apostolic workers and temporal resources. For the members of the people of God are called to share these goods in common, and of each of the 115
Churches the words of the Apostle hold good: "According to the gift that each has received, administer it to one another as good stewards of the manifold grace of God."[78]

---

[76] See S. Irenaeus, Adv. Haer. III, 16, 6; III, 22, 1–3: PG 7, 925 C-926 Aet 955 C-958 A; Harvey 2, 87 s. et 120–123; Sagnard, Ed. Sources Chret., pp. 290–292 et 372 ss.

[77] See S. Ignatius M., Ad Rom., Praef.: Ed. Funk, I, p. 252.

[78] *1 Peter* 4:10.

120 All men are called to be part of this catholic unity of the people of God which in promoting universal peace presages it. And there belong to or are related to it in various ways, the Catholic faithful, all who believe in Christ, and indeed the whole of mankind, for all men are called by the grace of God to salvation.

125 14. This Sacred Council wishes to turn its attention firstly to the Catholic faithful. Basing itself upon Sacred Scripture and Tradition*, it teaches that the Church, now sojourning on earth as an exile, is necessary for salvation. Christ, present to us in His Body, which is the Church, is the one Mediator and the unique way of salvation. In explicit terms He Himself affirmed the necessity of faith and bap-
130 tism[79] and thereby affirmed also the necessity of the Church, for through baptism as through a door men enter the Church. Whosoever, therefore, knowing that the Catholic Church was made necessary by Christ, would refuse to enter or to remain in it, could not be saved.

135 They are fully incorporated in the society of the Church who, possessing the Spirit of Christ accept her entire system and all the means of salvation given to her, and are united with her as part of her visible bodily structure and through her with Christ, who rules her through the Supreme Pontiff and the bishops. The bonds which bind
140 men to the Church in a visible way are profession of faith, the sacraments, and ecclesiastical government and communion. He is not saved, however, who, though part of the body of the Church, does not persevere in charity. He remains indeed in the bosom of the Church, but, as it were, only in a "bodily" manner and not "in his
145 heart." All the Church's children should remember that their exalted status is to be attributed not to their own merits but to the special grace of Christ. If they fail moreover to respond to that grace in thought, word and deed, not only shall they not be saved but they will be the more severely judged.[80]

---

[79] See *Mark* 16:16; *John* 3:5.

[80] Dieitur. Saneta (catholica apostolica) Romana Ecelesia .: in Prof. fidei Trid., 1. c. et Concl. Vat. I, Sess. III, Const. dogm. de fide cath.: Denz. 1782 (3001).

Catechumens who, moved by the Holy Spirit, seek with explicit   150
intention to be incorporated into the Church are by that very intention joined with her. With love and solicitude Mother Church already
embraces them as her own.

15. The Church recognizes that in many ways she is linked with
those who, being baptized, are honored with the name of Christian,   155
though they do not profess the faith in its entirety or do not preserve
unity of communion with the successor of Peter.[81] For there are
many who honor Sacred Scripture, taking it as a norm of belief and
a pattern of life, and who show a sincere zeal. They lovingly believe
in God the Father Almighty and in Christ, the Son of God and Sav-   160
ior.[82] They are consecrated by baptism, in which they are united with
Christ. They also recognize and accept other sacraments within their
own Churches or ecclesiastical communities. Many of them rejoice
in the episcopate, celebrate the Holy Eucharist and cultivate devotion toward the Virgin Mother of God.[83] They also share with us in   165
prayer and other spiritual benefits. Likewise we can say that in some
real way they are joined with us in the Holy Spirit, for to them too
He gives His gifts and graces whereby He is operative among them
with His sanctifying power. Some indeed He has strengthened to the
extent of the shedding of their blood. In all of Christ's disciples the   170
Spirit arouses the desire to be peacefully united, in the manner determined by Christ, as one flock under one shepherd, and He prompts
them to pursue this end.[84] Mother Church never ceases to pray, hope
and work that this may come about. She exhorts her children to

---

[81] S. Augustinus, Civ. Dei, XVIII, 51, 2: PL 41, 614.

[82] See Leo XIII, Epist. Encycl. Satis cognitum, 29 iun. 1896: ASS 28 (1895–96) p. 738. Epist. Encycl. Caritatis studium, 25 iul. 1898: ASS 31 (1898–99) p. 11. Pius XII, Nuntius radioph. Nell'alba, 24 dec. 1941: AAS 34 (1942) p. 21.

[83] See Pius XI, Litt. Encycl. Rerum Orientalium, 8 sept. 1928: AAS 20 (1928) p. 287. Pius XII, Litt. Encycl Orientalis Ecclesiae, 9 apr. 1944: AAS 36 (1944) p. 137.

[84] See Inst. S.S.C.S. Officii 20 dec. 1949: AAS 42 (1950) p. 142.

175   purification and renewal so that the sign of Christ may shine more
brightly over the face of the earth.

16. Finally, those who have not yet received the Gospel are related
in various ways to the people of God.[85] In the first place we must
recall the people to whom the testament and the promises were given
180   and from whom Christ was born according to the flesh.[86] On
account of their fathers this people remains most dear to God, for
God does not repent of the gifts He makes nor of the calls He
issues;[87] But the plan of salvation also includes those who acknowledge the Creator. In the first place amongst these there are the
185   Mohammedans, who, professing to hold the faith of Abraham, along
with us adore the one and merciful God, who on the last day will
judge mankind. Nor is God far distant from those who in shadows
and images seek the unknown God, for it is He who gives to all men
life and breath and all things,[88] and as Savior wills that all men be
190   saved.[89] Those also can attain to salvation who through no fault of
their own do not know the Gospel of Christ or His Church, yet sincerely seek God and moved by grace strive by their deeds to do His
will as it is known to them through the dictates of conscience.[90] Nor
does Divine Providence deny the helps necessary for salvation to
195   those who, without blame on their part, have not yet arrived at an
explicit knowledge of God and with His grace strive to live a good
life. Whatever good or truth is found amongst them is looked upon
by the Church as a preparation for the Gospel.[91] She knows that it is
given by Him who enlightens all men so that they may finally have
200   life. But often men, deceived by the Evil One, have become vain in

---

[85] See S. Thomas, Summa Theol. III, q. 8, a. 3, ad 1.

[86] *Romans* 9:4–5.

[87] *Romans* 11:28–29.

[88] See *Acts* 17:25–28.

[89] See *1 Timothy* 2:4.

[90] See Epist. S.S.C.S. Officii ad Archiep. Boston.: Denz. 3869–72.

[91] See Eusebius Caes., Praeparatio Evangelica, 1, 1: PG 2128 AB.

their reasonings and have exchanged the truth of God for a lie, serving the creature rather than the Creator.[92] Or some there are who, living and dying in this world without God, are exposed to final despair. Wherefore to promote the glory of God and procure the salvation of all of these, and mindful of the command of the Lord,   205 "Preach the Gospel to every creature,"[93] the Church fosters the missions with care and attention.

17. As the Son was sent by the Father,[94] so He too sent the Apostles, saying: "Go, therefore, make disciples of all nations, baptizing them in the name of the Father and of the Son and of the Holy Spirit,   210 teaching them to observe all things whatsoever I have commanded you. And behold I am with you all days even to the consummation of the world."[95] The Church has received this solemn mandate of Christ to proclaim the saving truth from the apostles and must carry it out to the very ends of the earth.[96] Wherefore she makes the words   215 of the Apostle her own: "Woe to me, if I do not preach the Gospel,"[97] and continues unceasingly to send heralds of the Gospel until such time as the infant churches are fully established and can themselves continue the work of evangelizing. For the Church is compelled by the Holy Spirit to do her part that God's plan may be fully realized,   220 whereby He has constituted Christ as the source of salvation for the whole world. By the proclamation of the Gospel she prepares her hearers to receive and profess the faith. She gives them the dispositions necessary for baptism, snatches them from the slavery of error and of idols and incorporates them in Christ so that through charity   225 they may grow up into full maturity in Christ. Through her work,

---

[92] See *Romans* 1:21,25.

[93] *Mark* 16:16.

[94] See *John* 20:21.

[95] *Matthew* 21:18–20.

[96] See *Acts* 1: 8.

[97] *1 Corinthians* 9:16.

230 whatever good is in the minds and hearts of men, whatever good lies latent in the religious practices and cultures of diverse peoples, is not only saved from destruction but is also cleansed, raised up and perfected unto the glory of God, the confusion of the devil and the happiness of man. The obligation of spreading the faith is imposed on every disciple of Christ, according to his state.[98] Although, however, all the faithful can baptize, the priest alone can complete the building up of the Body in the eucharistic sacrifice. Thus are fulfilled

235 the words of God, spoken through His prophet: "From the rising of the sun until the going down thereof my name is great among the gentiles, and in every place a clean oblation is sacrificed and offered up in my name."[99] In this way the Church both prays and labors in order that the entire world may become the People of God, the Body

240 of the Lord and the Temple of the Holy Spirit, and that in Christ, the Head of all, all honor and glory may be rendered to the Creator and Father of the Universe.

http://www.vatican.va/archive/hist_councils/ii_vatican_council/
documents/vat-ii_const_19641121_lumen-gentium_en.html,
consulted 15 April 2005 (revised).

---

[98] See Benedictus XV, Epist. Apost. Maximum illud: AAS 11 (1919) p. 440, praesertim p. 451 ss. Pius XI, Litt. Encycl. Rerum Ecclesiae: AAS 18 (1926) p. 68–69. Pius XII, Litt. Encycl. Fidei Donum, 21 apr. 1957: AAS 49 (1957) pp. 236–237.

[99] *Malachi* 1:11; see Didache, 14: ed. Funk I, p. 32. S. Iustinus, Dial. 41: PG 6, 564. S. Irenaeus, Adv. Haer. IV 17, 5; PG 7, 1023; Harvey, 2, p. 199 s. Conc. Trid., Sess. 22, cap. 1; Denz. 939 (1742).

DISCUSSION QUESTIONS

1. According to *Lumen gentium,* in what ways is the Church like a sacrament? In what ways unlike? How is the Church like the incarnation* of the Word of God in a human nature? How unlike?

2. According to *Lumen gentium,* where is the true Church of Christ? Can one point to it?

3. According to *Lumen gentium,* how is a church catholic? How is the Roman Catholic Church related to other Christian churches and communities? How is it related to various sorts of people who are not Christian?

4. According to *Lumen gentium,* if one can be saved without being in a church or believing in the Gospel, why do either, and why preach the Gospel?

III
Appendices

"Christ blessing enthroned between four angels, Church of San Apollinaire Nuovo, Ravenna, Italy. © Scala/Art Resource

Lists and Prayers

A. SOME TRADITIONAL LISTS:

1. Biblical Patriarchs

Antediluvian fathers of the human race, beginning with Adam; plus Abraham, Isaac, Jacob, and Jacob's 12 sons: Reuben, Simeon, Levi, Judah, Issachar, Zubulun, Joseph, Benjamin, Dan, Naphtali, Gad, and Asher. Acts 2:29 names David a "patriarch" as well.

2. Great Women of the Bible

Eve, Sarah, Rebecca, Rachel, Miriam, Rahab, Deborah, Jael, Ruth, Hannah, Bathsheba, Huldah, Judith, Esther, Mother of 7 Sons in *II Maccabees,* Elizabeth, The Blessed Virgin Mary, Mary Magdalen, Mary and Martha.

3. "The Law and the Prophets"

Symbolically represented by the figures of Moses and Elijah.

4. The Four Major Prophets

Isaiah, Jeremiah, Ezekiel and Daniel.

5. The Twelve Minor Prophets

Hosea, Joel, Amos, Obadiah, Jonah, Micah, Nahum, Habakkuk, Zephaniah, Haggai, Zechariah, and Malachi.

6. The Twelve Apostles

Peter, James, John, Andrew, Thomas, Matthew (Levi), Bartholomew, Philip, James (the Lesser), Simon the Zealot, Judas son of James (Jude/Thaddeus), Matthias.

7. The Ancient Patriarchates

Jerusalem, Antioch, Rome, Alexandria and Constantinople.

8. Four Great Fathers of the Eastern Church

Sts. Athanasius, Basil the Great, Gregory of Nazianzen and John Chrysostom.

9. Four Great Fathers of the Western Church

Sts. Ambrose, Jerome, Augustine and Gregory I ("the Great").

10. Thirty-three "Doctors of the Church"

Sts. Albert the Great, Alphonsus Liguori, Ambrose, Anselm, Anthony of Padua, Athanasius, Augustine, Basil the Great, Bede the Venerable, Bernard of Clairvaux, Bonaventure, Catherine of Siena, Cyril of Alexandria, Cyril of Jerusalem, Ephraem, Francis de Sales, Gregory Nazianzen, Gregory I ("the Great"), Hilary of Poitiers, Isidore of Seville, Jerome, John Chrysostom, John Damascene, John of the Cross, Lawrence of Brindisi, Leo I ("the Great"), Peter Canisius, Peter

Chrysologus, Peter Damian, Robert Bellarmine, Teresa of Jesus (Avila), Thérèse of Lisieux and Thomas Aquinas.

11. Ecumenical Councils

1.	325	Nicaea I
2.	381	Constantinople I
3.	431	Ephesus
4.	451	Chalcedon
5.	553	Constantinople II
6.	680–81	Constantinople III
7.	787	Nicaea II
8.	869–70	Constantinople IV
9.	1123	Lateran I
10.	1139	Lateran II
11.	1179	Lateran III
12.	1215	Lateran IV
13.	1245	Lyons I
14.	1274	Lyons II
15.	1311–12	Vienne (France)
16.	1414–18	Constance
17.	1438–45	Ferrara-Florence (1431–38 Basel)
18.	1512–17	Lateran V
19.	1545–63	Trent
20.	1869–70	Vatican I
21.	1962–65	Vatican II

(The Orthodox Church recognizes as truly ecumenical, and therefore binding on itself, only the first seven councils listed above. See Timothy Ware [Bishop Kallistos], *The Orthodox Church*[2] [London, 1993] 251–54.)

12. Popes Through the Centuries

1. St. Peter (32–67)
2. St. Linus (67–76)
3. St. Anacletus (Cletus) (76–88)
4. St. Clement I (88–97)
5. St. Evaristus (97–105)
6. St. Alexander I (105–115)
7. St. Sixtus I (115–125)—also called Xystus I
8. St. Telesphorus (125–136)
9. St. Hyginus (136–140)
10. St. Pius I (140–155)
11. St. Anicetus (155–166)
12. St. Soter (166–175)
13. St. Eleutherius (175–189)
14. St. Victor I (189–199)
15. St. Zephyrinus (199–217)
16. St. Callistus I (217–22)
17. St. Urban I (222–30)
18. St. Pontain (230–35)
19. St. Anterus (235–36)
20. St. Fabian (236–50)
21. St. Cornelius (251–53)
22. St. Lucius I (253–54)
23. St. Stephen I (254–257)
24. St. Sixtus II (257–258)
25. St. Dionysius (260–268)
26. St. Felix I (269–274)
27. St. Eutychian (275–283)
28. St. Caius (283–296)—also called Gaius
29. St. Marcellinus (296–304)
30. St. Marcellus I (308–309)
31. St. Eusebius (April–August 309 or 310)
32. St. Miltiades (311–14)
33. St. Sylvester I (314–35)
34. St. Marcus (January–October 336)
35. St. Julius I (337–52)
36. Liberius (352–66)
37. St. Damasus I (366–83)
38. St. Siricius (384–99)
39. St. Anastasius I (399–401)
40. St. Innocent I (401–17)
41. St. Zosimus (417–18)
42. St. Boniface I (418–22)
43. St. Celestine I (422–32)
44. St. Sixtus III (432–40)
45. St. Leo I (the Great) (440–61)
46. St. Hilarius (461–68)
47. St. Simplicius (468–83)
48. St. Felix III (II) (483–92)
49. St. Gelasius I (492–96)
50. Anastasius II (496–98)
51. St. Symmachus (498–514)
52. St. Hormisdas (514–23)
53. St. John I (523–26)
54. St. Felix IV (III) (526–30)
55. Boniface II (530–32)
56. John II (533–35)
57. St. Agapetus I (535–36)—also called Agapitus I
58. St. Silverius (536–37)
59. Vigilius (537–55)
60. Pelagius I (556–61)
61. John III (561–74)
62. Benedict I (575–79)
63. Pelagius II (579–90)

64. *St. Gregory I (the Great) (590–604)*

65. *Sabinian (604–606)*

66. *Boniface III
    (February–November 607)*

67. *St. Boniface IV (608–15)*

68. *St. Deusdedit (Adeodatus I)
    (615–18)*

69. *Boniface V (619–25)*

70. *Honorius I (625–38)*

71. *Severinus (May–August 640)*

72. *John IV (640–42)*

73. *Theodore I (642–49)*

74. *St. Martin I (649–55)*

75. *St. Eugene I (655–57)*

76. *St. Vitalian (657–72)*

77. *Adeodatus (II) (672–76)*

78. *Donus (676–78)*

79. *St. Agatho (678–81)*

80. *St. Leo II (682–83)*

81. *St. Benedict II (684–85)*

82. *John V (685–86)*

83. *Conon (686–87)*

84. *St. Sergius I (687–701)*

85. *John VI (701–05)*

86. *John VII (705–07)*

87. *Sisinnius (January–February 708)*

88. *Constantine (708–15)*

89. *St. Gregory II (715–31)*

90. *St. Gregory III (731–41)*

91. *St. Zachary (741–52)*

92. *Stephen II (March 752)*

93. *Stephen III (752–57)*

94. *St. Paul I (757–67)*

95. *Stephen IV (767–72)*

96. *Adrian I (772–95)*

97. *St. Leo III (795–816)*

98. *Stephen V (816–17)*

99. *St. Paschal I (817–24)*

100. *Eugene II (824–27)*

101. *Valentine (August–September 827)*

102. *Gregory IV (827–44)*

103. *Sergius II (844–47)*

104. *St. Leo IV (847–55)*

105. *Benedict III (855–58)*

106. *St. Nicholas I (the Great) (858–67)*

107. *Adrian II (867–72)*

108. *John VIII (872–82)*

109. *Marinus I (882–84)*

110. *St. Adrian III (884–85)*

111. *Stephen VI (885–91)*

112. *Formosus (891–96)*

113. *Boniface VI (April 896)*

114. *Stephen VII (896–97)*

115. *Romanus (August–November 897)*

116. *Theodore II
     (November–December 897)*

117. *John IX (898–900)*

118. *Benedict IV (900–03)*

119. *Leo V (July–December 903)*

120. *Sergius III (904–11)*

121. *Anastasius III (911–13)*

122. *Lando (913–14)*

123. *John X (914–28)*

124. *Leo VI (May–December 928)*

125. *Stephen VIII (929–31)*

126. *John XI (931–35)*

127. *Leo VII (936–39)*

128. *Stephen IX (939–42)*

129. *Marinus II (942–46)*

130. *Agapetus II (946–55)*

131. *John XII (955–63)*

132. *Leo VIII (963–64)*

133. *Benedict V (May–June 964)*

134. *John XIII (965–72)*

135. *Benedict VI (973–74)*

136. *Benedict VII (974–83)*

137. *John XIV (983–84)*

138. *John XV (985–96)*

139. *Gregory V (996–99)*

140. *Sylvester II (999–1003)*

141. *John XVII (June–December 1003)*

142. *John XVIII (1003–09)*

143. *Sergius IV (1009–12)*

144. *Benedict VIII (1012–24)*

145. *John XIX (1024–32)*

146. *Benedict IX (1032–45)*

147. *Sylvester III (January–March 1045)*

148. *Benedict IX (April–May 1045)*

149. *Gregory VI (1045–46)*

150. *Clement II (1046–47)*

151. *Benedict IX (1047–48)*

152. *Damasus II (July–August 1048)*

153. *St. Leo IX (1049–54)*

154. *Victor II (1055–57)*

155. *Stephen X (1057–58)*

156. *Nicholas II (1058–61)*

157. *Alexander II (1061–73)*

158. *St. Gregory VII (1073–85)*

159. *Blessed Victor III (1086–87)*

160. *Blessed Urban II (1088–99)*

161. *Paschal II (1099–1118)*

162. *Gelasius II (1118–19)*

163. *Callistus II (1119–24)*

164. *Honorius II (1124–30)*

165. *Innocent II (1130–43)*

166. *Celestine II (1143–44)*

167. *Lucius II (1144–45)*

168. *Blessed Eugene III (1145–53)*

169. *Anastasius IV (1153–54)*

170. *Adrian IV (1154–59)*

171. *Alexander III (1159–81)*

172. *Lucius III (1181–85)*

173. *Urban III (1185–87)*

174. *Gregory VIII (1187)*

175. *Clement III (1187–91)*

176. *Celestine III (1191–98)*

177. *Innocent III (1198–1216)*

178. *Honorius III (1216–27)*

179. *Gregory IX (1227–41)*

180. *Celestine IV (October–November 1241)*

181. *Innocent IV (1243–54)*

182. *Alexander IV (1254–61)*

183. *Urban IV (1261–64)*

184. *Clement IV (1265–68)*

185. *Blessed Gregory X (1271–76)*

186. *Blessed Innocent V (January–June 1276)*

187. *Adrian V (July–August 1276)*

188. *John XXI (1276–77)*

189. *Nicholas III (1277–80)*

190. *Martin IV (1281–85)*

191. *Honorius IV (1285–87)*

192. *Nicholas IV (1288–92)*

193. *St. Celestine V (July–December 1294)*

194. *Boniface VIII (1294–1303)*

195. *Blessed Benedict XI (1303–04)*

196. *Clement V (1305–14)*

197. *John XXII (1316–34)*

198. *Benedict XII (1334–42)*

199. *Clement VI (1342–52)*

200. *Innocent VI (1352–62)*

201. *Blessed Urban V (1362–70)*

202. *Gregory XI (1370–78)*

203. *Urban VI (1378–89)*

204. *Boniface IX (1389–1404)*

205. *Innocent VII (1406–06)*

206. *Gregory XII (1406–15)*

207. *Martin V (1417–31)*

208. *Eugene IV (1431–47)*

209. *Nicholas V (1447–55)*

210. *Callistus III (1445–58)*

211. *Pius II (1458–64)*

212. *Paul II (1464–71)*

213. *Sixtus IV (1471–84)*

214. *Innocent VIII (1484–92)*

215. *Alexander VI (1492–1503)*

216. *Pius III (September–October 1503)*

217. *Julius II (1503–13)*

218. *Leo X (1513–21)*

219. *Adrian VI (1522–23)*

220. *Clement VII (1523–34)*

221. *Paul III (1534–49)*

222. *Julius III (1550–55)*

223. *Marcellus II (April 1555)*

224. *Paul IV (1555–59)*

225. *Pius IV (1559–65)*

226. *St. Pius V (1566–72)*

227. *Gregory XIII (1572–85)*

228. *Sixtus V (1585–90)*

229. *Urban VII (September 1590)*

230. *Gregory XIV (1590–91)*

231. *Innocent IX (October–November 1591)*

232. *Clement VIII (1592–1605)*

233. *Leo XI (April 1605)*

234. *Paul V (1605–21)*

235. *Gregory XV (1621–23)*

236. *Urban VIII (1623–44)*

237. *Innocent X (1644–55)*

238. *Alexander VII (1655–67)*

239. *Clement IX (1667–69)*

240. *Clement X (1670–76)*

241. *Blessed Innocent XI (1676–89)*

242. *Alexander VIII (1689–91)*

243. *Innocent XII (1691–1700)*

244. *Clement XI (1700–21)*

245. *Innocent XIII (1721–24)*

246. *Benedict XIII (1724–30)*

247. *Clement XII (1730–40)*

248. *Benedict XIV (1740–58)*

249. *Clement XIII (1758–69)*

250. *Clement XIV (1769–74)*

251. *Pius VI (1775–99)*

252. *Pius VII (1800–23)*

253. *Leo XII (1823–29)*

254. *Pius VIII (1829–30)*

255. *Gregory XVI (1831–46)*

256. *Ven. Pius IX (1846–78)*

257. *Leo XIII (1878–1903)*

258. *St. Pius X (1903–14)*

259. *Benedict XV (1914–22)*

260. *Pius XI (1922–39)*

261. *Pius XII (1939–58)*

262. *John XXIII (1958–63)*

263. *Paul VI (1963–78)*

264. *John Paul I (August–September 1978)*

265. *John Paul II (1978–2005)*

266. *Benedict XVI (2005–)*

13. Seven Gifts of the Holy Spirit

1. Wisdom, 2. Understanding, 3. Counsel, 4. Fortitude, 5. Knowledge, 6. Piety, 7. Fear of the Lord—Isaiah 11: 2.

14. Nine Fruits of the Holy Spirit

1. Charity, 2. Joy, 3. Peace, 4. Patience, 5. Kindness, 6. Goodness, 7. Faith, 8. Modesty, 9. Continency—Galatians 5:22.

15. Seven Sacraments of the Church

1. Baptism, 2. Confirmation, 3. Eucharist, 4. Holy Orders, 5. Marriage, 6. Reconciliation, 7. Anointing of the Sick.

16. The General Roman Calendar
(including saints proper to U.S.A.)

Date	Saint or Feast of the Lord (Patron Saint of . . .)	Rank
	First of four Sundays prior to Christmas:	
	FIRST SUNDAY OF ADVENT	Sunday
December 3:	Francis Xavier, S. J., priest	
	(. . . all foreign missions, Borneo)	Memorial
4:	John Damascene, priest and doctor	
6:	Nicholas, bishop (. . . Russia, merchants, children, sailors, pawnbrokers)	
7:	Ambrose, bishop and doctor	Memorial
8:	IMMACULATE CONCEPTION	
	(U.S. Holy Day of Obligation)	
	(. . . the United States of America)	Solemnity
9:	Juan Diego (U.S.A.)	
11:	Damasus I, pope	
12:	OUR LADY OF GUADALUPE (U.S.A.)	
	(. . . Mexico, Americas);	Feast
13:	Lucy, virgin and martyr (. . . eye diseases)	Memorial
14:	John of the Cross, O. C., priest and doctor	Memorial
21:	Peter Canisius, S. J., priest and doctor, "The second Apostle of Germany"	
23:	John of Kanty, priest	
25:	CHRISTMAS (U.S. Holy Day of Obligation)	Solemnity
26:	STEPHEN, FIRST MARTYR (. . . stonemasons)	Feast
27:	JOHN, APOSTLE AND EVANGELIST (. . . bookbinders, papermakers)	Feast

28:	HOLY INNOCENTS, MARTYRS (. . . *foundlings*)	Feast
29:	Thomas Becket, bishop and martyr	
31:	Sylvester I, pope	
	Sunday within octave of Christmas or, if no Sunday falls	
	within the octave, December 30: HOLY FAMILY	Feast
January 1:	Octave of Christmas—SOLEMNITY OF MARY,	
	MOTHER OF GOD (U.S. Holy Day of Obligation)	Solemnity
2:	Basil the Great and Gregory Nazianzen, bishops and doctors	Memorial
4:	Elizabeth Ann Seton, religious (U.S.A.)	Memorial
5:	John Neumann, C.S.S.R., bishop (U.S.A.)	Memorial
6:	EPIPHANY	Solemnity
7:	Raymond of Peñafort, O. P., priest (. . . *canonists*)	
13:	Hilary of Poitiers, bishop and doctor	
17:	Anthony, abbot (. . . *skin rashes*)	Memorial
20:	Fabian, pope and martyr; Sebastian, martyr (. . . *lacemakers*)	
21:	Agnes, virgin and martyr (. . . *chastity*)	Memorial
22:	Vincent, deacon and martyr (. . . *vine dressers*)	
24:	Francis de Sales, bishop and doctor, co-founder of	
	Order of the Visitation	Memorial
25:	CONVERSION OF PAUL, APOSTLE	Feast
26:	Timothy and Titus, bishops	Memorial
27:	Angela de' Merici, virgin, foundress of the	
	Order of St. Ursula ("Ursulines")	
28:	Thomas Aquinas, O. P., priest and doctor,	
	"The Angelic Doctor" (. . . *Catholic schools, theologians*)	Memorial
31:	John Bosco, priest, founder of Salesians	Memorial
	Sunday after January 6:BAPTISM OF OUR LORD	
	(End of the Christmas Season)	Feast
February 2:	PRESENTATION OF OUR LORD	Feast
3:	Blase, bishop and martyr; Ansgar, bishop	
	(. . . *animals, throat diseases*)	
5:	Agatha, virgin and martyr	
	(. . . *wet nurses, bell founders and jewelers, fire*)	Memorial
6:	Paul Miki, S. J., and companions, martyrs	Memorial
8:	Jerome Emiliani (. . . *orphans and abandoned children*)	
10:	Scholastica, virgin	Memorial
11:	Our Lady of Lourdes	
14:	Cyril, monk; Methodius, bishop;	
	(brothers) "Apostles of the Slavs" (. . . *Moravia, Europe*)	Memorial
17:	Seven Founders of the Order of Servites	
21:	Peter Damian, O.S.B., bishop and doctor	Memorial
22:	CHAIR OF PETER, APOSTLE	Feast

23: Polycarp of Smyrna, bishop and martyr   Memorial
Wednesday of the seventh week prior to
Easter: Ash Wednesday, Beginning of THE SEASON OF LENT
March 3: Katharine Drexel, virgin (U.S.A.)
4: Casimir *(. . . Poland, Lithuania)*
7: Perpetua and Felicity, (married women) martyrs   Memorial
8: John of God, religious, founder of Brothers Hospitalers
(. . . of the sick and of hospitals)
9: Frances of Rome, religious *(. . . motorists)*
17: Patrick, bishop, "Apostle of Ireland" *(. . . Ireland)*
18: Cyril of Jerusalem, bishop and doctor
19: JOSEPH *(. . . the Universal Church, Belgium,*
a happy death, China)   Solemnity
23: Turibius de Mongrovejo, bishop
25: ANNUNCIATION   Solemnity
Sunday after first full moon after vernal equinox: Solemnity with an Octave
SUNDAY of the EASTER TRIDUUM
April 2: Francis of Paola, hermit, founder of
Order of Minim Friars *(. . . seafarers)*
4: Isidore of Seville, bishop and doctor
5: Vincent Ferrer, O. P., priest
7: John Baptist de la Salle, priest, founder of
Brothers of the Christian Schools (Christian Brothers)   Memorial
11: Stanislaus, bishop and martyr
13: Martin I, pope and martyr
21: Anselm of Canterbury, O.S.B., bishop and doctor
23: George, martyr, "Protector of England"
(. . . England, Portugal, soldiers)
24: Fidelis of Sigmaringen, O.F.M. Cap., priest and martyr
25: MARK, EVANGELIST *(. . . notaries)*   Feast
28: Peter Chanel, S. M., priest and martyr
29: Catherine of Siena, O. P., virgin and doctor *(. . . Italy)*   Memorial
May 1: Joseph the Worker *(. . . laborers, carpenters)*
2: Athanasius, bishop and doctor, "Father of Orthodoxy"   Memorial
3: PHILIP AND JAMES, APOSTLES   Feast
12: Nereus and Achilleus, (Roman soldiers) martyrs; Pancras, martyr
14: MATTHIAS, APOSTLE   Feast
15: Isidore the Farmer (married) *(. . . Madrid)*
18: John I, pope and martyr
20: Bernardine of Siena, O.F.M., priest *(. . . advertising)*
25: Venerable Bede, O.S.B., priest and doctor;
Gregory VII, O.S.B., pope; Mary Magdalene de Pazzi, virgin
26: Philip Neri, priest, founder of Congregation of the Oratory Memorial

27: Augustine of Canterbury, O.S.B., bishop, "Apostle of the English"

31: VISITATION   Feast

The fortieth day of Easter: ASCENSION THURSDAY

(U.S. Holy Day of Obligation)   Solemnity

The fiftieth day of Easter: PENTECOST SUNDAY

(End of Easter Season)   Solemnity

First Sunday after Pentecost: HOLY TRINITY   Solemnity

Sunday after Holy Trinity: CORPUS CHRISTI   Solemnity

Friday following Second Sunday after Pentecost:

SACRED HEART *(. . . Ecuador)*   Solemnity

Saturday following Second Sunday after Pentecost:

Immaculate Heart of Mary

June 1: Justin, martyr   Memorial

2: Marcellinus and Peter, martyrs

3: Charles Lwanga and companions, martyrs (Uganda)   Memorial

5: Boniface, O.S.B., bishop and martyr, "Apostle of Germany"   Memorial

6: Norbert, bishop, founder of the Norbertines (Premonstratensians)

9: Ephraem the Syrian, deacon and doctor

11: Barnabas, apostle   Memorial

13: Anthony of Padua, O.F.M., priest and doctor

    (. . . lost objects)   Memorial

19: Romuald, abbot, founder of Camaldolese Benedictines

21: Aloysius Gonzaga, S.J., religious *(. . . youth)*   Memorial

22: Paulinus of Nola, bishop; John Fisher, bishop and martyr;

    Thomas More, (married) martyr

24: BIRTH OF JOHN THE BAPTIST *(. . . tailors)*   Solemnity

27: Cyril of Alexandria, bishop and martyr

28: Irenaeus, bishop and martyr Memorial

29: PETER AND PAUL, APOSTLES

    (Paul: *. . . ropemakers)*   Solemnity

30: First Martyrs of the Church of Rome

July 1: Blessed Junipero Serra, priest (U.S.A.)

3: THOMAS, APOSTLE *(. . . East Indies, masons)*   Feast

4: Elizabeth of Portugal, religious

5: Anthony Zaccaria, priest

6: Maria Goretti, virgin and martyr

11: Benedict, abbot, founder of Order of St. Benedict,

    "Father of Western Monasticism" *(. . . Europe)*   Memorial

13: Henry (II, Holy Roman Emperor), *(. . . Benedictine Oblates)*

14: Camillus de Lellis, priest, founder of Minister of the Sick

    (. . . the sick and of their nurses)

15: Bonaventure, O.F.M., bishop and doctor,

    "The Seraphic Doctor"   Memorial

16:	Our Lady of Mount Carmel	
21:	Laurence of Brindisi, O.F.M. Cap., priest and doctor	
22:	Mary Magdalene *(. . . reformed prostitutes)*	Memorial
23:	Bridget of Sweden, religious, foundress of Order of the Most Holy Savior ("Bridgettines") *(. . . Sweden)*	
25:	JAMES (the Greater), APOSTLE *(. . . Spain, Chile)*	Feast
26:	Joachim and Ann (parents of Blessed Virgin Mary) *(Ann: . . . houseworkers, cabinet makers, Canada)*	Memorial
29:	Martha *(. . . housewives, cooks)*	Memorial
30:	Peter Chrysologus, bishop and doctor	
31:	Ignatius of Loyola, priest, founder of Society of Jesus ("Jesuits")	Memorial
August 1:	Alphonsus Liguori, bishop and doctor, founder of Congregation of the Most Holy Redeemer	Memorial
2:	Eusebius of Vercelli, bishop	
4:	John Baptist Vianney, priest *(. . . parish priests)*	Memorial
5:	Dedication of the Basilica of Saint Mary Major	
6:	TRANSFIGURATION of Our Lord	Feast
7:	Sixtus II, pope and martyr, and companions, martyrs; Cajetan, priest, founder of Theatines	
8:	Dominic, priest, founder of Order of Preachers ("Dominicans")	Memorial
10:	LAURENCE, DEACON AND MARTYR *(. . . Sri Lanka)*	Feast
11:	Clare, virgin, foundress of Poor Clares *(. . . television)*	Memorial
13:	Pontian, pope and martyr, and Hippolytus, priest and martyr	
15:	ASSUMPTION of the Blessed Virgin *(. . . India, airplane pilots)* (U.S. Holy Day of Obligation)	Solemnity
16:	Stephen of Hungary (king) *(. . . Hungary)*	
18:	Jane Frances de Chantal, religious (U.S.A.)	
19:	John Eudes, Orat., priest, founder of Sisters of our Lady of Charity, of Society of Jesus and Mary ("Eudists")	
20:	Bernard, O.S.B., Cist., abbot and doctor	Memorial
21:	Pius X, pope	Memorial
22:	Queenship of Mary	Memorial
23:	Rose of Lima, O.P., virgin *(. . . South America; Americas)*	
24:	BARTHOLOMEW, APOSTLE	Feast
25:	Louis IX (king); Joseph Calasanz, priest	
27:	Monica	Memorial
28:	Augustine of Hippo, bishop and doctor	Memorial
29:	Beheading of John the Baptist, martyr	Memorial
September 3:	Gregory (I) the Great, pope and doctor *(. . . singers and scholars)*	Memorial
8:	BIRTH OF MARY	Feast

9:	Peter Claver, S.J., priest (U.S.A.)	Memorial
13:	John Chrysostom, bishop and doctor	Memorial
14:	TRIUMPH OF THE CROSS	Feast
15:	Our Lady of Sorrows	Memorial
16:	Cornelius, pope and martyr, and Cyprian of Carthage, bishop and martyr	Memorial
17:	Robert Bellarmine, S.J., bishop and doctor	
19:	Januarius, bishop and martyr (. . . *volcanic eruptions*)	
21:	MATTHEW, APOSTLE AND EVANGELIST	Feast
26:	Cosmas and Damian (brothers, physicians), martyrs (. . . *medical doctors*)	
27:	Vincent de Paul, priest, founder of the Congregation of the Mission (. . . *all charitable societies*)	Memorial
28:	Wenceslaus (duke of Bohemia), martyr (. . . *Bohemia*)	
29:	MICHAEL (. . . *Germany*), GABRIEL, AND RAPHAEL, ARCHANGELS	Feast
30:	Jerome, priest and doctor (. . . *students*)	Memorial
October 1:	Thérèse of the Child Jesus, O.C.D., virgin, doctor, "Co-Protectress of France" (. . . *foreign missions*)	Memorial
2:	Guardian Angels	Memorial
4:	Francis of Assisi, deacon, founder of Order of Friars Minor (. . . *Italy*)	Memorial
6:	Bruno, priest, founder of Carthusians; Blessed Marie rose Durocher, virgin (U.S.A.)	
7:	Our Lady of the Rosary	Memorial
9:	Denis, bishop and martyr, (. . . *France*) and companions, martyrs; John Leonardi, priest	
14:	Callistus I, pope and martyr	
15:	Teresa of Jesus (Avila), O.C.D., virgin and doctor (. . . *Spain*)	Memorial
16:	Hedwig, religious (. . . *Silesia*); Margaret Mary Alacoque, virgin	
17:	Ignatius of Antioch, bishop and martyr	Memorial
18:	LUKE, EVANGELIST (. . . *painters, artists*)	Feast
19:	Isaac Jogues, John de Brebeuf, priests, & companions S.J., martyrs (U.S.A.);	Memorial
20:	Paul of the Cross, priest	
23:	John of Capistrano, O.F.M., priest	
24:	Anthony of Claret, bishop, founder of the Missionary Sons of the Immaculate Heart of Mary ("Claretians")	
28:	SIMON AND JUDE (Jude: . . . *hopeless cases*), APOSTLES	Feast
November 1:	ALL SAINTS (U.S. Holy Day of Obligation)	Solemnity
2:	ALL SOULS	

3:	Martin de Porres, O.P., religious	
4:	Charles Borromeo, bishop	Memorial
9:	DEDICATION OF THE BASILICA OF SAINT JOHN LATERAN	Feast
10:	Leo the Great, pope and doctor	Memorial
11:	Martin of Tours, bishop	Memorial
12:	Josaphat, bishop and martyr	
13:	Frances Xavier Cabrini, virgin, foundress of Missionary Sisters of the Sacred Heart (U.S.A.)	Memorial
15:	Albert the Great, O.P., bishop and doctor, "The Universal Doctor" (. . . *students*)	
16:	Margaret of Scotland (queen); Gertrude the Great, O.S.B., virgin	
17:	Elizabeth of Hungary (queen), religious	Memorial
18:	Dedication of the Basilicas of Peter and Paul, apostles; Rose Philippine Duchesne, virgin (U.S.A.)	
21:	Presentation of Blessed Virgin Mary	Memorial
22:	Cecilia, virgin and martyr (. . . *musicians*)	Memorial
23:	Clement I, pope and martyr; Columban, abbot; Blessed Miguel Augustín Pro, S.J., priest and martyr (U.S.A.)	
30:	ANDREW, APOSTLE (. . . *Scotland, Russia and Greece, fishermen*)	Feast
	Last Sunday in Ordinary Time: CHRIST THE KING	Solemnity

17. Theological Virtues

Faith, Hope, and Charity (Love)

18. Moral or Cardinal Virtues

Prudence, Justice, Temperance and Fortitude

19. Ten Commandments (Catholic Listing)

I, the Lord, am your God.

1. You shall not have other gods besides me.

2. You shall not dishonor the name of the Lord.

3. Remember to keep holy the Sabbath day.

4. Honor your father and your mother.

5. You shall not kill.

6. You shall not commit adultery.

7. You shall not steal.

8. You shall not bear false witness against your neighbor.

9. You shall not covet your neighbor's spouse.

10. You shall not covet your neighbor's goods.

20. Six Commandments of the Church

1. To assist at Mass on all Sundays and holy days of obligation.

2. To fast and abstain on the days appointed.

3. To confess our sins at least once a year.

4. To receive Holy Communion during the Easter time.

5. To contribute to the support of the Church.

6. To observe the laws of the Church concerning marriage.
   (Taken from: The New Baltimore Catechism, No. 2)

21. Seven Corporal Works of Mercy

1. To feed the hungry

2. To give drink to the thirsty

3. To clothe the naked

4. To shelter the homeless

5. To visit the imprisoned

6. To visit the sick

7. To bury the dead

22. Seven Spiritual Works of Mercy

1. To convert the sinner

2. To instruct the ignorant

3. To counsel the doubtful

4. To comfort the sorrowful

5. To bear wrongs patiently

6. To forgive injuries

7. To pray for the living and the dead.

23. Seven Deadly or "Capital" Sins (Inclinations to Evil)

1. Pride,

2. Covetousness,

3. Lust,

4. Anger,

5. Gluttony,

6. Envy,

7. Sloth.

24. Seven Penitential Psalms

Psalms 6, 32, 38, 51, 102, 130, 143.

25. Four Last Things

Death. Judgment. Heaven. Hell.

B. SOME TRADITIONAL PRAYERS

1. Shema (oldest Jewish prayer)

Hear, O Israel, the Lord is our God, the Lord is One.
Blessed be the name of his glorious majesty forever and ever.
You shall love the Lord your God with all your heart, and with all
your soul, and with all your might. And these words which I command you today shall be in your heart. You shall teach them
diligently to your children, and you shall speak of them when you are
sitting at home and when you go on a journey, when you lie down

and when you rise up. You shall bind them for a sign on your hand, and they shall be for frontlets between your eyes. You shall inscribe them on the doorposts of your house and on your gates (*Deuteronomy* 6:4–9).

2. *Liturgy of St. John Chrysostom <u>Monogenés</u> Prayer (Eastern Church)*

Only begotten Son and Word of God, Thou who art immortal, and didst deign for our salvation to become incarnate of the holy Theotokos and Ever-virgin Mary, without change becoming man, and Who wast crucified, O Christ God, trampling down death by death: Thou Who art one of the Holy Trinity, glorified together with the Father and the Holy Spirit, save us.

3. *A General Confession (Anglican/Episcopalian)*

Almighty and most merciful Father; we have erred, and strayed from thy ways like lost sheep. We have followed too much the devices and desires of our own hearts. We have offended against thy holy laws. We have left undone those things which we ought to have done; And we have done those things which we ought not to have done; And there is no health in us. But thou, O Lord, have mercy upon us, miserable offenders. Spare thou those, O God, who confess their faults. Restore thou those who are penitent; According to thy promises declared unto mankind In Christ Jesus our Lord. And grant, O most merciful Father, for his sake; That we may hereafter live a godly, righteous, and sober life. To the glory of thy holy Name. Amen.

4. *A General Thanksgiving (Lutheran)*

Almighty God, Father of all mercies, we your unworthy servants give you humble thanks for all your goodness and loving-kindness to us and to all whom you have made. We bless you for our creation, preservation, and all the blessings of this life; but above all for your immeasurable love in the redemption of the world by our Lord Jesus

Christ, for the means of grace, and for the hope of glory. And, we pray, give us such an awareness of your mercies that with truly thankful hearts we may show forth your praise, not only with our lips, but also in our lives, by giving up ourselves to your service, and by walking before you in holiness and righteousness all our days; through Jesus Christ our Lord, to whom, with you and the Holy Spirit, be honor and glory throughout all ages.

5. A Prayer of Susanna Wesley (Methodist)

You, O Lord, have called us to watch and pray. Therefore, whatever may be the sin against which we pray, make us careful to watch against it, and so have reason to expect that our prayers will be answered. In order to perform this duty aright, grant us grace to preserve a sober, equal temper, and sincerity to pray for your assistance. Amen.

6. Prayers of the Rosary

The Sign of the Cross
†In the Name of the Father, and of the Son, and of the Holy Spirit. Amen.

The Apostles' Creed
I believe in God the Father Almighty, Creator of Heaven and Earth, and in Jesus Christ, His only Son, our Lord, Who was conceived by the Holy Ghost, born of the Virgin Mary, suffered under Pontius Pilate, was crucified, died, and was buried. He descended into hell, and on the third day He rose again from the dead. He ascended into Heaven and sits at the Right Hand of God the Father Almighty; from thence He shall come to judge the living and the dead. I believe in the Holy Spirit, the Holy Catholic Church, the Communion of Saints, the forgiveness of sins, the resurrection of the body, and life everlasting. Amen.

The Glory Be

Glory be to the Father, and to the Son, and to the Holy Spirit, as it was in the beginning, is now, and ever shall be, world without end. Amen.

The O My Jesus (The Fatima Prayer)

O, my Jesus, forgive us our sins, save us from the fires of Hell, and lead all souls to Heaven, especially those in most need of Thy mercy.

The Our Father

Our Father, Who art in Heaven, hallowed be Thy Name, Thy Kingdom come, Thy Will be done on Earth as it is in Heaven. Give us this day our daily Bread, and forgive us our trespasses, as we forgive those Who trespass against us. And lead us not into temptation, but deliver us from evil. Amen.

The Hail Mary

Hail Mary, full of grace, the Lord is with thee. Blessed art thou among women, and blessed is the Fruit of thy womb, Jesus. Holy Mary, Mother of God, pray for us sinners now and at the hour of our death. Amen.

The *Salve Regina*

Hail Holy Queen, Mother of Mercy, our life, our sweetness, and our hope. To thee do we cry, poor, banished children of Eve. To thee do we send up our sighs, mourning, and weeping in this vale of tears. Turn, then, most gracious advocate, thine eyes of mercy upon us, and after this our exile show unto us the blessed Fruit of thy womb, Jesus. O clement, O loving, O sweet Virgin Mary. Pray for us, O holy Mother of God, that we may be made worthy of the Promises of Christ.

Let us pray.

Almighty and ever-living God, Who by the cooperation of the Holy Spirit, didst prepare the body and soul of the glorious Virgin-Mother, Mary, to be a fit dwelling for Thy Son, grant that we who rejoice in her memory may be freed by her kindly prayers both from present ills and from eternal death. Through the same Christ our Lord. Amen.

20 Mysteries of the Rosary:

Joyful:

1) Annunciation
2) Visitation
3) Birth of Our Lord
4) Presentation in the Temple
5) Finding of Jesus in the Temple

Luminous:

1) Baptism in the Jordan
2) Wedding Feast at Cana
3) Proclamation of the Kingdom
4) Transfiguration
5) Institution of the Eucharist

Sorrowful:

1) Agony in the Garden
2) Scourging at the Pillar
3) Crowning with Thorns
4) Carrying of the Cross
5) Crucifixion

Glorious:

1) Resurrection
2) Ascension
3) Descent of the Holy Spirit
4) Assumption
5) Crowning of Our Lady Queen of Heaven

7. The Angelus (Outside Eastertime)

(Announced by the church bells at 6:00 or 7:00 A.M., Noon, and 6:00 P.M.)

V- The Angel of the Lord declared unto Mary.

R- And she conceived of the Holy Spirit.

Hail Mary. . . .

V- Behold the handmaid of the Lord.

R- Be it done unto me according to thy word.

Hail Mary. . . .

V- And the Word was made Flesh.

R- And dwelt among us.

Hail Mary. . . .

V- Pray for us, O Holy Mother of God.

R- That we may be made worthy of the promises of Christ.

Let us pray:

Pour forth, we beseech Thee, O Lord, Thy grace into our hearts, that we, to whom the Incarnation of Christ, Thy Son, was made known by the message of an Angel, may by His Passion and Cross be brought to the glory of His Resurrection. Through the same Christ our Lord. Amen.

The *Regina Coeli* (Easter to Pentecost)
Queen of Heaven rejoice, Alleluia,
For he whom you deserved to bear, Alleluia,
Has risen as he said, Alleluia.
Pray for us to God, Alleluia.
V. Rejoice and be glad, O Virgin Mary, Alleluia,
R. Because our Lord is truly risen. Alleluia.
Let us pray:

O God, Who by the resurrection of Thy Son, Our Lord Jesus Christ, has vouchsafed to make glad the whole world, grant, we beseech Thee, that, through the intercession of the Virgin Mary, His Mother, we may attain the joys of eternal life. Through the same Christ Our Lord. Amen.

8. The Memorare of St Bernard

Remember, O most gracious Virgin Mary, that never was it known that anyone who fled to thy protection, implored thy help, or sought thy intercession was left unaided. Inspired by this confidence, I fly unto thee, O Virgin of virgins, my Mother. To thee I come, before thee I stand, sinful and sorrowful. O Mother of the Word Incarnate, despise not my intentions, but in thy mercy, hear and answer me. Amen.

9. The Come Holy Ghost

V. Come, Holy Ghost, replenish the hearts of Thy faithful,
R. And enkindle in them the Fire of Thy Divine Love.

V. Send forth Thy Spirit, and they shall be re-created;

R. And Thou shalt renew the face of the earth.

Let us pray:

O God, Who by the light of the Holy Spirit didst instruct the hearts of Thy faithful, grant us by that same Spirit a love and relish of what is right and just, and a constant enjoyment of his divine consolations. Through Christ our Lord. Amen.

10. A Blessing Before Meals

Bless us, O Lord, and these Thy gifts, which we are about to receive from Thy bounty, through Christ our Lord. Amen.

11. A Blessing After Meals

We give thee thanks for all Thy benefits, O Almighty God, who lives and reigns forever;

May the souls of the faithful departed, through the mercy of God, rest in peace. Amen.

12. An Act of Faith

O my God, I firmly believe that Thou art one God in three divine Persons: Father, Son, and Holy Ghost. I believe that Thy divine Son became man, died for our sins, and that He will come to judge the living and the dead. I believe these and all the truths which the Church teaches, because Thou hast revealed them, Who can neither deceive nor be deceived. Amen.

13. An Act of Hope

O my God, relying on Thine almighty power and infinite mercy and promises, I hope to obtain pardon of my sins, the Help of Thy Grace, and Life Everlasting through the merits of Jesus Christ, our Redeemer and Lord. Amen.

14. An Act of Love

O my God, I love Thee above all things, with my whole heart and soul, because Thou art all-good and worthy of all love. I love my neighbor as myself for love of Thee. I forgive all who have injured me and ask pardon of all whom I have injured. Amen.

15. An Act of Contrition

O my God, I am heartily sorry for having offended Thee, because I dread the loss of heaven and the pains of hell, but most of all because they offend Thee, my God, Who art all-good and deserving of all love. I firmly resolve, with the Help of Thy Grace, to confess my sins, do penance and amend my life. Amen.

16. Prayer to One's Guardian Angel

Angel of God, my guardian dear, to whom God's love commits me here, ever this day be at my side, to light and guard, to rule and guide. Amen.

17. Morning Prayer

Live, Jesus, live,
    so live in me,
That all I do
    be done by Thee.
And grant that all
    I think and say,
May be thy thought
    and word today.
        Amen.

18. A Prayer of St. Patrick

Christ be with us, Christ before us, Christ behind us,
Christ within us, Christ beneath us, Christ above us,
Christ on our right, Christ on our left,

Christ where we lie, Christ where we sit, Christ where we arise,
Christ in the heart of every one who thinks of us,
Christ in every eye that sees us,
Christ in every ear that hears us.
Salvation is of the Lord,
Salvation is of the Christ,
May your salvation, O Lord, be ever with us. Amen.

19. Prayer of St. Francis of Assisi

Lord, make me an instrument of your peace.
Where there is hatred, let me sow love;
where there is injury, pardon;
where there is doubt, faith;
where there is despair, hope;
where there is darkness, light;
and where there is sadness, joy.
Divine Master, grant that I may not so much seek to be consoled
    as to console;
to be understood as to understand;
to be loved as to love.
For it is in giving that we receive;
it is in pardoning that we are pardoned;
and it is in dying that we are born to eternal life.

20. St. Ignatius' Prayer for Generosity

Dearest Lord, teach me to be generous.
Teach me to serve you as you deserve:
To give and not to count the cost;

To fight and not to heed the wounds;
To toil and not to seek for rest;
To labor and not to ask for reward,
Save knowing that I do your holy will. Amen.

21. The Morning Offering

O JESUS
Through the Immaculate Heart of Mary
I offer you my prayers, works, joys and sufferings of this day
For all the intentions of your Sacred Heart,
In union with the Holy Sacrifice of the Mass throughout the world,
In reparation for my sins,
In thanksgiving for your many gifts,
For the needs of the Church and the reunion of all Christians,
And in particular for. . . . . (Pope's monthly intention)

Glossary

A. D.—(Latin *Anno Domini* = "in the year of the Lord") Christian designation for human history extending from the birth of Christ up to the present time. See Common Era.

Ambrose (ca. 339–397)—A bishop of Milan, saint and Doctor of the Church, whose preaching contributed to St. Augustine's decision to embrace Christianity. A staunch defender of orthodoxy against paganism and Arianism.

anchoress—a female hermit or recluse.

apostle—(Gr. *apostolos* = "one who is sent out") Someone called and sent by God to preach the gospel. Used most often of "the Twelve" of the gospels who witnessed Jesus' earthly life and preaching and were commissioned by the risen Christ to be founders of his church.

Apostolic Succession—According to Catholic faith, the unbroken continuity through history of the God-given ministry of the college of bishops, in union with the bishop of Rome, to teach, safeguard, and celebrate the basic beliefs and practices of the church received from the Apostles, doing so under the guidance of the Holy Spirit.

asceticism—(Gr. *askesis* = "exercise") The practice of a religious discipline directing one's entire life toward intimacy with God and the doing of God's will. It emphasizes self-control in order to combat vices and develop virtues, as well as a moderation in, or complete renunciation of, various facets of customary social life and personal comfort.

B. C. "Before Christ": The Christian designation for that time in human history before the putative date for the birth of Christ.

B. C. E. "Before the Common Era": An alternative designation for "B.C." See Common Era.

bishop—(Anglo-Saxon corruption of Gr. *episcopos* = "overseer") A member of the highest order of ministers in the church, those established through sacramental ordination as successors of the Apostles and entrusted by God with responsibility both for coordinating the charisms of the members of a local church and, in concert with all other bishops, for guaranteeing the unity of faith and practice of the universal church. Thus, *a personal sacramental symbol* of the church's unity of faith and love: "The bishop is in the church and the church is in the bishop" (St. Cyprian of Carthage [ca 210–258]).

catechesis—(Gr. *kat chein* = "to sound in the ear," "to instruct") Originally used to refer to instruction given to catechumens, those being prepared for baptism. It now refers to any instruction in the faith throughout the life of the Christian.

C. E.—See Common Era

Christology—(Gr. *Christos,* translation of Hebrew *"mashiach,"* meaning "Anointed One") The study of Jesus Christ, his humanity and divinity, and his saving mission with all its implications.

Common Era (C. E.)—A contemporary alternative designation for "A. D." (see above). The basis for its calculation is the same as "A. D.," i.e., the putative date of the birth of Christ.

consubstantial—(= *consubstantialis,* the Latin translation of the Council of Nicaea's Gr. *homoousios:* "of the same substance or being") A technical theological term developed to identify the ontological unity of the three Persons of the Blessed Trinity.

covenant—A voluntary bond uniting two or more parties in mutual love and involving some agreed upon common agenda and purpose.

deacon—(Gk. *diakonos* = "servant," "minister") The sacramentally ordained minister in the church third in order to the bishop and priest (presbyter). As personal aides to the bishop deacons were traditionally entrusted with overseeing the church's care for, and distribution of alms to, the poor. In the liturgy deacons accompanied the presiding bishop or priest, oversaw good order in the church, read the Gospel, announced the prayers of the faithful, and distributed the precious Blood of Christ at Communion. Deacons today in the Catholic Church read the Gospel at the Eucharist and, in the absence of a priest, perform baptisms, witness Christian marriages, and preside at Christian burials.

decalogue—(Gr. "ten words" or "statements") The Ten Commandments delivered by God to Moses on Mt. Sinai revealing to the Israelites the basic demands of their God-given human nature for its proper fulfillment, leading ultimately to full human happiness and union with God.

diaspora—(Gr. "dispersion"—the equivalent of the Hebrew, *galuth* or *golah,* meaning "exile.") The scattering of the Israelite/Jewish people from their homeland. Initially applied to deportees under the Assyrian (722 B.C.) and Babylonian (597 B.C.) conquests, it eventually came to designate all Jewish people living outside of Palestine. In Biblical times Diaspora Jews remained in close touch with their home country, paying the Temple taxes and keeping religious observances.

Doctor of the Church—Title given since the Middle Ages to certain theologian saints whose teachings and lives provide the church with a deeper understanding of her faith. Originally applied to Sts. Ambrose, Augustine, Jerome and Gregory I ("the Great"). A complete current list of those proclaimed "Doctors of the Church" appears in the "*Lists and Prayers*" section above.

doctrine—(Latin *doctrina* = "teaching") Any official teaching of the church interpreting her traditional belief in Jesus Christ in a way designed to speak to the world today. Not necessarily an infallible teaching.

dogma—(Gk. = "opinion" or "decree") A religious truth that the church has defined as divinely revealed. Every dogma is a doctrine, but not every doctrine is a dogma.

dualism—Any philosophical or religious system holding that all reality originates from or consists in two irreducible principles or gods. E.g., Manichaeism.

ecclesiastic—Someone who speaks for or represents the church in an official way, usually a person with Holy Orders (bishop, priest, or deacon).

ecclesiology—(Gr. from *ekklesia* = "convocation" or "assembly") That branch of theology which studies the church, her origin, nature, structures and mission.

ecumenism—(derived from Gr. *oikoumene* = "the housed [world]") The modern movement across various Christian denominations to unite divided Christianity into the overall unity intended by Christ for his church.

the elect—Those people effectively "chosen" by God for salvation. In the Catholic R.C.I.A., those who are ritually approved at the beginning of Lent for baptism at the Easter Vigil.

encyclical—(Gr. "circular letter") Formal pastoral letter addressed by the pope to the whole Catholic Church, and often to all people of good will, to convey timely teachings and instructions on matters of Christian faith and morals.

eschatology—(Gr. *eskhatos* = "the last") A study of the "*eschata*," the last things; in theology the study of the ultimate destiny both of the individual soul and of the whole created order.

Eucharist—(Gr. *eukharistia* = "thanksgiving") The sacramental celebration of the Paschal Mystery—Christ's Passion, Death and Resurrection—the central worship of the church. In addition to a blessing prayer over bread and wine and a sharing in them (now become the body and blood of Christ), it is also comprised of Scripture readings and additional prayers, and is presided over by an ordained bishop or priest, who normally delivers a homily as well.

exegesis—(Gr. *exegeisthai* = "to draw out or explain") The act of explaining a sacred text. It attempts, among other tasks, to establish what the authors of the Bible intended to say in their original context and to interpret their message so as to allow God to speak through it today in the fullest possible way to contemporary readers.

faith—According to Scripture, that loving trust in God based upon God's wondrous Self-manifestation in creation and his saving deeds in the past. It includes obedience, the readiness to hear and do God's will (*ob-audire* = "listen to"). This ability to believe in God is only possible as part of God's free Self-gift in Christ dwelling within the believer (grace), communicating the saving faith of Jesus himself (see Hebrews 12:1–3), and thus leading to salvation. "Faith" can also refer to *what* is believed, the doctrinal content of faith. Thus Christ, through the Holy Spirit, is both the sharing *source* and the *content* of the church's faith.

Free Church—A term which originated within the 17th century Church of England designating groups that refused to conform to its discipline and liturgical practice: Society of Friends (Quakers), Puritans, Presbyterians and Methodists. Used today to include as well other denominations that are also without highly formal liturgical traditions. E.g., Baptists.

friar—(ME *frere* from Latin *frater* = brother) A member of a mendicant (begging) religious order in the church, vowed to radical poverty and dedicated to preaching and instructing the faithful. E.g., Dominicans, Franciscans.

Gnosticism—(Gr. *gnōsis* = knowledge) a complex religious movement in the 2nd century A.D., in general teaching that salvation comes only through divinely-bestowed esoteric knowledge and only to those sufficiently endowed with the divine spark to be able to receive it.

grace—(Latin *gratia* = "gift;" Gr. *kharis*) God's gift of Self freely given ("uncreated grace") to human beings in a way that transforms them into daughters and sons of God in Christ, endowed with God's own divine life ("created grace"), bringing with it pardon and healing and participation in Christ's saving work in the world.

Hellenized—(Gr. *Hellas* = "Greece") The state of having become Greek or Greek-like in customs, ideals, form, and/or language.

heresy—(Gr. *hairesis* "choice" or "thing chosen") In its Catholic meaning: the denial by a baptized person of any defined doctrine of the Catholic faith. "Formal heresy" refers to the willful and persistent adherence to false doctrine; "material heresy," the holding of heretical doctrines without fully realizing it.

homoousios—(Gr. = "of the same substance") A non-biblical term used at the Council of Nicaea to describe the equal ontological status of Jesus Christ with God the Father. See consubstantial.

Incarnation—(Latin *caro* = "flesh"; hence, "enfleshing") The assumption of a full human nature by the Second Person of the Blessed Trinity with the result that Jesus Christ is, from the first moment of conception, both truly human and fully divine. The central and defining mystery of the Christian faith.

Judah—The name of one of the two tribes that remained faithful to the Davidic throne in Jerusalem when the Northern Kingdom broke itself off. Also known as the Southern Kingdom.

justification—(Gr. *dikaioo* = "to justify:" i.e., "to make holy," "declare righteous," and/or "acquit") The event or process by which sinful human beings are made acceptable to God. See grace.

liturgy—(Gr. *leitourgia* "a work for or of the people") The official public worship of the church. "Official" here signifies that the texts and rites have been approved by ecclesial authority. Along with *martyria*, Christian witness, and *diakonia*, Christian service, one of the three primary realizations and manifestations of Christian life in the world.

Logos—(Gr. = "word," "message," "discourse," "reason") The Word of God, through whom creation was formed independently of any pre-existing matter or substrate (See *Colossians* 1:15–20). Used with reference to the Second Person of the Trinity.

Magisterium—(Latin *magister* = "master, teacher") Within Catholicism: the pope and bishops in union with him, considered either separately or (especially) in unison, in their function as official, sacramentally ordained teachers of the faith of the Catholic Church. "The Ordinary Magisterium" designates their every-day explication of the Catholic faith; "the Extraordinary Magisterium" refers to the pronouncement by the pope alone or in union with the universal episcopate of any point of faith as demanding unconditional assent by all Catholics, that is, as infallible. E.g., The Immaculate Conception of the Blessed Virgin Mary, 1854, Pope Pius IX.

Manichaeism—The complex dualistic religion developed by Manes (c. 216–276), a Persian, on the basis of various gnostic and Judeo-Christian teachings. Severely ascetic, it envisions life as a constant struggle between two eternal principles: the Spirit of God, the source of all good, and the Spirit of Evil, the cause of all evil in the world, usually identified with matter. The end time will bring the final separation between Light and Darkness and the escape of the soul from the body.

Mass—(ME *missae* = "dismissals") A traditional Catholic name for the Eucharist deriving from solemn dismissal rites during and at the end of the Eucharist in which penitents, catechumens and then the faithful were given special blessings. See Eucharist.

Messiah—(*messias* = Gr. rendering of Hebrew *mashiach,* "Anointed One") In the Old Testament anointing is bestowed on persons for one of three different roles: prophet, priest, and king. The title is most frequently used of a reigning king. In later OT books the term encapsulates the hope that a perfect king would come as God's instrument of human and cosmic fulfillment. The New Testament identifies this figure with Jesus Christ of Davidic lineage who fulfilled God's promise beyond all expectation.

modalism—(Latin *modus* = "aspect, facet") The exaggerated emphasis on the oneness of God which reduces the three "Persons" in God to three ways or "modes" in which a mono-personal God acts in the world.

monasticism—(Gr. *monos* = "one, alone") That living of Christian life defined by vows of poverty, celibate chastity, and obedience in order to pursue both one's own salvation and deeper union with God and the salvation of others through prayer and witness to the faith, most often including some form of loving service. The two basic forms of monasticism are that of the *anchorite,* a hermit, and of the *cenobite,* a member of a stable religious community.

Monophysitism—(Gr. *monos*—"one, alone" + *physis*—"nature") The doctrine that in the Person of the Incarnate Jesus Christ there is but a single, divine, nature, in contrast to the orthodox Christian teaching that in Christ is one divine Person in two natures, one human and one divine.

numerology—A study in a supposed deeper significance and power of numbers.

parable—A short fictitious story from ordinary life that illustrates in a parallel way a moral attitude or religious truth.

Passion—(Latin *passio* = "suffering,") The saving transition of Jesus through suffering and death into resurrected life. Understood in the ancient church to include the Last Supper in which Jesus symbolized and explicitated the inner freedom and love that animated those saving events.

Neo-Platonism—A revival and religious interpretation of the philosophy of Plato (427?–347 B.C.), developed by Plotinus (A.D. 205–270), which flourished from the third to the sixth century A.D. It teaches that all reality has emanated from "The One," the supreme reality to which human beings must return through purification, knowledge and love in order to be saved.

patristics—(Latin *pater* = "father") Study of the history and the theology of "the Fathers," those ancient Christian writers, mostly bishops, whom mainstream Christian tradition has always regarded as highly authoritative witnesses to the authentic faith and practice of the church. Historians give various dates for the "Patristic Age," typically beginning with St. Irenaeus (fl. ca. 185) and extending as late as to St. John Damascene (ca. 675–ca. 749).

Pelagianism—A Christian heresy identified with a wandering British monk, Pelagius (ca. 350–425), teaching that human beings can achieve salvation through their own sustained efforts, independently of divine grace. Opposed by St. Augustine and condemned by the Council of Ephesus in A. D. 431.

Platonism—The philosophy of Plato (427?–347 B.C.). It asserts the existence of a higher intelligible world of eternal, changeless, and universal ideas or forms. Physical objects of the sensible world are "real" only to the degree that they image, and thereby participate in, the forms.

pneumatology—(Gr. *pneuma* = "spirit") The branch of theology, developed in the fourth century, which studies the Person and work of the Holy Spirit, the Third Person of the Blessed Trinity.

predestination—(Latin *praedestinare* = "to foreordain") That theological understanding according to which God knows and even foreordains from all eternity which human persons are to be saved.

priest—(Gk. *presbyter* = "elder" Ger. *priester*) A sacramentally ordained member of a bishop's advisory body, co-responsible with and under him for the guidance and leadership of the church by personal example and teaching of the faith, and by presiding at liturgy. A term which through history came also to translate the Greek *hiereus* = "one who deals with the sacred," i.e., one who offers sacrifice—leading to the mistaken notion that only priests and bishops, and not the assembly as a whole under the leadership of bishop or priest, truly offer the Eucharist.

Providence—(Latin *providere* = "to have foresight," "to provide for") The divine plan by which God lovingly works for the ultimate good of all of creation, including his guiding the course of individual lives.

redaction—The work done by those biblical authors who, in editing earlier textual material, introduced changes according to the messages they wished to communicate to their particular audiences.

redemption—(Latin *redemptio* = "buying back") God's saving activity which delivers humankind from sin and evil into communion with God.

The Reformation—(Latin *reformare* = "to renew, give new form") The religiously motivated movement of the sixteenth century responding to abuses in the Catholic Church by reliance solely on the scriptural word of God. Although not its original intention, it separated large sections of Western Christendom from the institutional Catholic Church and resulted in the establishment of various Protestant ecclesial communions.

retreat—A period of withdrawal—either in a group or individually—for prayer and meditation, often under the guidance of a director.

revelation—(Latin *revelare* = "to take away the veil") God's self-disclosure both through the created world and human events (see

Wisdom 13:1–9, Romans 1:20), and in a special, full and definitive way in the person, words and actions of Jesus Christ.

righteousness—The state of union with God through grace in which we are acceptable to God.

sacramentals—Sacred symbols of the church's faith through which God manifests and realizes his saving presence but which individually are not, like the seven Sacraments, essential to the church's continuing existence and mission in the world. Examples include: blessings of persons (including the sign of the cross), of meals, and of objects which are thereby set aside for holy activities—such as holy water, metals, palms, rosaries, crucifixes, Ash Wednesday ashes, candles, etc., and officially sanctioned holy activities such as Benediction with the Blessed Sacrament, Stations of the Cross, pilgrimages, etc.

Sacraments—(Latin *sacramentum* = "sacred reality," "oath," "pledge"—The Latin equivalent of Gr. *mysterion* = "mystery," "sacred rite") The essential liturgical rites of the church in which God acts through the church's faith to communicate his divine life to people and through which participants experience the love and power of God (grace) that flows from Christ's passion, death, and resurrection. The Catholic Church officially recognizes and celebrates seven Sacraments: Baptism, Confirmation, Eucharist, Holy Orders, Marriage, Penance/Reconciliation, and Anointing of the Sick.

salvation—(Latin = "making safe," "rescuing") Complete and eternal union with God, delivering humanity and all creation from the destructive power of sin and death.

sanctification—(Latin = "being made holy," "making holy") The holiness of union with God realized in and through God's self-gift in Jesus Christ ("uncreated grace") to human beings, bringing about interior personal transformation ("created grace"), that which the Eastern church calls "illumination" and "divinization."

schism—A formal institutional division in or separation from a church or religious body.

scholasticism—(Gr. *skhol* "leisure" Latin *schola* "school") A medieval method of theological inquiry using aristotelian approaches to ordering and analyzing reality and applying them to the truths of the church's faith. So named because it was developed in the various *schools* maintained in European universities by religious orders (e.g., Dominicans, Franciscans).

Scripture—Sacred writings so inspired by God as to be normative, when taken as a whole, of the faith of the church.

Semi-Pelagianism—A teaching, eventually condemned by the church, first articulated by certain fifth-century monastic theologians who opposed the extreme predestination theology of St. Augustine. Although these theologians did not deny that God's grace is necessary for salvation, they insisted that human beings must make the first step without the help of grace, in order to make themselves open to receive the necessary grace.

Septuagint—(Gr. *septuaginta* "seventy"). A third-century B.C. Greek translation of the Old Testament which, according to legend, was completed in seventy days by seventy translators, each of the entire text, working independently of one another and yet arriving at completely identical results, thereby confirming that their mutually agreeing Greek translations themselves were divinely inspired. Often designated, when cited, by the Roman numerals for seventy: LXX.

soteriology—(Gr. *sōtēr* = "savior") The branch of theology which investigates the church's faith in Christ as Savior of the world.

subordinationism—An understanding of God in which the Son is seen as inferior in divinity to the Father, and the Holy Spirit inferior to both the Son and the Father.

tabernacle—(Latin *tabernaculum* = "tent") The sacred container, normally found in the sanctuaries of church buildings, which holds the consecrated hosts for Holy Communion. It has its origin in the tent in which the Israelites housed the Ark of the Covenant which itself was a sacred receptacle and a kind of throne of the invisible God.

theology—(Gr. *theos* = "God") Literally, the "study of God." It is "faith seeking understanding" (St. Anselm of Canterbury [1033–1109]). It begins with the church's faith and proceeds in methodical ways, developing an organized body of knowledge, to understand and interpret that faith in relationship to contemporary understandings of the world and human life.

Tradition—(Gr. *paradosis* Latin *traditio* = "transmission") Seen from various perspectives as (1) the church's inner *life* in Christ, (2) the *truth content* of that life as manifested in the church's (a) dogmas, (b) ritual worship and (c) customs, and (3) the *process* by which that true life is handed on in the church to each successive generation.

Trinity—The fundamental article of the church's faith in one God in three Persons.

virtue—(Latin *virtus* = "force") A habit of good behavior which enables one to do what is right with increasing ease, joy, and consistency. The opposite of a virtue is a vice, the humanly destructive habit that facilitates our continuing to do evil.

Zion—A biblical poetic name for the city of Jerusalem. The hill on which the temple of Solomon was located is sometimes called Mount Zion. Jerusalem/Zion is often allegorically seen as a woman (e.g., see *Galatians* 4:25–27); in Christian allegory, the heavenly city of the just. Nineteenth century "Zionism" was the movement of Jews to migrate to the Holy Land.

Index

love, 10, 14, 30–31, 71–73, 78,
80–81, 98–99, 102,
117–118, 121, 123, 125,
128, 152, 165–173, 180,
182, 184, 186, 196,
199–201, 205, 207, 210,
227, 238–239, 242, 246,
256, 267, 271, 292,
294–295, 299–302
Luther, Martin, 175, 223–225,
227, 239, 246
Lutheran, 28, 95, 105, 177, 295

M

Major Prophets, 280
Manichaeism, 139
martyr, 69, 85, 92, 102, 147,
286–292
Mass, 105, 111, 122, 134, 192,
227, 250, 254, 256–257,
293, 303
memorial, 94–95, 286–292
mercy, 132, 135, 151, 167,
169–172, 206, 220, 293,
295, 297, 299–300
Messiah, 33, 36, 43, 68
Minor Prophets, 280
miracles, 60, 72
Miriam, 279
monasticism, 289
Moses, 9, 26–27, 36, 47, 54, 69,
279
mysteries, 89, 95, 121, 165, 256,
298
mystery, 3, 82, 151, 166–167,
200, 219, 248, 250,
252–254, 263, 265–267

N

Nathan, 35–36
natural law, 233

O

Origen, 144, 185
Orthodox Church, 281

P

Pain, 15, 122, 128, 172,
193–194, 219, 235
parable, 42, 61
Passion, 58, 93–96, 117, 169,
200, 204, 252, 298
Patriarch, 22, 141–142, 279
Patriarchates, 280
Patrick, St., 301
Paul VI, Pope, 247, 262, 264
peace, 86, 100, 102, 139, 141,
147, 151, 188, 212, 216,
235–236, 242, 246, 270,
286, 300, 302
penance, 121, 177, 196, 198,
267, 301
Pentateuch, 7, 9–11, 29
philosophy, 68, 158–159,
161–162, 217, 238
piety, 166, 210, 256, 286
Platonists, 119
pleasure, 122, 127, 134, 144,
180, 182, 184
Polycarp, 78, 86, 288
popular devotions, 257
poverty, 189, 202–204, 212,
232, 266
power, 17, 23, 27, 31, 35, 54,
60, 71–72, 80, 86, 89, 95,

W

Wickedness, 170–171
widow, 92, 142, 195, 219
wills, 124, 132–135, 144, 272
witness, 14, 28, 122, 220, 230,
    243, 249, 293
worship, 4, 10, 29, 31, 35, 87,
    94–95, 119, 124, 141, 145,
    240–241, 248–249, 252,
    255

Z

Zion, 45–46